THE WORLD
AND THE
PROPHETS

The Collected Works of Hugh Nibley

The Collected Works of Hugh Nibley will
include volumes on the following subjects:

The Old Testament and related Studies
Ancient History
The Pearl of Great Price
Early Christianity
The Book of Mormon
The Doctrine and Covenants and Mormonism
Education, Politics, and Society

Other volumes in this series:

Old Testament and Related Studies
Enoch the Prophet

The Collected Works of Hugh Nibley: Volume 3
Mormonism and Early Christianity

THE WORLD
AND THE
PROPHETS

Hugh Nibley

Edited by
John W. Welch
Gary P. Gillum
Don E. Norton

Foreword by
R. Douglas Phillips

Deseret Book Company
Salt Lake City, Utah
and
Foundation for Ancient Research and Mormon Studies
Provo, Utah

Chapter 18, "Easter and the Prophets," and chapter 19,
"Two Ways to Remember the Dead," were reprinted in Gordon
Allred, ed., *Immortality* (Salt Lake City: Hawkes, 1974).

Library of Congress Cataloging-in-Publication Data

Nibley, Hugh, 1910–
    The world and the prophets.

    (The Collected works of Hugh Nibley ; v. 3)
    Bibliography: p.
    Includes index.
    1. Prophets (Mormon theology)   2. Prophets.
3. Church history—Primitive and early church,
ca. 30–600.   4. Church of Jesus Christ of Latter-Day
Saints—Doctrines.   5. Mormon Church—Doctrines.
I. Title.   II. Series: Nibley, Hugh, 1910–   . Works.
1986 ; v. 3.
BX8643.P7N53   1987   231.7′45   87–620
ISBN 0-87579-078-X

First edition 1954
Second edition 1962
Third edition, first printing April 1987

To my mother

Contents

Foreword

At a time when the strident voices of members of the clergy are again heard challenging the right of Mormons to call themselves Christians and denying the divine origin of The Church of Jesus Christ of Latter-day Saints, the republication of Hugh Nibley's *The World and the Prophets* can only be most welcome, not only to members of the Church but to fair-minded people everywhere.

The first thirty chapters in this volume were originally delivered as a series of weekly lectures broadcast on KSL Radio from March 7 to October 17, 1954, under the title "Time Vindicates the Prophets." Several of these lectures, therefore, are seasonal, as they were delivered on or around Easter, Indepenence Day, or Pioneer Day. They were published in book form that same year, and an enlarged second edition appeared in 1962 with the two concluding chapters added at that time. In those editions, as in this one, the character of these presentations as talks has been retained. Just as the Church's beliefs and institutions were under attack when these lectures were first given, so today critics of the Church are again attacking the conception of God held by the Latter-day Saints, their claim to continuous revelation, their belief in Joseph Smith as a prophet of God and in the Book of Mormon as divine scripture, and their insistence that The Church of Jesus Christ of Latter-day Saints is the true church of Jesus Christ. The answers given by Professor Nibley then are just as valid today as they are timely.

Among the long line of defenders of the Restored Church, Hugh Nibley was the first to equip himself with the knowledge of all the ancient languages, especially Hebrew, Greek, and Latin, together with the historical training needed to read the scriptures in their original tongues and to deal with the other documents of the Early Christian Church. At the same time, he gained a command of the studies of church history and theology, not only in English but also in French, Dutch, and German. I vividly remember, as a young student in his Early Christian Church History course, the impression he made as he brought to class the imposing tomes of Migne's *Patrologia*, that vast corpus of the writings of the Fathers of the Church, and read to us from the original Greek and Latin.

With this background, he was uniquely qualified to chart the developments of the early Church, both historical and theological, through that period known to Mormons as "the Great Apostasy." He was further able to show that many beliefs of the Restored Church, though totally different in most respects from those of conventional Christianity, are virtually identical with those of the Primitive Church. His purpose, as he himself states, is simple:

> We make no attempt to argue out the position of the Church of Jesus Christ of Latter-day Saints. Here we are simply indicating briefly that for better or for worse, the Mormons consistently find themselves in the company of the ancient saints and, accordingly, far removed from the ways of conventional Christians. . . . It is an historical, not a theological or philosophical, vindication of our prophets. [1]

It is, of course, gratifying to Latter-day Saints to learn that they share the same attitudes and beliefs regarding God, prophets, revelation, death, miracles, free agency, martyrs, and tradition, among others, with the Early Christian Church. But Professor Nibley does far more than point out such identities of doctrines, practices, and institutions between Latter-day Saint Christians and the early Christians. He also describes with great clarity the process by which the Church changed from an organization with inspired prophets into a thoroughly different and alien institution built upon the learning of men. He shows how prophets were replaced by scholars, revelation by philosophy, inspired preaching by rhetoric; how the testimony of the Holy Ghost was replaced by a self-induced mystical experience, and how for the spiritual gifts and miracles was substituted the magical wonder-making of the pagans. For example, in his masterful analysis of the Council of Nicaea, he describes clearly how the inspired pronouncements of the Apostles were replaced by a creed worked out under the political pressure of the emperor. We learn also how the freedom to believe, which was so highly valued in the Primitive Church, gave way to the stifling authoritarianism of the Byzantine and Medieval churches.

But his most important contribution lies in showing us the tragic consequences entailed in the loss of living prophets, particularly as seen in his not unsympathetic treatment of Clement of Alexandria, Origen, and Augustine as they wrestle with the great theological questions of their time and grope for answers, succumbing in the end to the seduction of Greek philosophy. The systematic working out of doctrines by these learned schoolmen and their successors, far from being the colossal achievement often claimed for it, represents in fact a great failure. As Maurice Wiles, Dean of Clare College, Cambridge, equally reminds us concerning the introduction of the most famous of all theological formulas—the unscriptural *homoousios*—into the Nicene Creed:

> To generations of Christians the description of the Son as "of one substance" with the Father has served as a joyous affirmation of the faith in a creed sung at one of the highest moments of Christian worship. Yet that is very far from being the way in which it found entrance into the vocabulary of Christian doctrine. Rather it was admitted with reluctance as being the only available means of excluding Arianism. [2]

It is thus abundantly clear that the whole philosophical theological enterprise, however well intended, is incompatible with the existence of continuing revelation. For that reason there can never be a theology, a systematic theology as such, in the true Church, and thus we should be overwhelmingly grateful for our living prophets.

Many people have helped prepare this volume for publication, including Rebecca Bishop, Stephen Callister, John Gee, Gary Gillum, Darrell Matthews, Mari Miles, Phyllis Nibley, Don Norton, Stephen Ricks, and Morgan Tanner; their work is greatly appreciated. Funding from Ronald E. Tew and the Brigham Young University Religious Studies Center facilitated this work and is gratefully acknowledged. Professor John W. Welch and the Foundation for Ancient Research and Mormon Studies deserve our deep appreciation for making this new edition of this important work available once more.

R. Douglas Phillips

1

"How Will It Be When None More Saith 'I Saw'?"

In the realm of the mind, in letters, the arts, and in most of the sciences, it was the ancient Greeks, most educated people will concede, who walked off with nearly all the first prizes. It is hard to say anything on any but the most specialized and technical of matters that some Greek many centuries ago did not say better. If any people ever knew and lived life well and fully, it was the chosen spirits among the Greeks. They explored every avenue of human experience; they inquired into every possibility of broadening and improving the mind; they sought the truth as persistently and as honestly as men can ever be expected to seek; and, sounding the depths and skirting the outmost bounds of man's wisdom, came to the unanimous conclusion that the wisdom of man is as nothing.

The man to whom the Greeks themselves always gave first place among their wisest, Solon of Athens, sums up his own experience in unambiguous elegiacs:

"Like gaping fools we amuse ourselves with empty dreams. . . . Do not doubt it, insecurity follows all the works of men, and no one knows, when he begins an enterprise, how it will turn out. One man, trying his best to do the right thing, steps right into ruin and disaster, because he cannot see what is ahead; while another behaves like a rascal and not only escapes the penalty of his own folly but finds himself blessed with all kinds of success."[1]

The greatest of their lyric poets told the Greeks in one of
his greatest odes:

"The hopes of men are often exalted in one moment only
to be dashed down in the next, as they roll helplessly in a sea
of false expectations and miscalculations. For no mortal man
ever got an absolute guarantee from the gods that his affairs
would turn out as he thinks they would. There is always
some unknown quantity that vitiates any attempt to predict
the future."[2]

The soberest and noblest of the dramatists, that poet
who "saw life steadily and saw it whole," told the Greeks of
Oedipus, who was all that a man could possibly be: great-
hearted, noble, idealistic, intelligent, well-informed, clever
and resourceful, perfectly courageous, and determined to do
all in his power to help others. To these virtues Oedipus
added an attribute that most men worship but few enjoy—
luck, the most fabulous luck. Oedipus always got the "breaks."
And what was his end? Trusting in the perfection of his
human endowments, Oedipus found himself at the end of
the play in the ghastliest situation that a mortal could imagine, having perpetrated not only the most colossal blunders,
but also having unwittingly committed the most monstrous
crimes against family and society. We need not dwell upon
his fate but can sum it up in the last words of the tragedy:

"Here, people, you have Oedipus—look at him! He knew
the riddle of the Sphinx; he was the ablest man of his time;
there wasn't a man who didn't envy his career—but look
what he has come to! Don't think for a moment that you can
call anybody happy until you know for sure exactly what is
going to happen to him right up till the end—that is, until he
goes down into the grave without having tasted misery."[3]

A final instance. The most popular Greek dramatist,
Euripides, had a little ditty of which he was rather fond; he
introduced it into a number of his plays to sum up the human
situation:

"The gods take many forms indeed, they bring surprising things to pass. And that which we have confidently believed in goeth into fulfillment, while the gods manage to bring about the one thing that nobody expected. That's the way things are."[4]

The early Christian apologists made use of this confessed limitation of the wisest pagans, this fatal obstacle not only to human perfection but even to the enjoyment of a few brief hours and weeks of unsullied happiness, to display what they regarded as the peculiar advantage of their own religion. "Neither by nature nor by any human skill," wrote Justin Martyr to the Greeks, "is it possible for men to know such high and holy things; but only by a gift that descends from above upon holy men from time to time." Justin explains elsewhere that these men are called prophets and are a type of human entirely unknown to the heathen world. "They do not need training in speech or skill in controversy and argument," he continues here, "but only to keep themselves pure to receive the power of the Spirit of God, so that the divine plectrum can express itself through them as on the strings of a lyre, making use of righteous men and revealing to them the knowledge of sacred and heavenly things. Wherefore they all speak as with a single mouth and a single tongue . . . concerning all things which is needful for us to know. . . . The fact that they all agree, though speaking at widely separated times and places, is the proof of their divinity."[5]

Note the interesting musical analogy of sympathetic vibration. The holy men can receive God's revelations because they are in tune to the proper wavelength, so to speak. God can play on them as a plectrum plucks the strings of a lyre because they are prepared to vibrate to his touch—not by virtue of any special training, and not whenever *they* choose to respond, but whenever it pleases God "from time to time" to move them from heaven. Such is the nature of the prophetic gift, says Justin. The early Christians felt that without this gift of direct revelation from heaven such as is received only by prophets, they would be no better than the heathen—well-meaning but bankrupt. The gift of prophecy—while it remained—was the boast and glory of the church. Thus when Justin wishes to prove to a Jewish friend that the truth has now passed from the Jewish to the Christian community, his one argument is that the gift of prophecy, once enjoyed by the Jews, has now been transferred to his own people, the proof of which, he says, is "that prophetic gifts are to be found among us to the present day, . . . such as were anciently shared among you."[6] Note well: the church boasts the possession of prophetic gifts a hundred and fifty years after Christ, and not merely the written words of the prophets of old—for the Jews had those—but the words of living prophets, no longer had among the Jews.

Origen, some eighty years later, used the same argument: "It can be shown [he tells Celsus] that the Jews were entirely abandoned [by God] after the earthly sojourn of Jesus, and that they no longer possessed those things in which their former sanctity was thought to reside; nay, that not the slightest indication of divinity was to be had among them. For they no longer have prophets or wonders, of which some traces may still be found among the Christians."[7]

For Origen, when it comes to a showdown, the possession of prophets and wonders is what proves a divine church. But note that Origen can claim only lingering traces of the gift of prophecy for his church. Apparently the Jews were not the only people who could lose the holy gifts on which all depended, and at an early day the Christians were reminded of this fact again and again by the so-called Apostolic Fathers, the first important church writers after the Apostles themselves. "Let us never relax and take it easy," wrote Barnabas, "secure in the knowledge that we are the elect, . . . especially when we consider that after all those great signs and wonders were wrought in Israel they were at length abandoned in just such a manner."[8] Barnabas, Clement, Ignatius, and others remind the saints repeatedly that what the Jews have lost the Christians can lose just as easily.

As the true church gloried in the possession of prophets as the surest sign of its divinity, even so, when prophecy ceased, as it did all too soon, the church sorely missed it. We shall tell of this at a later time. For the present we may quote some lines from Browning's "A Death in the Desert," which no less an authority than Kirsopp Lake has recommended as "the best preparation for understanding" the mood of the church after the passing of the Apostles.[9] As the poet describes it, the passing of John, last of the witnesses, leaves the Christians with an overpowering sense of loss—without a real prophet they are no better than other men; without a prophet all is doubt and misgiving; without an eyewitness there can be no final certainty.

> Still, when they scatter, there is left on earth
> No one alive who knew (consider this!)
> —Saw with his eyes and handled with his hands
> That which was from the first, the Word of Life.
> How will it be when none more saith "I saw"?

And the poet with characteristic presumption imputes his own doubts to John, too old to be a prophet!

> Grasping the while for stay at facts which snap
> Till I am found away from my own world,
> Feeling for foothold through a blank profound,
> Along with unborn people in strange lands,
> Who say—I hear said or conceive they say—
> Was John at all, and did he say he saw?
> Assure us, ere we ask what he might see!

But must the church always have *living* prophets in its midst? Is it not enough that we have the words of the prophets of old preserved in holy writ? The answer to that is clear enough in the few passages we have cited. The true church must and will always have living prophets. But that is unwelcome news to the world. It has always been poison. It is the one teaching that has made the restored gospel unacceptable to the wisdom of men. A *dead* prophet the world dearly desires and warmly cherishes; he is a priceless tradition, a spiritual heritage, a beautiful memory. But woe to a living prophet! He shall be greeted with stones and catcalls even by pious people. The men who put the Apostles to death thought they were doing God a favor, and the Lord tells us with what reverence and devotion men adorn the tombs of the prophets whom they would kill if they were alive (Luke 11:47-48).

Men can read the words of a dead prophet and apply his heavy charges to that dead generation to which the prophet spoke, piously shaking their heads the while and repeating, "If we had been in the days of our fathers, we would not have been partakers with them in the blood of the prophets." By that very statement, the Lord tells those devout lovers of dead prophets, "Ye be witnesses unto yourselves, that ye are the children of them which killed the prophets" (Matthew 23:30-31). Christ predicted that he, too, like the other prophets, would be eagerly sought after once he had left the earth—but then it would be too late:

"When once the master of the house is risen up, and hath shut the door, and ye begin to stand without, and to knock at the door, saying, Lord, Lord, open unto us; and he shall answer and say unto you, I know you not whence ye are:

"Then shall ye begin to say, We have eaten and drunk in thy presence, and thou hast taught in our streets.

"But he shall say, I tell you, I know you not whence ye are; depart from me, all ye workers of iniquity" (Luke 13:25-27).

After the Lord is gone, men will gladly knock on the door, but it will not be opened. "In vain do they worship *me*," he says (Matthew 15:9, Mark 7:7), speaking of times to come—not "in vain do they worship idols." Once the Lord has departed this earth, men will number him among the prophets and march under the banner of his name, saying on every side, "Lo, here is Christ! and Lo, there!" And when that time comes, the Master warns, "if any man shall say unto you, Lo, here is Christ, or there; believe it not" (Matthew 24:23). At the time when all shall be calling upon his name just as their predecessors painted the tombs of other prophets, he will refuse to recognize any of them.

Here we have something in the nature of a general principle. The rejection of living prophets and the veneration of dead ones is not a folly limited to one nation or to one generation. It meets us throughout the long history of Israel as a sort of standard procedure. Nor did it cease with the coming of Christ, who promised his disciples that they would be treated as badly and rejected as completely as he. The wise men of his time had a ready answer to Jesus: "Abraham is our father" (John 8:39), they protest. "We be not born of fornication; we have one Father, even God (John 8:41). "We are Moses' disciples. We know that God spake unto Moses: as for this fellow, we know not from whence he is" (John 9:28-29).

God had visited the earth in remote times; he had spoken to Abraham and to Moses. Venerable traditions burdened with a magnificent weight of art, poetry, scholarship, and ritual attested the sincere devotion of the race to the memory of God's visits to men in times past. But to ask men to believe that that same God had spoken in their own day, and to a plain man who walked their streets—that was simply too much to take! That was the test that Christ's generation could not pass.

It was a test that few have ever passed: the humiliating test of recognizing a true prophet and taking instruction from the weak and humble things of the earth. Was the wondrous modern age of applied science that began in the nineteenth century to be excused from taking the same test of authority? Remember that the prophets of old came to generations

that were very modern in their thinking, smart and sophisticated, advanced, liberated, intellectual; the Hellenistic world,
if anything, surpassed our own in those qualities of social
advancement. But to come to our own age, do you think the
God of heaven is going to come unannounced by prophets?
God's declared policy of testing the world by the sending of
prophets from time to time was not abrogated two thousand
years ago. Men have not so changed, and God has not so
changed but that this sure touchstone of past ages can be
employed with full effect in our own day. It is precisely
those ages which think themselves beyond such things that
are most eligible for the warning voice of the prophets. Our
message is that God has called prophets again in these days
and that the world might well heed their words.

2

A Prophet's Reward

We quoted in the previous chapter from Justin Martyr on the importance of living prophets for a true church. In an autobiographical account, Justin recalls that his own conversion to Christianity began when a certain old man addressed the following words to him in the course of a philosophical conversation:

"A long time ago there lived certain men—much older than any of those so-called philosophers we have been talking about; blessed and righteous men, beloved of God. And they spoke by the Holy Spirit, foretelling those very things which are now coming to pass. They are called prophets. They are the only men who have ever seen the truth of things and told it to men without making any timid concessions to public opinion, without seeking to make an impression on people, and without being in the least influenced by concern for what other people might think of them. But, being filled with the Holy Ghost, they simply reported those things which they had seen and heard. The writings of those men survive to this day, and anyone can derive the greatest benefit from them, and learn from them about the beginnings and endings of things, and all such matters as philosophers are supposed to know. For it was not their wont to build up a case by formal argument, but simply to report the truth as *reliable witnesses*, without any disputation at all."[1]

When Justin reported this conversation to a group of philosophy students, at this point of the story, he recounts, they burst out laughing—it was just too funny for words.

But Justin remained unmoved, for he saw clearly that only
by revelation from outside could man be freed from his fear-
ful confinement within the narrow cell of his own limited
experience.

Years before, the mysterious Clement had reached the
same conclusion. "Wishing to learn something," he recalls in
the first part of the so-called *Clementine Recognitions*, "I frequented the schools of the philosophers, where, however, I
heard nothing but dogmatic assertions and equally dogmatic
refutations endlessly put forth—formal disputations, artfully
constructed syllogisms, and subtle conclusions. . . . Neither
side ever brought forth proof that really convinced me inside,
because the statements and definitions of things passed as
true or false not from the actual nature of things or the real
truth, but always according to the skill and cleverness of the
people putting them forth."[2] It is like manna from heaven
when this Clement has his first gospel conversation with
Peter, who begins by explaining to him why a prophet is
necessary. Peter compares the world in which we live to a
great house filled with dense smoke—blinding smoke produced by human unbelief, malice, ambition, greed, etc.
Because of this smoke, the people who live in the house can
see nothing clearly, but we must imagine them groping about
with weak and running eyes, coughing and scolding, bumping into each other, tripping over furniture, trying to make
out a bit of reality here and there—a corner, a step, a wall—
and then trying to fit their desperate and faulty data together
to make some kind of sense.[3]

The image is a good one. It reminds us of Plato's comparison of this world to a cave in which men see only shad-
ows, and to Aristotle's comparison, in the first book of the
Metaphysics, of the human mind to the eyes of a bat that
can see only the most crassly obvious things and them only
in a sort of half-light. Especially it recalls Job's declaration
that we can know nothing in this world, where our days are
only a shadow (Job 8:9). In the same sense, Origen compares

the human intellect at its brilliant best with a tiny little can-
dle, a feeble spark that can hardly light a foot of the way
ahead.[4] And Tertullian likens the philosophers to men stumbling and groping about in the dark. Once in a while, he
says, they do "stumble on the truth by a happy accident,"
but it is inexcusable for a Christian to follow such blind and
unreliable guides, since he has something far better—a revelation from heaven.[5] That is exactly the moral of Peter's lecture to Clement in the *Recognitions*. There is only one possible way to get any sure knowledge either of the building or
its builder, and that is to consult one who has come from the
pure air of the outside where he has viewed the house with
clear detachment and spoken with its builder. Such a clear
view comes only by revelation and can only be conveyed to
men, Peter insists again and again, by a true prophet. As an
example, he cites the case of Abraham. (We cannot here
examine the nature of the document from which we are quoting; suffice it to say for the present that it is a genuine fragment of very early Christian belief.) At a time when the
whole world was plunged into darkness because of sin (Peter
is reported as telling Clement), a righteous man, Abraham,
attempted to gain a knowledge of the Creator by studying
"the reason and order of the stars."

"Wherefore an angel, assisting him by vision, taught him
more fully in the things he had begun to understand. . . .
Now as this Abraham, desiring to know the cause of things,
was deeply pondering upon them in his mind [lit. revolving
them with intense concentration], the True Prophet appeared
to him, even he who alone knows the hearts and minds of
men; and he taught him the knowledge of godhead *(divini-
tatis scientiam)*, and he showed him both the origin and the
end of the world, and the immortality of the spirit *(animae)*,
and the ordinances *(instituta)* by which men must live to
please God; and he showed him the resurrection of the dead
which was to come, and the judgment which is to come,
with the reward of the good and the punishment of the bad,

explaining to him how all things are governed by a just law. And having instructed him correctly and fully in all things, he returned again to his invisible dwelling-places."[6]

This true prophet, Peter explains, was Jesus Christ, the same who had brought this knowledge to the earth in his own day. He insists before all things that "faith in religious and holy matters requires the presence of a true prophet, so that he might tell us also how we are to understand everything."[7] Someone is almost sure to protest that this smacks of authoritarianism, and Peter sees the point. In the dealings of men with each other, any assumption of infallibility or even superiority is sheer arrogance; we mortals are all highly fallible. For that very reason, Peter insists, it is all-important to prove that a prophet is a *true* prophet and not one of the swarming impostors. We must, he says, "before all things try the faith of the prophet by every possible test." A prophet is no ordinary person; he makes no ordinary claim; and he does not ask people to believe him, but to test him. God is not authoritarian: He asks no one to believe; but invites the world, as his prophets do, "Prove me herewith."

When the Lord was upon his earthly mission, he greatly angered and upset men by forcing them to decide whether he was a true prophet or not. Early in his mission he was met by certain devils who begged him to leave them alone: "They cried out, saying, What have we to do with thee, Jesus, thou Son of God? Art thou come hither to torment us before the time?" The devils could not ignore him; his mere presence was a "torment" to them. And it was the same with men, for when the people of a nearby town heard what had happened, "behold, the whole city came out to meet Jesus: and when they saw him, they besought him that he would depart out of their coasts" (Matthew 8:29, 34). Apparently his presence made men as uncomfortable as it did the devils, for while the Lord was in their midst, they could not be neutral regarding him. Only after he had left the earth could Christians have an "open mind" regarding Christ's mission. Of such people he said through his prophet John, "So then because thou art lukewarm, and neither cold nor hot, I will spue thee out of my mouth" (Revelation 3:16). The Lord insists that we make up our minds one way or another regarding his calling.

Before considering the test of a true prophet, we must make clear the fact that a prophet is a witness, not a reformer. Criticism of the world is always implicit in a prophet's message of repentance, but he is *not* sent for the purpose of criticizing the world. Men know the world is wicked, and the wickedest ones often know it best. To denounce human folly has been the avocation of teachers and philosophers in every age, and their reward, surprisingly enough, has not been death but usually a rather handsome fee. The age of Christ, like the nineteenth century, was a remarkably tolerant one as far as ideas were concerned. On the one hand we find quacks, impostors, and miracle mongers flourishing throughout the Roman empire; and on the other, traveling philosophers and high-powered professors indulging in the most unsparing and outspoken criticism of all established institutions, sacred and profane, while the world applauded. It was *not* the Sermon on the Mount that drove men to crucify the Lord. It was not for their moral tirades that the prophets of old and the Apostles were stoned. In the age of Apollonius and Dio Chrysostom people liked nothing better than to sit in fashionable congregations while being scolded by picturesque crackpots. No Christian writer ever made such devastating attacks on prevailing manners and morals as the pagan satirists did; no Christian apologist ever debunked heathen religion as effectively as Cicero did—with perfect safety. Ovid was banished, not for criticizing the corruption of the times, but for being too lenient toward it, thereby thought the authorities, encouraging vice.

What, then, did Christ and the Apostles do and say that drove men into paroxysms of rage? They performed tangible miracles such as could not be denied, and they reported

what they had seen and heard. That was all. It was as witnesses endowed with power from on high that they earned
the hatred of the world, of which John speaks so much: "We
speak that we do know, and testify that we have seen; and
ye receive not our witness" (John 3:11).

"Many good works have I shewed you from my Father
[says the Lord on one occasion]; for which of those works
do ye stone me?

"The Jews answered him, saying, For a good work we
stone thee not; but for blasphemy; and because that thou,
being a man, makest thyself God.

"Say ye of him, whom the Father hath sanctified, and
sent into the world, Thou blasphemest; because I said, I am
the Son of God?

"Therefore they sought again to take him: but he escaped
out of their hand" (John 10:32-33, 36, 39).

On another occasion the enraged multitude cried, "Art
thou greater than our father Abraham, which is dead? and
the prophets are dead: whom makest thou thyself?" (John
8:53.) When Christ in reply said that Abraham had actually
seen His day and rejoiced, while he was before Abraham,
"Then took they up stones to cast at him" (John 8:53-59).

And as soon as the Apostles said, "We are his *witnesses*
of these things," the council and the high priests "were cut to
the heart, and took counsel to slay them" (Acts 5:32-33; italics added). Again, we are told that the multitude "were cut
to the heart" when Stephen accused them of rejecting what
had been brought "by the disposition of angels" (Acts 7:53-54).
But the last straw was when he had the effrontery to say,
"Behold, I see the heavens opened, and the Son of man
standing on the right hand of God. *Then* they cried out with
a loud voice, and stopped their ears, and ran upon him with
one accord, and cast him out of the city, and stoned him"
(Acts 7:56-58). If Stephen had spent his life, as innumerable
philosophers have, denouncing the vices and follies of the
age, he might have died peacefully in bed. But those fatal

words, "I see," were his death warrant. And what did Paul
say to make the Jews cry out in utter horror: "Away with
such a fellow from the earth: for it is not fit that he should
live," as "they . . . cast off their clothes, and threw dust into
the air?" (Acts 22:22-23.) What indeed? These were the
unforgivable words that made him unfit to live: "Suddenly
there shone from heaven a great light round about me. And I
fell unto the ground, and heard a voice saying unto me,
Saul, Saul, why persecutest thou me? And I answered, Who
art thou, Lord? And he said unto me, I am Jesus of Nazareth,
whom thou persecutest" (Acts 22:6-8). Paul could have won
his audience over by speaking as a scholar, but when he bore
witness to what he had seen and heard, he was asking for
trouble.

To come down to modern times, why were people so
furiously angry with Joseph Smith? It was not for being a
reformer or rebuking a naughty world. In his day, the most
popular preacher was the one who could denounce the manners of the times most fiercely and paint the most lurid picture of the wrath to come. Nobody led militant campaigns
against even the most rabid preachers of hellfire or swore to
drink their blood. We have said that the world in which
Jesus lived was full of quacks and impostors who carried on
unmolested. So in the time of Joseph Smith, the country was
full of strange separatist cults with strange social programs
and strange moral practices such as the Mormons were falsely
accused of, but no one thought it virtuous to burn their set-
tlements or shoot them on sight. In what did the modern
prophet's deadly offense consist? In the summer of 1833 a
much-publicized mass meeting was held in Missouri to protest the admission of Mormon immigrants into Jackson
County, and this was the official objection: "The committee
express fears that . . . they will soon have all the offices in
the county in their hands; and that the lives and property of
other citizens would be insecure, under the administration of
men who are so ignorant and superstitious as to believe that

they have been the subjects of miraculous and supernatural cures; hold converse with God and his angels, and possess and exercise the gifts of divination and unknown tongues." [8] Charles Dickens, as is well known, was very favorably impressed by the Mormons he saw both in America and England, but one thing about them he could not tolerate: "What the Mormons do," he wrote in 1851, "seems to be excellent; what they *say* is mostly nonsense," because "it exhibits fanaticism in its newest garb," namely, "seeing visions in the age of railways." [9] That put them in the same class with the prophets and Apostles of old. "We know Abraham is our father, and Moses is our prophet, but who is this guy?" "Abraham is dead, and the prophets are dead—who do you think you are?"

Before we even consider the question of whether Joseph Smith was a true prophet or not, the uniqueness of his position deserves respectful attention. Because, true or false, he was the first man since the days of the Apostles to claim the things that real prophets claim. The modern prophets who excited the laughter and contempt of the world exactly as the ancient prophets shocked and amused the friends of Justin were the first men since ancient times to talk of what they had seen and heard in the presence of God and angels. What could they expect but a prophet's reward?

3

Prophets and Preachers

Let us consider the common claim that a prophet is just another preacher. In every age there have been men and women claiming prophetic gifts and supernatural experiences. Some of these have been true prophets, but most of them, as the scripture reminds us again and again, have been false. To avoid the labor of distinguishing the true from the false, it has been the practice of historians simply to lump all such claimants together in a single class. To do this is to perpetrate a grave injustice against real prophets, just as to lump all professing healers together (as some people do) is a grave injustice to honest doctors. If there were only three real physicians in the world, it would still be unfair to put all doctors together in one category; and if there were only three honest prophets in history, it would be wrong to class all prophets together.

For example, Christ has been charged by ancients and moderns alike with being just another traveling healer and wonderworker, a wandering wiseman, a teacher of virtue, a thoroughly typical representative of the "lunatic fringe." Generations of scholars have been quick to point to the remarkable parallel between his wanderings, sufferings, and teachings and those of his near-contemporary, Apollonius of Tyana. The old traveling quack Peregrinus impressed the shrewd and discerning Lucian as being a typical Christian disciple. At an early period men began collecting stories and affidavits about Jesus' early life showing him to be a simple country boy with an inordinate desire to impress people. The

conscientious and intelligent Celsus published one of these
accounts in all good faith. According to this version Jesus
made up the story about being born of a virgin because he
was really ashamed of having been born in a miserable Jewish village to a poor working woman of the lowest class. "He
says she was actually thrown out by her husband, a carpen-
ter by trade, when he found that she had been guilty of adul-
tery. Then, he says [Celsus is quoting his Jewish informant],
since she had been kicked out, she wandered around like a
tramp and bore Jesus in disgrace. And he, having no means
of support, went off to Egypt looking for work. There he
became acquainted with certain skills on which the Egyptians pride themselves. As his adeptness in these increased,
he began to get exalted ideas about himself and ended up
announcing that he was God."[1] The same local authority can
furnish specific data for this story: We even know the name
of the soldier by whom Mary was pregnant—it was Panthera;
and everybody always admitted that the child was not
Joseph's.[2] This, Celsus finds far more plausible than any far-
fetched tales about virgin birth; the whole thing seems to
ring true to him, he says, and easily accounts for all the
events that otherwise have to be explained by miracles. We
must admit that Celsus has a point. The low-class origin, the
poverty, loose morals, odd jobs, magic and hocus-pocus,
mounting ambition, and supernatural claims are all very plausible. One could furnish many parallels from the world in
which Jesus lived. Ever since Celsus, men have seized upon
superficial resemblances of Christ to other religious men of
his age to prove that he was simply one of many. That makes
him easy to explain. By diligent search one can match all his
teachings with the teachings of others—the earliest Apologists actually used to do that, asking the pagans, "Why do
you persecute us when we teach only what you do?" Christ
was a homeless man followed about by disciples, so were the
traveling Sophists; he was a great moral teacher, so were
they; he was persecuted and reviled, so were the Stoics and

Pythagoreans; his followers claimed that he was the Messiah, so did the followers of Bar Kochba and Bar Nephele; he was crucified, so were Mani and many other religious fanatics. Even his resurrection easily suggests the victory over death in the year-drama rituals of many oriental people, when the king emerges from the underworld after having been overwhelmed in combat with death. All these things have been pointed out repeatedly in order to bring Christ down to the level of everyday experience and supplant the miraculous and embarrassing by the commonplace and reassuring. But all to no avail. One does not compose music with a slide rule, and the divinity and truthfulness of Christ were never meant to be proved by history, since we are told from the beginning that that knowledge comes to one only by direct revelation from the Father in heaven.

But even on historic grounds the accidental resemblances between the Lord and other teachers are superficial and trivial compared with the great fundamental *differences* between them. There is a huge classic literature dealing with the activities of traveling wise men and religious teachers in late antiquity. These men all had certain well-marked characteristics. After the manner of the seven wise men, they wandered unattached through the world as spectators of God's works; Christ always stayed within a few miles of home and never evinced any interest in natural philosophy. They were all seekers after wisdom; Christ had it to give. They lived in complete detachment from society and were tolerated by rulers and governments as harmless dreamers; *his* organizing activities alarmed Roman and Jewish authorities. They emancipated themselves from family and friends; he lived intimately with them all his days. They performed interesting experiments and theatrical tricks to delight and impress the multitude; his miracles were all useful ones, never meant to be eye-catching. They attended the schools of others and sought to sit at the feet of great teachers; he spoke as one *having* authority. They did everything to attract the largest possible following; he forbade his disciples to do what would make them popular. They gained or lost students as disciples chose to follow or leave them; he chose his own disciples and bound them to him by bonds and covenants. They all (as Professor Jaeger has shown) gave political counsel and advice, seeking official advisory positions and corresponding widely with government officials by mail; he gave no such advice and wrote no such letters. The only proper place for them to deliver their discourses was in the theater, the official assembly place; he always avoided holding forth in such places. They cultivated peculiarities of dress and appearance; his disciples were criticized for not doing so. We could go on and on, but the point is clear: Christ was in all essentials the very opposite to the men with whom he is classed. In a word, he was a true prophet, and they were not: if they sometimes resembled him, it was because of their own efforts to make a noise like true prophets. The great difference was that they were only *looking* for what Christ *had*. They spoke as scribes and pharisees, hypocrites; he as one having authority. There is all the difference in the world between the two. Amid a host of like-minded seekers—many of them devout and honest men—one alone was *not* a seeker.

Bearing this in mind, let us turn to criticisms of our modern prophets, especially of Joseph Smith. I am sure that as we read the "official" account of Jesus, most of our listeners thought of the usual Gentile stories of Joseph Smith. More familiar even than the sly, sordid details and the air of superior knowledge and sophistication in the teller is the characteristic insinuation that Jesus and his family were not really the sort of people with whom respectable men and women associate. This tone runs through all the early anti-Christian as it does through the anti-Mormon literature. Men have not been slow to point out superficial resemblances of the modern prophet to other men around him: he founded a church, so did other men; he claimed revelation from heaven, so did they; he was persecuted, so were they; he read the Bible, so

did they; and since they were impostors, so accordingly was
he. This last is what you cannot say. One might build up an
endless list of resemblances between Joseph Smith and
Gladstone, but what would it prove save that they both were
men? What we must ask in the case of the modern prophet is
what we must ask in the case of Jesus: where was he *essentially* different from all the rest?

On this question, one man's opinion is deserving of particular attention. Eduard Meyer was one of the most learned
men of modern times. Ancient history was his field, and the
origin of religions was his special interest. He wrote authoritative works on the origin of religions, and singled out the
Latter-day Saints as one of the great original religions. Most
other churches and sects are really only episodes in the history of a going concern, variations on an accepted theme,
reforms or innovations undertaken by men who, though they
may have felt aware of a special calling or a special talent for
the job, were simply doing what other men did. But three
religions—primitive Christianity, Islam, and Mormonism—
actually claim to have been founded not by men but by
direct revelation from heaven.

Meyer finds the closest resemblance between the Mormon Church and the primitive Christians. They resemble
each other in every detail, even to their defects. He also finds
resemblances between Joseph Smith and Mohammed, but
these are superficial and incidental compared with the essential points on which the two men, both claiming to be prophets, stand in complete antithesis to each other. Since it has
long been a popular indoor sport among the Gentiles to
compare Joseph Smith to Mohammed, it will not be amiss at
this time to list the points of difference between the two as
observed by one of the few scholars, perhaps the only scholar,
who has ever had a firsthand knowledge of both Mormons
and Mohammedans:

(1) First of all, Meyer dwells at considerable length on
the doubts and misgivings that so long beset Mohammed,

his long periods of self mistrust and black despair, especially that period known as the *fatra* when he meditated and, according to some sources, even attempted suicide. For the Prophet of Islam, being an honest man, was greatly worried over the possibility that he might be insane, or that what he had seen might have been a devil rather than an angel. In contrast to this, "it is for Joseph Smith very significant," wrote Meyer, "that there is in his case absolutely no question of any such doubts and misgivings."[3] Meyer congratulates Mohammed for having the normal human reaction and chides Smith for not having it.

(2) Second, in contrast to Joseph Smith's behavior, Meyer holds up the exemplary caution, restraint, and shrewdness of Mohammed, showing how he gained confidence with practice and through the years carefully worked out his doctrine and his story, correcting, revising, and building it up. Unlike Joseph Smith, *or the Old Testament prophets*, Meyer observes, Mohammed never actually sees anything in his revelations, but reads slowly and very painfully from a book.[4] Smith finds himself in company with the ancient prophets of Israel. Mohammed does not.

(3) The most important difference between the two purported prophets, according to Eduard Meyer, is "that Joseph Smith has a belief in the continuation of direct prophetic inspiration, speaking in tongues, etc., and along with that, of personal inspiration which *every* believer can receive. . . . Mohammed, on the other hand, knows only of one single book, that is the Bible, with which he has a vague acquaintance."[5]

(4) Joseph Smith views spiritual and supernatural things "much more crassly and materially" than does Mohammed. For Joseph, the manifestations of the other world are something quite real and matter-of-fact. "For Mohammed, on the other hand, there is only one miracle—the revelation of the words of the divine book and the appearance of angels. He denied any power to do miracles, and his followers have no

special power of any kind."[6] Modern Mohammedans rather pride themselves on their cool and rational attitude toward all other-worldly things.

(5) The most obvious point of resemblance between these two men is their common claim to have given the world a revealed book. But precisely on this point Meyer finds the completest (if not the most important) difference between them. After all, hundreds of men have claimed to have given inspired writings to the world—there is nothing in the mere *claim* to justify or condemn a prophet. But Smith's book is like no other. Whereas "for Mohammed the book always remains in the hands of the angel," Smith not only read but also translated his book, which he carried around from place to place; he actually copied out characters of the book and circulated them around for all, including his worst enemies, to look at—has any impostor ever displayed such absolute confidence in his work? "Any such thing," says Meyer, "would never have occurred to Mohammed."[7]

Mohammed's accounts of heavenly visitors are vague and conflicting. Usually his visions came in sleep—he looks above him and sees something in the air, or he sees Gabriel standing on the horizon, or filling the sky with his gigantic size, or confronting him whichever way he turns his head, or standing a bowshot away. There is a dream-like quality in it all. Smith's reports, on the other hand, are clear, specific, and precise. The writer's great-grandfather was a Jew, and a very hardheaded and practical man. He tells in his journal, writing on the very day that the event took place, of how he cross-examined Joseph Smith on every minute detail of the First Vision and of how the Prophet satisfied him promptly and completely. From that day he never doubted the calling of the Prophet. Apparently Mohammed is not exactly sure just what an angel is. But what could be more clear and concrete than Joseph Smith's description of Moroni?

Eduard Meyer's final conclusion is that "Mohammed's revelations stand higher than those of Joseph Smith, because

in his case we feel . . . something of the power of a conviction wrung out by hard mental toil, and even at times we
feel something of a poetic inspiration."[8] Of this, not the
minutest trace in Joseph Smith. Meyer can respect the mental effort of the founder of Islam wrestling with his human
limitations, but Joseph Smith remains an enigma. Meyer has
no patience with this upstart who never doubts in the face of
the most appalling persecution, and amid all his terrible trials
and struggles never struggles for inspiration. Meyer's impa-
tience with Joseph Smith is actually a strong witness to his
prophetic calling, for Meyer treats Ezekiel in exactly the same
way. Of this great prophet he says:

"The prophetic apparatus has sunk to the most literal
form. Ezekiel is a literary hack-worker. He does not work
through the living word such as Isaiah and Jeremiah strug-
gled to bring out of the depths of the soul, but simply reels
off the contents of a book which he is supposed to have
swallowed in a vision. . . . Ezekiel is narrow-minded,
cramped, without sweep or power, devoid of any creative
imagination (Phantasie), and hence marked by unendurable
pedantry and monotony."[9]

Here we have an interesting test. Meyer likes and understands Mohammed who, though a remarkable man to say
the least, is after all just a man who reacts as one would
expect any normal man to react if he were trying to work
himself into a state of religious conviction. The vagueness,
the mystery, the struggle, the doubt—every religious leader
experiences them, and we all have some idea of what Mohammed went through. He is, so to speak, just another preacher,
though a great one. But not so Joseph Smith! Meyer finds
him, like Ezekiel, crass, literal, unpoetic, devoid of power of
fantasy, unmoved by doubts, unennobled by despairing struggles. Here are men that cannot by any effort be fitted into
Meyer's catalogue of religious thinkers. If the nature of his
prophetic claims placed him completely apart from all the
other religious men of his day, it also disqualified Joseph

Smith for classification with any other type of prophet than that represented by Ezekiel, Christ, and the ancient Apostles. However much he may have resembled other men in other things, when it came to his prophetic calling, Joseph Smith was not a Mohammed struggling to convince himself and find poetic expression; he was not a scholar of divinity seeking to unriddle the scriptures for his less-educated or less-inspired fellows; and certainly he was not just another preacher. *He was a true Prophet of God.*

4

Prophets and Scholars

What is a prophet? On one thing the Jewish and Christian doctors have always seen eye to eye, namely that "Abraham is dead, and the prophets are dead." The prophets being thus disposed of, the word *prophet* has been liberated in our own day for almost unlimited use. Almost any individual of more than ordinary insight, learning, or rhetorical gifts is sure at some time or other to be called a prophet. So loosely has the word come to be used that we must, before proceeding, reach an agreement on a few things that a prophet is not.

The ancient and valuable *Didaché*, which revolutionized the study of church history after its discovery in 1883, gives— among its most valuable contributions to a very obscure field of study—priceless information on the nature of priesthood and prophecy in the early church. On one subject in particular it is clear and specific—the tests for distinguishing between a true and a false prophet, for in those early days there were still prophets, both true and false, in the church. If anyone who claimed to be a prophet attempted to *teach* anything of his skill to another, he was *not* a true prophet, the saints were advised. Prophecy is a direct gift from God; it cannot be conveyed from one man to another; it cannot be transmitted through any courses of instruction. (*Didaché* XI, 11-12.)

Peter, for example, had the certain knowledge that Jesus Christ was the Son of God. Did he get that knowledge from Jesus, his master and teacher? No, he did not. "Blessed art thou, Simon Bar-jona: for flesh and blood hath not revealed it unto thee, but my Father which is in heaven" (Matthew 16:17). Here was Peter taking direct instruction from the mouth of the Lord himself, in the flesh; yet it was not from him but from his Father that Peter got the testimony of Christ. The same held true of all those disciples of the Lord who received a testimony of his divinity. "All that the Father giveth me shall come to me; and him that cometh to me I will in no wise cast out." (John 6:37.) It is the revelation of the Father that brings souls to Christ: "And the Father himself, which hath sent me, hath borne witness of me" (John 5:37). The knowledge of salvation is not transmitted from one man to another horizontally, as it were; it is not passed from one generation to the next as a great earthbound tradition. A *testimony*, that is, the sure knowledge that Jesus is the Christ, the Savior and Redeemer of the world, is received not by horizontal but by vertical descent, or, to use Justin Martyr's expression, it is "a gift that descends from above on holy men at a certain time."[1]

No man who has a testimony is dependent on any other man for that testimony. Everyone must know for himself that Jesus is the Christ. No one is expected to believe the gospel is true because some official or board or synod says it is. At the end of the great King Follett discourse, the Prophet Joseph Smith said, "I don't blame any one for not believing my history; if I had not experienced what I have, I could not believe it myself." And the Lord repeatedly insisted that if anyone would have a witness of him, that witness must come not from him but from his Father. Every man must have his own experience in these things. "No man can say that Jesus is the Lord, but by the Holy Ghost," Paul tells us (1 Corinthians 12:3), and no amount of instruction by other men will suffice. "Without revelation direct from heaven," said Brigham Young, "it is impossible for any person to understand fully the plan of salvation. We often hear it said that the living oracles must be in the Church, in order that the Kingdom of God may be established and prosper on the earth. I will give another version of this sentiment. I say that the living oracles of God, or the Spirit of revelation must be in each and every *individual*, to know the plan of salvation and keep in the path that leads them to the presence of God."[2]

Obviously, then, the prophetic gift, the highest form of revelation, coming directly from above cannot be transmitted through any courses of instruction, however valuable they may be as preparation; it cannot be acquired in any school. In a word, the prophet is not a scholar. As surely as the words of a prophet are written down in books, they become the object of specialist study. Once the true prophet has been duly rejected and passed to his reward, swarms of experts descend upon his words to begin the learned business of exegesis. The words of the dead prophets become the peculiar possession of armies of specially trained and carefully conditioned scholars. In a very old text, Peter is reported as saying in a letter to James regarding the use of his own writings in the church: "They think they are able to interpret my own words better than I can, telling their hearers that they are conveying my very thoughts to them, while the fact is that such things never entered my mind. If they take such outrageous liberties while I am alive, what will they do after I am gone!"[3] Much later, Clement of Alexandria expressed much the same sentiment.[4] You see the point: The scholar and learned divine must necessarily get their knowledge from the written word, and then trouble begins. The prophet, on the other hand, who may well be illiterate, gets his knowledge by direct intercourse with heaven. The orientation of the two is entirely different.

This is well illustrated in the case of the Lord himself. We will recall that he was accused by the learned of blasphemy for claiming tangible contact with the Father in heaven who, he insisted, was not just his symbolic but his real Father. Now the men who opposed Jesus were learned in the scripture: He said, "The Son of man must suffer many things, and be rejected of the elders and chief priests and scribes, and be slain" (Luke 9:22), specifically singling out as his opponents the most learned segment of the society. These men could cite scripture for everything they did or said, and in all things the scripture was their authority. Of Christ, on the other hand, we read: "They were astonished at his doctrine [*didaché*—way of teaching]: for he taught them as one that had authority, and not as the scribes" (Mark 1:22). What he spoke *was* scripture. And the same holds for every true prophet. That fact is admitted by the whole Christian world, which is willing to accept as holy writ any syllable that can be shown to be the genuine utterance of an Apostle, no matter how trivial the matter discussed, as, for example, when Paul asks Timothy to bring him his books and overcoat.

There is much to indicate that the Corinthians were altogether too much taken up with the reputations and opinions of scholars—a weakness which ultimately proved fatal. Paul took them to task for this in the beginning of his first letter to them:

"Where is the wise? where is the scribe? where is the disputer [*syzetetés*—we would say committee-member] of this world . . . ?

"For after that in the wisdom of God the world by wisdom knew not God, it pleased God by the foolishness of preaching to save them that believe.

"The foolishness of God is wiser than men; and the weakness of God is stronger than men.

"For ye see your calling, brethren, how that not many wise men after the flesh, not many mighty, not many noble, are called" (1 Corinthians 1:20-21, 25-26).

And Paul explains that this is done so "that, according as it is written, he that glorieth, let him glory in the Lord," not being beholden to any man or to any human instruction. The attitude of the early church on this subject is well-expressed in a remarkable passage from Clement, one of the oldest fragments of genuine early Christian literature in existence, as it has been preserved for us by Eusebius:

"Those inspired and, one might truly say, divine men, by which I mean the Apostles of Christ, having purified their lives to the highest degree and adorned their minds with every virtue, spoke only the common tongue; but they were emboldened by the possession of a supernatural power, which had been bestowed upon them as a gift by the Savior himself. They neither knew nor made any effort to know anything about the art of persuasion or skill with words as taught in the schools. The only power they ever made use of was the assurance of the Holy Ghost and the miraculous power of Christ operating through them, by which they preached the kingdom of God throughout the world. They gave little thought to writing anything down. What they did they did with the aid of a power beyond that of men. Paul, for example, the most skillful speaker and the best educated man of them all, left nothing in writing but a few extremely short letters; yet he was in a position to utter marvelous things without number, as one having actually been in contact with visions of the third heaven, caught up even to God's paradise, where he was deemed worthy to hear unutterable things. But the other disciples of our Savior were not without experience of these things, either: the twelve Apostles, the Seventy disciples, and countless others under their instruction."[5]

From this passage it is perfectly clear that the early church depended wholly on the inspired teaching of living prophets and would have nothing to do with that formal instruction in rhetoric and dialectic which, by the fourth century, had become a "must" for any candidate for the office of bishop.

Of course, God can choose a learned man for a prophet if he wants to, but we are told in no uncertain terms that such is not the type of man he prefers. To the pagan Celsus, who made merry over the poor education and bad grammar of the Apostles, Origen replied that the obviously defective education of the prophets was a most powerful argument in their favor, for if they had acquired the learning of the schools, then their great gifts of leadership and persuasion might possibly be attributed not to direct instruction from above, but to their years of training.[6]

The prophet recognizes the merit of study; there *is* a spirit in man, Paul tells us, and we know that the spirit of Jesus Christ enlightens every man that comes into the world. The prophet recognizes the scholar for what he is, but the scholar does not return the compliment. He cannot conceive how anyone could possibly acquire knowledge by any method other than his. He cannot believe that any man has experienced anything which he has not experienced. The great Dutch scholar Quispel is at present engaged in showing how this narrow prejudice of the experts has rendered them incapable of comprehending the true nature of the Primitive Church. "I have never seen a vision," says the scholar, "therefore Joseph Smith never had one. I *have* seen dreams, therefore I will allow him that."

The world will not admit that there can be more than one kind of inspiration, but the saints have always known better. The multitude that heard the voice of God speaking at the baptism of Jesus did not on that occasion see the Holy Ghost, as John did. Paul's companions on the road to Damascus had a miraculous manifestation, but it was not the same that Paul had, and they could not lay claim to his calling (Acts 22:9). And while many worshiped Christ as he ascended to heaven before their eyes, "some doubted" (Matthew 28:17). We cannot agree with the Talmudist who says that any opinion expressed by a clever scholar is to be received exactly as if it were the word of God to Moses on Sinai—they are not the same at all. We cannot agree with the fourth-century fathers that the learned man who reads the scripture is conversing with God just as literally as did Adam in the garden. Nor can we agree with the popular academic platitude that since the gospel contains all truth, whatever is taught anywhere, provided only it is true, is the gospel. This is of a piece with that other cliché, that since God is mind, any mental activity whatever is to be regarded as a direct revelation from heaven. All knowledge does come, as Brigham Young assures us, by a kind of revelation, but the idea that all things are equally holy, provided only they are true, is a cheap and easy fallacy that would be the ruin of any science or discipline. Physics and chemistry become meaningful only when facts are presented in a definite order and with a definite priority of importance—otherwise everything is chaos. So it is with the gospel: "Woe unto you, scribes and Pharisees, hypocrites," cried the Lord, addressing the scholars on this very theme. Nothing is unimportant, he tells them, but some things must come first: "These ought ye to have done, and not leave the other undone"—but he calls them "blind guides," specifically because they "strain at a gnat and swallow a camel" (Matthew 23:23-24). The man who makes his own mental processes the equivalent of revelation from heaven is straining at a very little gnat, while he swallows a camel.

In closing let us return to Paul, by far the best-educated, Clement assures us, of all the disciples of Christ. "But I certify you, brethren, that the gospel which was preached of me is not after man. For I neither received it of man, *neither was I taught it,* but by the revelation of Jesus Christ" (Galatians 1:11-12; italics added). Compared with such knowledge, he says, "I count all things but loss for the excellency of the knowledge of Christ Jesus my Lord: for whom I have suffered the loss of all things, and do count them but dung, that I may win Christ" (Philippians 3:8). That is indeed knowledge worth having, and it is to be had only by revelation. It is our happy duty to announce that since the restoration of the gospel such revelation is again available to mankind, provided they heed the words of the prophets, and do not regard their own discoveries and conclusions as the end of knowledge.

5

Prophets and Philosophers

A top-ranking savant from the East recently made the observation to this speaker, that the unique thing about Mormonism is that it is a *nonspeculative* religion in a world of purely speculative religions. That remarkable characteristic establishes at once the identity or kinship of The Church of Jesus Christ of Latter-day Saints with the original, primitive Christian church, which in ancient times also had the unique distinction of being a nonspeculative religion in a world completely "sold" on philosophy.

During the course of these discussions, we have touched lightly, if often, on the subject of philosophy. It is a theme with which we are not competent to deal, but what we can do is to indicate the attitude of the early Christians to the philosophers. This is a very significant thing in any consideration of the gift of prophecy, for the early Christian Apologists were fond of contrasting the certainty and concreteness of their revealed prophetic religion with the vagueness and disunity of the philosophers; that was one of their favorite talking points, as we have indicated before. So deeply rooted in the Christian teaching was the complete antithesis between philosophy and true religion that, to quote Gilson, "even in the twelfth and thirteenth centuries, the terms *philosophi* and *sancti* signified directly the opposition between the views of the world elaborated by men devoid of the illumination of the faith and those of the Fathers of the church speaking in the name of Christian revelation."[1] That is, in

Christian traditions, philosophy is the opposite of revelation. But to avoid the charge of philosophizing, speaking in
the name of revelation is not enough: one must speak *by*
revelation, and this the Fathers could not do.

One of the most arresting and convincing stories that has
come down to us from the earliest days of the Christian
church is the account of the conversion of Clement in the
first part of the *Clementine Recognitions*. The so-called
Tübingen School regarded this text as the most valuable single
record of life in the primitive church outside the New Testament itself. Its value has been raised or lowered by various
schools and scholars in proportion as the text has confirmed
or weakened the position of their various churches. The piece
is devoid of any trace of exaggeration or partisan pleading.
Indeed, Rufinus of Aquileia, who translated it into Latin at
the end of the fourth century, said that it was full of queer
and puzzling things that no one in the church of his day
understood, and that it preached doctrines, especially concerning the nature of God, which were totally strange to the
church of Rufinus' day. [2] This is very strong evidence that we
have here a genuine old Christian text, for this was not the
sort of thing that anybody would forge, and numerous papy-
rus fragments discovered in the last fifty years fully bear out
the picture that Clement has given us in the first part of the
Recognitions. If the least be said for it, the story is Christian
and very early Christian. It merits its place in the first volume of the *Patrologia*. Quite recently R. M. Grant has
described the *Clementine Recognitions* as "a favorite piece of
'Sunday afternoon literature'" among the orthodox church
members of the second century. [3]

Clement tells us that he was a very serious-minded child,
perplexing himself at an early age about the great questions
of life: whether he would live after death; whether he existed
before his birth; whether, as he puts it, the immensity of
time had ever been for him just a vast oblivion and silence in
which he never was and, hereafter, never would be (put in

those terms, incidentally, the question is a very moving one). "But this also was being ever turned over in my mind," he writes, "when was this universe (*mundus*) made? Or, what was there before it existed? Or, has it really always existed? For it seemed certain, that if it was created it must surely in time be dissolved again, and if it was to pass away, what would be then? Unless only complete oblivion and silence should ensue, there would have to be something else totally beyond the present comprehension of the human mind." Clement was no fool. "Therefore," he said, "since I was from my earliest youth engaged in such searchings of the mind, eager to learn something, I attended the schools of the philosophers,"—they being the people who are supposed to answer such questions. In an earlier talk we told what Clement found there: "Nothing at all," in his own words, "but an endless asserting and refuting of opinions (*dogmatum*)—formal disputations, artfully constructed syllogisms, and subtle conclusions. And whenever the argument in favor of the soul's immortality won the day, I congratulated myself; but whenever it was maintained that the soul was mortal, I left the room with a heavy heart. But neither side ever brought forth a proof that really convinced me, because the statements and definitions of things passed as true or false not from the actual nature of things or the real truth, but always according to the skill and cleverness of the people putting them forth."[4]

So the philosophers did not satisfy him, but they did scare him: "According to the conclusions (*sententias*) of some of the philosophers," he writes, "I would be put into the fiery stream of Pyriphlegethon or into Tartarus (the fiery lake), to suffer, like Sisyphus or Tityus or Ixion or Tantalus, eternal torments in hell (*in inferno*)."[5] This, he says, worried him greatly, not because he was convinced that it was true, but because the probability of the thing constantly rankled. It is interesting here to note in passing that this boy was kept in line by some of his teachers by threats of hellfire; the fiery

inferno (the word Rufinus actually uses) appears here as doctrine of the pagan schools before Christianity was heard of
in Rome.

   In this unhappy state of doubt and perplexity, Clement
began to pay some attention to growing rumors of strange
happenings in far away Judaea, and then one day he happened on a Christian street meeting being held by the local
branch in Rome: "There was a man standing in a very much
frequented part of the town," as he tells it, "calling out to the
people and saying: 'Hear me, Romans, the Son of God is in
the Judaean country, promising eternal life to all who will
hear him, provided they will do certain things conformant to
the will of Him who sent him, namely God the father. . . .'
Now this man who was telling these things to the populace,
was an easterner, a Jew by nationality, whose name was
Barnabas. He declared that he was one of that man's disciples, and had been sent out by him for the express purpose
of making these things known to any who wanted them.
When I heard that much, I decided to stop and join the
crowd that was listening to him, to hear what he had to say.
For I could see right off that there was nothing of the dialectical art in the man, but that he spoke simply and without
the slightest trace of affectation *fucus*, reporting the things
he had heard from the Son of God, or what he had seen. He
did not support his assertions with skill of argument, but
called up out of the people who were standing about many
witnesses to the words and miracles which he was reporting.
   "Well, the people began to give a favorable hearing to
things spoken in such sincerity and to receive the simple sermon. But there were those present who seemed to be educated men or philosophers who began to laugh at the man
and check him, throwing out the snares of syllogistic arguments like irresistible weapons against him. But he, unper-
turbed and acting as if he considered their sharp attacks as
not worth noticing, didn't even bother to give them an answer,
but went right on fearlessly giving the discourse he had

promised." But there was one clever fellow in the crowd who kept interrupting with the same question over and over again: "Why was a gnat, tiny thing that it is, created with six feet and wings to the bargain, while an enormous elephant has no wings and only four legs?" This man made so much noise that Barnabas finally addressed him: "We come here under a mandate of Him who sent us to announce to you his marvellous words and deeds. And in support of what we say we do not produce carefully worked out arguments, but call up witnesses from among your own number."

Note that this is a sort of testimony meeting: not only do the Apostles and disciples of Christ bear witness to what they have seen and heard, but the simple members of the branch are called upon to do the same. They are all witnesses, not arguers. This impressed and amazed Clement, for this was not the sort of thing they did in the schools. "I recognize standing right here in the crowd," Barnabas continued, according to Clement, "quite a number whom I remember to have heard what we have heard and to have seen what we have seen. Now it is entirely in your power to receive or reject our message. But we cannot keep back those things which we know will be for your good, for if we are silent, the condemnation will be ours, but if we speak and you don't receive it, the loss will be yours. As for your ridiculous propositions, we could answer them easily enough, and we would if you were asking them in a sincere desire to know the truth—I mean all that stuff about the difference between elephants and fleas."

In reply to this, all the smart boys guffawed and yelled, trying to drown Barnabas out and make him stop talking, calling him a crazy barbarian, for he spoke with an accent. At that point, Clement himself, animated by that zeal for fair play which characterizes all the first part of the *Clementine Recognitions* but soon disappears from Christian writing, leaped into the melee and addressed the crowd with great boldness: "Most rightly, I said, has the omnipotent

God hidden his will from you, knowing you to be unworthy from the first—as should be clear to any thinking person from your present behavior. For when you see preachers of the will of God coming to you, if their speech displays no familiarity with the grammatic art, but instead they tell you God's commands in simple unpolished phrases, so that anyone who hears them can follow and understand what they say, you make fun of these ministers and messengers of your salvation, forgetting . . . that a knowledge of the truth may be found among rustics and barbarians; yet you won't accept it unless it comes by one of your town and in your vernacular; and that is proof enough that you are not friends of truth and philosophers [seekers after wisdom] at all, but the dupes of men with big mouths, babblers yourselves, who believe that truth must dwell not in simple words but in shrewd and clever language." This sort of talk on Clement's part led to a near riot, and he and Barnabas had a narrow escape.[6]

It appears here that at this early day, Christianity and philosophy are on opposite sides of the fence, as Gilson indicated—but it was not to be so for long. S. V. McCasland has recently noted that "the older unspeculative conception of the creation of man in the image of God" was the original Christian doctrine, as witnessed "by unambiguous passages in the Clementine Homilies," which show us how early that doctrine fell into disrepute.[7] Still more recently, J. Morris has written, "In the half-century from 130 to 180 a succession of university teachers published elaborate and elegant Apologiae for Christianity [the very type of thing, incidentally, that Clement had condemned in the pagans], which tended to emphasize the Holy Spirit or Logos." He notes that at that time Theophilus of Antioch "altogether avoided mentioning that God had a son [just as still earlier Churchmen avoided mentioning that he has a body], let alone that a Crucifixion was involved."[8] "With perfect impunity and the greatest of ease they proceeded to do violence to the

scriptures," writes Eusebius of the period, "blithely disregard-
ing the original teaching. . . . They never consulted the scriptures, but busily worked out elaborate structures of syllogisms. . . . They deserted the holy scripture for Euclid,
Aristotle, and Theophrastus. . . . They cultivated the arts of
the unbelievers and took to hair-splitting discussions about
the once simple faith of the Holy Writ."[9] They became imitators of Seneca, whose specialty, as Cochrane describes it,
was "clothing in scintillating phrases the commonplaces of a
shallow optimism, the beautiful day-dream of human perfect-
ability and brotherhood under the Caesars"[10]—later, we might
add, under the imperial church.

Justin Martyr, though he recognized the superiority of
prophecy to philosophy, never gave up his philosopher's garb,
of which he was very proud, and went all out to show that
Plato, after all, taught no differently than Moses and Christ,
that Heraclitus taught the same morality as Moses, and even
that Plato's areté is nothing other than the Holy Ghost![11]

At the same time, Irenaeus accused the Gnostics of drag-
ging philosophy into the church. Their works, he says, "read
like a patchwork made up from the philosophers as all those
call themselves who do not know the true God, piecing
together a doctrine from philosophical shreds and tatters with
high-sounding eloquence." All the attributes of God, he notes,
they derive from the philosophers, "and they hold forth with
hairsplitting subtlety on philosophical questions, introducing, as it were, Aristotle into the faith."[12]

"O miserable Aristotle!" cried Tertullian shortly after,
"who taught them [the Christians] dialectic, the art of proving and disproving, the cunning turn of sentences, forced
conjectures, tough arguments, contrary even to itself."[13] All
heresies are suborned by philosophy, he says: from the philosophers they get the idea that the flesh is not resurrected—
a thing on which all philosophers agree; hence, too, they get
the doctrine of the baseness of matter and such set questions
as whence is evil and why?—old chestnuts in the schools.

Paul knew philosophy at Athens, Tertullian observes, and was not impressed by it. "What have Athens and Jerusalem in common?" he asks in a famous passage. "What the Academy and the Church?"

But by the next century, Minucius Felix sees no difference between the teaching of the prophets and those of the philosophers and concludes "either that the Christians are now philosophers, or that the ancient philosophers were already Christians."[14] And Clement of Alexandria sees in philosophy God's preparation of the human race for the gospel: "Philosophy prepares the work that Christ completes."[15] Yet that work having been consummated, it is not philosophy but the gospel that bows out of the picture, for Clement himself never mentions the millennium, softpedals the second coming of Christ, and allegorizes the resurrection. In a new but already famous book on Clement of Alexandria, Walter Voelker writes: "In Clement of Alexandria, Stoic, Platonist, Mystic, etc., constantly shove against and overlap on each other and entangle themselves often in a narrow compass into a completely inextricable mess (Knäuel)."[16] Origen was just as bad, completely rejecting the old faith, as Schmidt notes, in favor of philosophy. "In his way of life," wrote Porphyry of Origen, "he lived like a Christian, which was misleading, since in actual fact and in his teachings about God he was a thoroughgoing Hellenist."[17] It was he who introduced logic and dialectic into the church—those two obsessions of declining antiquity of which the early church had so prided itself of being free. It was he, we will recall, who told the pagan Celsus that all Christians would do nothing but study philosophy if they did not have to take time off to earn a living. Step by step we can trace the infiltration of philosophy into the church, but that is another story.

Let us summarize briefly some of the objections of the early Christians to philosophy (the same objections, incidentally, which scientists today make to philosophy):

(1) The philosophers disagree constantly among themselves. "It is impossible to learn anything true concerning religion from your teachers," says Justin, "who by their mutual disagreement have furnished you with sufficient proof of their own ignorance."[18] One of the very earliest Christian writers, Tatian, says, "Tear yourself away from the solemn conventions of these self-styled philosophers who do not agree among themselves."[19] Even the pagan Caecilius admits this in the *Octavius* of Minucius Felix, "One is confused by the numerous and reputable sects of philosophy that only show how far beyond *human mediocrity* the exploration of divine things really is."[20]

(2) This meant that there was no reliable norm in philosophy to which all men could be held. Reason should indeed qualify for the position but has a fatal weakness: "O what a powerful reasoner self-interest is!" says Tertullian.[21] And modern psychology has shown us, as the study of literature and historiography have long ago, that when men have honestly thought themselves free of all prejudice, are perfectly detached and impersonal in their judgments and impartial in their conclusions, all their thinking has actually been not merely colored but predetermined by their conditioning. They cannot escape that.

(3) What they really deal with is not evidence but opinion. "They announce a doctrine as truth the moment it pops into their heads," says Tatian,[22] and though the statement seems exaggerated, yet a brief consideration will show that if the great maxims of philosophy *can* be proved, they certainly never *have* been: *Panta Rhei* (all things flow), *Die Welt Ist Meine Vorstellung*, Man is the measure of all things, *Cogito ergo sum*, etc. Did the men who expounded these famous doctrines even begin to exhaust the evidence necessary to prove them? On what do they rest? In the end, on their proclaimer's personal mental equipment!

(4) Hence, another constant objection to the philosophers, as Tatian states it: "They are full of mutual hatred and jealousy and ambition." A large literature has descended to us from antiquity on this theme. It is a case of man versus man. Recall Clement's experience in the schools: They would argue endlessly back and forth, he says, and the prize went not to the truth but to the man who was able to wear his opponent down. The ball was knocked back and forth, back and forth, and the game ended when one of the players had a lapse of memory, or got tired or rattled and was not able to come back with a quick answer. But that, as the early Christians observed, has nothing to do with truth. This disdain for evidence and passion for method guaranteed that the philosophers never got anywhere. Terrence and Galbunugus, we are told, argued for fourteen days and nights on whether *ego* has a vocative case. For every question there is an answer, the Arabs say, and if one cannot find the answer at the moment, he can always think of it later. And so the squirrel cage goes round and round. When Erasmus was being shown through the Sorbonne, his guide took him into a great hall and announced in an awed voice: "In this chamber the doctors of philosophy have disputed for four hundred years," to which Erasmus replied, "And what have they ever settled?"

(5) A remarkable aspect of the undue prominence of personalities in what should be the impersonal search for truth is the wonderful way in which philosophers of every age, more than any other humans, display an irresistible urge to form themselves into schools. The fluidity of the open mind is a rare and momentary thing in the history of thought. As Rashdall says of the great philosophical movement of the twelfth and thirteenth centuries: "The wild outburst of intellectual ardor cooled very rapidly as it crystallized into the institutional machinery of the university system."[23] A John Dewey denouncing the tyranny of schools of thought promptly becomes a nucleus around which yet another school of thought—and a very stiff and orthodox one—crystallizes.

More than any other profession, philosophers subscribe themselves in schools which they defend with passion and to which they subject themselves with unquestioned submission. Socrates made sly fun of the followers of some of his great Sophist friends for this, for this whole-souled worship of individuals and this alignment in schools is the last thing that a really open mind would ever be guilty of.

(6) But the main objection of the early Christians to the philosophers was simply that they were superfluous. "Since the word Himself has come down from heaven to us," says Clement of Alexandria, "there is no point in our traveling far and wide to attend the schools of men any more, or in our going to Athens or somewhere else in Greece or Ionia to study. . . . There is nothing which the Word Himself has not now taught us, . . . answering the very questions that the philosophers have sought to answer all these years."[24] "Now either all these men . . . knew the truth or else they did not," says Irenaeus, speaking of the philosophers. "If they did, then the Savior's descent to the earth was superfluous; . . . if they did not, why do you . . . go to them for supernatural knowledge, since they do not know God?"[25] And Tertullian: "They indeed by a lucky chance might sometimes stumble on the truth, as men groping in the dark may accidentally hit upon the right path; but the Christian, who enjoys a revelation from heaven, is inexcusable if he commits himself to such blind and unreliable guidance."[26] In other words, whatever merit philosophy might have in the search for God has been superseded by a revelation from heaven. One may not choose to agree with that verdict, but such certainly was the teaching of the early Christians. For them, the true religion of Jesus Christ could only be a *non*speculative religion; and what appears at first sight as an astonishing defect in the restored church is actually a wonderful vindication of its prophets.

6

Prophets and Creeds

For a long time the world refused to look upon Mormons as Christians. Indeed most people still think of them as a *tertium quid*, unique and isolated from all other creatures. There is some justice in this viewpoint if one defines a Christian as one who subscribes to the creeds of Christendom, but the dictionary gives no such definition: for it, a Christian is simply one who believes in Christ, with nothing said about adherence to formulae describing his nature devised three hundred years after his death. The Latter-day Saints do *not* accept the ecumenical creeds because they were not given by the power of revelation but worked out by committees of experts. As we noted last week, the early church could not make too much of the inability of philosophers to discover the nature of God, yet the first and greatest of the councils, that of Nicaea, may be described without exaggeration as a philosopher's field day. Let us consider briefly a few steps that led to the formulation of the Nicene Creed.

It all began when Bishop Alexander of Alexandria "one day in a meeting of his presbyters and the rest of the clergy under him, theologized in a rather showy way (*philtimoteron*) on the subject of the Holy Trinity, *philosophizing* to the effect that in a triad was really a monad. Arius, one of the presbyters under his authority and a man not unskilled in *dialectic give and take*, . . . took the extreme opposite position just to show how much smarter he was (out of *philoneikias*) . . . and replied bitingly to the things the Bishop had said." Socrates, the historian, concludes a summary of

Arius' speech on this occasion by saying, "Constructing his *syllogism* by this novel reasoning, he attracted everybody's attention, and with a small spark lit a mighty blaze."[1] Now isn't this a perfect illustration of those very vices and follies for which the original Christians condemned philosophy? The bishop, philosophizing in a showy way, not seeking truth but just being smart, using technical terms—triad and monad—unknown to the scripture, is refuted by a clergy-man carefully trained in that dialectic art which the early Fathers so abhorred; he too, animated not by love of truth but by a desire to outshine the bishop—such is the spirit in which the great investigation begins.

The "mighty blaze" mentioned by Socrates divided the Christian world into warring factions, and the Emperor Constantine wrote a strong letter to the heads of both par-ties. In this letter he says among other things, "These and such like technical questions . . . are simply a sort of parlor game (*ereschalia*) for the passing of idle time, and albeit they may be justified as providing a kind of training for the wits, they are best kept locked and confined in your own minds, and not lightly aired in public places nor foolishly permitted to reach the ears of the masses. For just how many people are there who can understand such advanced and extremely puzzling matters, or have any clear idea what they are about, or give a correct explanation of them? And even if someone should suppose that he could understand it easily, how many of the common people will he be able to persuade? Or who would be able to carry on a disputation in the subtleties of such technical questions without running an appalling risk? Therefore a great outpouring of words in such matters should be prohibited, lest the problem presently carry us beyond the depths of our own limited understanding, or we go beyond the limited training of those who listen to our teachings, who can no longer understand what is said, and out of this dou-ble defect the whole society necessarily fall into blasphemy or schism. While you wrangle with one another over minor, nay, utterly trivial matters, it is not right that God's numerous people should be led by your minds; in view of your disunity, such a thing is utterly wrong, absolutely improper."[2] What a lecture to the leaders of the Church! And these were the men who were to make the creeds.

In the end, the emperor had to summon, as we all know, the great Council of Nicaea. While the gathering body of churchmen was waiting for the latecomers to arrive, some interesting preliminary discussions were held. These illustrate perfectly the spirit of the whole thing. We are told that a large number of laymen were there, experts in the art of dialectic, entering enthusiastically into the discussions on every side. "Meanwhile, not long before the general assembly was to take place, certain dialecticians were addressing the multitude and showing off in controversy. Great crowds being attracted by the pleasure of hearing them, one of the confessors, a layman with a clear head, stood up and rebuked the dialecticians and said to them that Christ and the Apostles did not give to us the dialectical art nor empty tricks, but straightforward knowledge preserved by faith and good works. When he said this, all those present were flabbergasted, and then agreed. And the dialecticians, hearing straight talk, became a good deal more sober and contained. Thus was abated the uproar which dialectic had stirred up."[3] There were still clear heads in the church, but they did not belong to the men who were about to make the creed. They are represented here by an aged layman, a martyr—that is, one who had refused to deny the faith in persecution—a link with the real old church, who here appears among the squabbling doctors as a "nine-days' wonder" when he reminds them how far from the track of Christ and the Apostles they have come. They were abashed for the time, but not repentant.

Let us skip to the closing speech of the mightiest of councils. It was delivered, fittingly, by the emperor, "who was first to bear witness to the correctness of the creed," according to Eusebius in a letter to his own flock, " . . . and he urged everyone to come to the same opinion and sign the statement of dogmas and to agree with each other by signing a statement to which but a single term had been added—the word, *homoousion*." The emperor then proceeded to explain with much technical language that word (which had been agreed on in committee) and the final verdict that the thing was really incomprehensible. "So in such a manner," Eusebius concludes, "our most wise and most devout (*eusebes*, blessed) Emperor *philosophized*; and the Bishops by way of explaining the *homoousios* prepared the following statement."[4]

In the statement that follows occurs an interesting admission: "We are well aware that the Bishops and writers of ancient times when discussing the theology of the Father and the Son never used the word *homoousios*." To allay the doubts of his flock Eusebius hastens to assure them that "the faith here promulgated . . . we all agreed upon, not without careful examination and according to opinions presented and agreed upon in carefully stated *logismoi*, and in the presence of the most devout Emperor." In other words, the committee had worked hard. All the trouble has been caused, according to this document "by the use of certain expressions not found in the Scripture. . . . Since the divinely inspired Scriptures never use such terms as 'out of nothing,' or 'that existed which at one time did not exist,' and such like terms; for it did not seem proper (*eulogon*) to say and teach such things, . . . never in times before have we thought it proper to use these terms."[5] The letter then proceeds to authorize the use of those very terms which it acknowledges to be unknown to the early Christians. Had God so changed his nature that he needed new terms to describe that nature? We left the word *logismoi* untranslated above, because Paul uses the very same word in 2 Corinthians 10:4-5 when he says that revealed knowledge, the *Gnosis*, invalidates or confounds all *logismoi*, that is, calculations of men. Now Eusebius takes comfort in the thought that the Nicene Creed is made up of carefully worded *logismoi*. You see how the foundations of doctrine had shifted from prophetic revelation to human reason. Latter-day Saints would regard such a change as fatal to the church, and in this they are in good company. For though conventional church histories pass over it in complete silence, the fact is that the early ecumenical councils of the church were viewed by the leading churchmen of the time and the general public alike as a most grave and alarming symptom. Let some of these men explain it in their own words.

Athanasius, one of the star performers at Nicaea, viewed with alarm the councils that immediately followed that one: "What is left to the Catholic church to teach of salvation if now they make investigations into the faith, and set up a present-day authority to give out official interpretations of what has already been said? . . . And why do the so-called clergy dash back and forth trying to find out how they should believe about our Lord Jesus Christ? If they had been believing all along they couldn't possibly be searching now for something they don't have!" Everyone is laughing at the Christian leaders, Athanasius says, and is saying, "These Christians don't know what to think of Christ!" which of course weakens their authority.[6] "What is the use of all these synods?" he asks. "In vain do they dash hither and yon under the pretext that synods are necessary to settle important matters of doctrine, for the Holy Scriptures are sufficient for all that."[7] (Note where Athanasius finds the court of last appeal—not in any episcopal see, but simply in the scripture.) "We contradict those who were before us, depart from the traditions of our fathers, and think we must hold a synod. Then we are seized by misgivings, lest if we simply come together and agree our diligence will be wasted; so we decide that the synod ought to be divided into two groups, so we can vote; . . . and so we render ineffective what was done at Nicaea under pretext of working for greater simplicity."[8] Could one ask for a better description of the strangely modern state of mind in which the early creeds of Christendom were hammered out—the zeal of the busy, self-important committeemen; the fussy, fuzzy preoccupation with procedure and busywork; the urge to hold meetings come what may? "All these synods are unnecessary," Athanasius repeats, "and they are unnecessary because we have the Scripture; and if the Scripture is a subject of disagreement in the synods, then we have the writings of the Fathers. The men at Nicaea were not unmindful of this. . . . As for these other synods, they simply don't make sense, and they never get anywhere."[9] And again: "Who can call such people Christians, or how can we speak of faith among men who have neither reason nor writings that aren't changing all the time, but to suit every circumstance are being everlastingly altered and reversed?"[10]

We turn next to Athanasius' great western contemporary St. Hilary: "It is a thing equally deplorable and dangerous," he writes in a famous passage, "that there are as many creeds as opinions among men, as many doctrines as inclinations, and as many sources of blasphemy as there are faults among us; because we make creeds arbitrarily, and explain them arbitrarily. . . . The *homoousion* is rejected, and received, and explained away by successive synods. . . . Every year, nay every month, we make new creeds to describe invisible mysteries. We repent of what we have done, we defend those who change their minds, we anathematize those whom we defended. We condemn either the doctrine of others in ourselves, or our own in that of others; and, reciprocally tearing one another to pieces, we have been the cause of each other's ruin."[11] And later to the emperor: "The faith has been corrupted—is reformation possible? The faith is sought after as if it were something not in our possession. The faith has to be written down, as if it were not in our hearts. Having been reborn by faith, we are now being taught the faith just as if our rebirth had been without faith. We learn about Christ *after* we have been baptized, as if there could be any baptism at all without a knowledge of Christ."[12] Here the synods and creeds are depicted as a declaration of bankruptcy, a clear indication that the faith is lost, a frantic attempt to fill a vacuum. And the filling was to be done with words, the endless talk of the philosophers.

Speaking of an episode of the Council of Nicaea, the historian Sozomen wrote, "It would be hard to say which is the more miraculous, to make a stone speak or to make a philosopher stop speaking."[13] But let us hear Hilary: "Since the whole argument is about *words,* and since the whole controversy has to do with the subject of innovation [i.e., the introduction of philosophical terms not found in the scripture], and since the occasion of the discussion is the presence of certain ambiguities, and since the dispute is about authority, and since we are quarreling about technical questions, and since our problem is to reach a consensus, and since each side is beginning to be anathema to the other, it would seem that hardly anybody belongs to Christ (or is on Christ's side) any more. We are blown about by winds of doctrine, and as we teach we only become more upset, and the more we are taught, the more we go astray."[14] What a commentary on Nicaea! "We avoid believing that of Christ which *He* told us to believe, so that we might establish a treacherous unity in the false name of peace, and we rebel with new definitions of God against what we falsely call innovations, and in the name of the Scriptures we deceitfully cite things that are not in the Scriptures: changeful, prodigal, impious, changing established things, abolishing accepted doctrine, presuming irreligious things."[15] Here Hilary is not denouncing heretics and separatists. Like Athanasius, Eusebius, Basil, Chrysostom, Akakius, Eleusius, Phoebadius, and a host of lesser lights, he is depicting not the folly of the few, but, as he puts it, "the faith of our miserable age. . . . Last year's faith," he asks, "what is the changeful stuff that it contains? First it silenced the *homoousion,* then it preached it, then it excused it, then it condemned it. And where does that sort of thing lead to? To this, that neither we nor our predecessors were in a position to be sure of preserving any sacred thing intact."[16] When men are left to their own resources, without the guidance of living prophets, even the great tradition will not preserve the true faith, for, as Hilary has just noted, men are not able of themselves to preserve that tradition.

We have quoted a few statements—by no means all the pertinent ones—of two of the most respected voices in Christendom, men who were present in person at the great councils of the fourth century in which the Christian creeds as we now have them received their definitive form. How these men miss the voice of the prophets! The fact that the church should hold councils to decide on basic doctrines centuries after Christ and the Apostles are supposed to have given these doctrines to the world greatly disturbs not only them but also, as they repeatedly tell us, the general membership of the church as well. The fact that those councils carry on their deliberations after the manner and in the artificial language of the schools of philosophy distresses them even more. Throughout the Middle Ages the ablest men labored mightily to comprehend and restate in intelligible terms those ever-illusive definitions of God, school succeeding school exactly as in the fourth century. The Reformation, striving to correct administrative abuses and restate moral principles, left the basic doctrines untouched, and to this day the whole Christian world, from the cool recesses of high-church Gothic to the torrid canvas of the revivalist, owes allegiance to the angry and perplexed churchmen of the fourth century. The long centuries have shown, and have shown exhaustively, that "man cannot by searching find out God." Unless dictated by God himself through revelation, any creed must necessarily be a compromise, to establish, as Hilary puts it, a treacherous unity in the false name of peace, and at the price of deliberately sacrificing truth. In the long history of the creeds, time has strikingly vindicated the prophets. If we are to have a creed, the living voice of prophecy alone can prescribe it, and in this, The Church of Jesus Christ of Latter-day Saints stands alone.

7

The Prophets and the Search for God

Through the long centuries, the "search for God" has been the program of the Christian churches. "The books have gone on piling up ever since St. John wrote his Gospel and still there is no end in sight," writes Rufus M. Jones of works on the life of Jesus; "hardly fewer are the books that undertake to tell us about the reality and the nature of God. They are almost as numerous as 'the leaves that strow the brooks in Vallombrosa. . . .' There is certainly no slackening of interest in this supreme quest."[1] In every sect and every age, the theologians describe themselves as engaged in this mighty quest, and repeatedly and increasingly the Latter-day Saints are held to be opinionated and narrow because they do not join in the search. Why should they? Consider the position of the early Christians on this subject. But first, perhaps, we should explain our practice in these talks of referring everything back to those early Christians as described in the Bible, the nine so-called apostolic fathers and the five early Apologists. We make no attempt at present to argue out the position of The Church of Jesus Christ of Latter-day Saints. Here we are simply indicating briefly, as we must, that for better or for worse, the Mormons consistently find themselves in the company of the ancient saints and, accordingly, far removed from the ways of conventional Christians. That does not necessarily prove that the Mormons are *right* on every or any issue, but it more than implies that if the ancient Christians were on the right track, so are the

Mormons. It is an historical, not a theological or philosophical, vindication of our prophets. It is merely one approach to the problem of the divine authenticity of the restored church, but it is an important one.

Take, for instance, this matter of the search for God. What did the early church think about it? For an answer we very properly go back to Justin, first and greatest of the early Apologists. In the famous dialogue with Trypho, one of the most valuable and often quoted of all Christian writings, Justin tells about his first conversation with a Christian. At the time, as he describes it, Justin himself was a professional philosopher who had never heard the gospel. The Christian, a venerable old man whom he met while out walking, asked Justin, "Do not the philosophers spend all their time talking about God? And don't all their investigations deal with the subject of his single rule and providence? Or is it not the proper business of philosophy to engage in the systematic search for God?" To all this, Justin, a philosopher and a pagan, be it remembered, unhesitatingly answers, "Yes."[2] So, you see, the search for God is *not* a peculiarly Christian thing. In fact, it is not Christian at all! Was Peter's confession the reflection of a man feeling his way forward bit by bit out of the dark? Was Paul's testimony the guarded utterance of a man speculating on the possible existence and nature of God? When Stephen was stoned, was his consolation that there might be a something somewhere? Did the Lord take Peter, James, and John up onto the mountain of the Transfiguration with him to speculate on the probable existence of an indefinable essence that might be called God? Did the resurrected Lord instruct the Apostles for forty days in syllogistic exercises to prove his existence?

The thought that the Apostles might be searching for God is simply laughable. Yet that was one of the first danger signals to appear in the church—the predicted activity of those intellectuals who would be "ever seeking and never coming to a knowledge of the truth." Already, at the end of the first century, Ignatius of Antioch writes to the Trallians: "There are some Christ-betrayers, bearing about the name of Christ in deceit, and corrupting the word of the Gospel. . . . They do not believe in his resurrection. They introduce God as being unknown."[3] And to the Smyrnaens he says: "Do ye, therefore, mark those who preach other doctrines, how they affirm that the Father of Christ cannot be known."[4] The great crime of the heretics in general, according to the *Apostolic Constitutions*, is "that they blaspheme God by saying that he is unknowable and not the Father of Christ . . . but is indescribable, unutterable, unnamable, self-begotten. We, the sons of God [it is supposed to be the Apostles speaking] declare that there is one God alone, the Lord of the law and the prophets, the creator of things that are, the Father of Christ, not self-caused and self-begotten, as the Gnostics say, but everlasting and without beginning, dwelling in inaccessible light. He is not two or three or many, but one eternally, not unknown or unnamed but proclaimed through the Law and the Prophets."[5] Irenaeus' first charge against the Gnostics is that "they say the Father cannot be known."[6]

On the other hand, nothing shocked or scandalized the pagans more than the Christian insistence in knowing God; Celsus is outraged at such presumption, and to his charge, Origen replies that God is indeed unknown—to bad men.[7] The fountain of all error in the world, according to Melito of Sardis, "is that man does not know God, and accordingly adores in his place something that is not God."[8] Hilary reports with dismay that "with the exception of Bishop Elusius and a few others, the greater part of the ten Asian provinces where I now stay are ignorant of the true God."[9] And those ten Asian provinces were the most populous Christian communities in the world. Whether Hilary's own knowledge of God was true or not is not the question—the point is that he feels it extremely important that Christians should know God. The first principle of the law which God has given to all men, says Lactantius, is to know God himself, and not to

know him is the greatest of all faults.[10] We have already
quoted Hilary and Athanasius in these talks as expressing
the feeling that lay like a shadow over the fourth century:
that there is something seriously wrong when Christians take
to looking for God. And we have also noted Tertullian's
remark that it is all right for philosophers to grope around
for answers to the great questions of the universe, but that
such behavior is unpardonable in a Christian, who is supposed to have the answers given to him direct from heaven.

To take as the basic assumption in one's search for God
the premise that God is unsearchable may seem incongru-
ous, yet the two propositions seem always to go together.
The claim that God can never be known, far from discouraging the search for him, seems to whet men's appetites like
nothing else. As surely as a theologian announces with ringing finality that God the Father and the Holy Trinity are
mysteries, even to hint at a solution of which is unspeakable
presumption, he will launch forthwith into deep researches
of his own into the subject, often extending for thousands of
pages. "The great Athanasius himself," wrote Gibbon in a
well-known passage, "has candidly confessed, that whenever
he forced his understanding to meditate on the divinity of
the Logos, his toilsome and unavailing efforts recoiled on
themselves; that the more he thought, the less he compre-
hended; and the more he wrote, the less capable was he of
expressing his thoughts. In every step of the inquiry, we are
compelled to feel and acknowledge the immeasurable dispro-
portion between the size of the object and the capacity of the
human mind."[11] But how many thousands of columns of the
Patrologia does Athanasius fill with his own speculations on
the subject and his ferocious denunciations of those who differ from those laboriously contrived opinions? "God's great-
ness is beyond all comprehension of rational minds and
spirits," says a liturgy attributed to Ignatius.[12] Precisely therein
lies the inescapable necessity for revelation; and precisely

therein lies the irresistible challenge of the problem to the invincible ambition and vanity of the human mind.

Both Origen and Irenaeus make as clear as they possibly can the fact that the human intellect cannot hope even to approach remotely the slightest inkling of an idea of the true nature of God, and each then composes volumes on the nature of God! The same is true of Hilary and Basil, the latter filling several books with determined discourses on the exact nature of God even after he rebuked the Eunomians for "daring to try to comprehend the divine nature, when they cannot comprehend the nature of even the smallest animal."[13] The nature of God is incomprehensible, according to Chrysostom, not only his *ousia* (substance) alone, but his wisdom also is incomprehensible even to the prophets. He is not to be compared even to the supernal virtues or to anything else; it is crime and folly to presume curiously to explore his nature; he is incomprehensible even to the angels, and so forth.[14] So what does Chrysostom do but devote the better part of seventeen volumes of the *Patrologia* to exploring and describing the nature of God! The Scholastic theologians were the worst offenders in this thing, but we will skip them to come down to the present, when Bishop Buchberger, in a new German Catholic *Lexicon of Theology*, declares as the official position of his church that "God cannot be 'seen,' but only known through the intellect. An adequate knowledge of God is impossible for us, since God is incomprehensible (*unbegreiflich*)."[15] Then he launches into a very long and interesting discourse on the various philosophical ways by which one must seek to comprehend God. We cannot in view of this be angry with Mr. J. B. S. Haldane, the great British biologist, when he writes, "It is also noteworthy that the God of Christianity is far more mysterious and self-contradictory than those of other religions," though we believe he might temper the charge if he looked more closely at the vagaries of the Moslem theologians. "Your solution," writes

Mr. Haldane to a worthy opponent who is defending conventional Christian ideas of God, "is to take all these contradictions, or as many as you can, and 'solve' them by the
hypothesis of a being who is at once self-explanatory and
utterly mysterious, out of time but everywhere in space, three
yet one, and so on. No wonder such a being is incomprehensible. It is incomprehensible because it is self-
contradictory."[16]

The churchmen have always insisted that since God is
incomprehensible to the mind, in the end our belief in him
and our knowledge of him rest on faith alone. We can never
know, says Hilary for example, how it was possible for Christ
as God to be born, suffer, die, be resurrected, and shed
tears—such things are totally beyond our comprehension.
Still, we are required to believe that they happened—we must
have faith.[17] "There is no use," says Chrysostom, "knocking
ourselves out [polypragmoneisthai] trying to comprehend these
mysteries, since they are incomprehensible; when God chooses
to reveal, then we know, and it is by faith and not by reason
that we come to know divine things."[18] The Catholic teaching regarding the Trinity today is Haec veritas revelata est
mysterium: it is a revealed truth and a mystery.[19]

Granting that, then, why the everlasting search? Why
the ceaseless quest that at best can only lead us back to what
we believe in the first place? Almost every great intellectual
search for God begins, significantly enough, with an apology for the undertaking. We are told that this investigation
is not being undertaken because the church requires it—
heaven forbid! How could a church claiming to have a true
revealed religion admit for a moment that it was actually
dependent on philosophy for its knowledge of God? No, we
are told that the search along philosophical lines is necessary
because there are unbelievers to be convinced who will not
listen to arguments based on the scriptures alone. It is further explained that even professing believers may derive real
benefit from a discipline by which, according to a famous

formula, the true religion is "rendered more efficacious (*saluberrima*), is nourished, defended, and strengthened."[20] Philosophy is not necessary, you understand, but it is a real help.

One cannot help asking at this point: Does the revealed truth require any such help at all? One of the great hallmarks of truth, as Milton teaches us, is that it can defend itself. It needs no special pleading, let alone battalions of technically trained experts, to render it effective. If men do not accept the gospel as it stands, there is no profit in dressing it up to make it more appetizing. "If they hear not Moses and the prophets," said the Lord, "neither will they be persuaded, though one rose from the dead" (Luke 16:31). The gospel needs no "adorning," to use St. Augustine's word. If it is the supreme truth, it cannot possibly be helped but only harmed by the officious activities and extraneous ornaments of professional pleaders and skillful salesmen. What about the missionaries? you ask. An excellent case in point: in ancient as in modern times, the missionaries of the church have impressed the world before everything by their notorious lack of any special training or talent. To survive in such hands, the gospel must be its own advocate, and it is—it can safely be trusted to delivery by the weak and unprepossessing. Only when men are entirely without pretense, even when that means being without education or polish, can the Holy Ghost speak for himself. That the heathen must be impressed and the believers reassured by the offices of philosophy is an unconvincing argument.

But the commonest defense of the intellectual quest for God is that it was forced on the church as a necessary tool with which to meet the onslaughts of learned pagans—the world had to be met with its own weapons, fire fought with fire. But the early Christians had fought fire with water, not fire. Do not try to meet the world on its own grounds, the Apostolic Fathers had advised the saints; its weapons are not our weapons. The philosophic backfires which later church-men set against heretic and pagan quickly spread and by the fourth century got completely out of hand—a mighty con-flagration, says the historian Socrates, with the Christians carrying the vices of the philosophers to greater extremes than the pagans ever had. To use another figure: when at an early time the intellectual virus threatened the church, cer-tain men took it upon themselves to inoculate the church against it, heedless of the warnings of the Apostolic Fathers that the untried serum would prove fatal—and so it did. The church promptly came down with a first class case of the *morbus scholasticus* which broke all records for virulence, and from which it never recovered.

Let us return to Justin's story with which we began. After Justin has admitted to the old Christian that the main busi-ness of philosophy is the search for God, the old man asks him point-blank: "What do you say God is?" Justin answers again without hesitation: "That which always has the same relationship to things and is always the same in itself, and which is the cause of all other things, that is God." Then the old man asks him how such a being can be known, leading him on with an interesting proposition: "If someone were to tell you," he says, "that there is in India an animal shaped like no other on earth, but of such and such nature, a com-plex and variegated beast, you wouldn't really know what it was like until you had seen it; and what is more you couldn't say anything at all about it unless you had talked with some-body who had seen it." To this Justin agrees. "Well then," says the old Christian, "how can the philosophers think cor-rectly about God, or say anything true about Him, since they don't have any actual knowledge of Him, having at no time either seen or heard?" To this crass bit of early Chris-tian literalism, our pagan Justin is quick to reply: "But my dear old man, God is not to be seen with the eyes, as are other living things, but only to be grasped with the mind, as Plato says, and I believe him." Then he goes on to explain how, according to Plato, God is seen with the mind's eye, "he being the cause of all perceptible things, (but himself) having no color, no shape, no dimension, none of such qualities as may be seen by the eye, but yet is that which exists, as I said, beyond all existence (*ousia, substantia*) unutterable, indescribable, and yet alone beautiful and good, coming as a direct intuition to properly disposed spirits because of their kinship and their desire to see him."[21]

Here surely is a strange state of things! Justin, the unenlightened heathen, defending what were to become strictly orthodox Christian ideas about God against a venerable Christian whose literal-mindedness was to become anathema to the churchmen of a later day! Justin, the pagan schoolman, devoting his life to the search for God while his first Christian friend with amused detachment comments on the obvious futility of such a course. Either Justin's account is confused or else the Christians did an about-face in their thinking about God. That the latter is the case is clearly proved by the behavior of Justin himself. "It is characteristic," wrote Heussi, "that after his conversion he retained the profession and even the costume of the travelling teachers of philosophy [the Sophists], and now as a Christian philosopher, sought to be effective through writing, teaching, and discussion. Thus the charismatic [that is, inspired] 'teachers' of the early Christian period were supplanted by a secular teaching profession."[22] That is what happened. Justin was only one of many who in their own and the following centuries were to come into the church bringing with them as their most precious possession and esteemed contribution the heritage of classic philosophy with its basic program of the search for God.

If the Latter-day Saints have never joined the bemused company, groping for God in the wan half-light of a pagan limbo, it is because they have had prophets to speak to them. God, said Paul to Timothy, "will have all men to be saved, and to come unto the knowledge of the truth" (1 Timothy 2:4). He predicts that the time is coming—and soon—when the church will harbor those who are "ever learning, and never able to come to the knowledge of the truth" (2 Timothy 3:7). These became the exponents of the endless search for God.

8

Prophets and Gnostics

The recent discovery of a complete Gnostic library in Egypt has not so much revived as accelerated the study of the most baffling and portentous episode in church history, the rise of the Gnostics. The latest survey of the whole field, an impressive corroborative work by a number of Dutch scholars, sees in the Gnostic crisis the end of the primitive church and the moment at which "Christianity enters upon a new phase of its history."[1] In this great revolution of the second century, the whole orientation of the church changed completely. What brought this about? It was the ceasing of prophetic voices. The continuing demand in the church for the spiritual gifts, especially the gift of prophecy, gave rise to an army of quacks and fakirs who, though discredited in time, left their mark permanently and conspicuously on the Christian church. These were the Gnostics, so-called.

Paul had prophesied that "whether there be prophecies, they shall fail; whether there be tongues, they shall cease; whether there be knowledge, it shall vanish away" (1 Corinthians 13:8). Here the so-called original text uses the identical word for the failing of prophecies and the vanishing of knowledge, *katargethesontai*, "to be taken out of circulation," "to be made inoperative," used both times in the future indicative. There is no sense of contingency here; the whole statement is simple and emphatic: "Such prophecies as there are shall be stopped; such tongues as there are shall be made to cease (*pausontai*); such gnosis as there is shall be done away with." These gifts were not simply to fade away; they were going to be taken away. They were already weak enough: We have these gifts now only in a limited form, Paul explains in the following verses, and then he makes the significant remark: But for the present time there remain "faith, hope, and love, these three." The colorless "and now" of the King James is not fair to the emphatic *nuni de*, *"but at this time"* of the "original," and while the "abideth" of our English Bible emphasizes the quality of lasting and reliable firmness the original *menei* does not mean "to be firm" at all, but simply to stay behind. The emphatic "these three" that remain is in obvious contrast to the three that are going to be taken away, namely, the gift of prophecy, the gift of tongues, and the *gnosis*—the greatest gift of all.

Gnosis means the act of knowing, and in some contexts it can be translated simply as "knowledge." But not when Paul uses it! His frequent use of the word leaves us in no doubt as to what it conveyed to the early Christians. For them it was exactly what we would translate as "a testimony of the gospel." "But I think any price is worth paying for the supreme value of the *gnosis* of Christ Jesus my Lord," writes Paul to the Philippians (3:8), "for which I have sacrificed everything, counting all but dung in comparison with acquiring Christ as my fortune." How often we have heard such expressions as that—"I would not exchange my testimony of the gospel of Jesus Christ for all the wealth in the world!" "God . . . hath shined in our hearts, in proportion to the illumination of the *gnosis* of the glory of God in the face of Christ," he writes to the Corinthians (2 Corinthians 4:6). Our spiritual weapons, he tells them (10:6), "cast down every high thing raised up against the *gnosis* of God, abolishing *logismoi* (human calculations) and bringing every *noema* (argument, reasoning) into conformity with obedience to Jesus Christ." Here we see that *gnosis* is not the normal fruit of human thought or reason or research—it confounds these *logismoi* and *noemata*. "I am an ordinary man," says Paul, "as far as *logos* (that is education, mental power) is concerned, but I am certainly *not* such with regard to the *gnosis*" (2 Corinthians 11:6). "How can I help you," he says again to the Corinthians (1 Corinthians 14:6), "if I don't speak to you in revelation or in *gnosis*, or in prophecy, or *didaché* (inspired teaching)?" Here the *gnosis* is plainly the knowledge acquired only by revelation and not in ordinary ways. Paul reminds the Colossians (2:3) that the *gnosis* is "hidden away," and that not everyone has it who claims to. This is the famous "science falsely so-called" of 1 Timothy 6:20, where Timothy is really told to avoid arguing with those who claim to have the *gnosis* but don't have it.

The title of Irenaeus' one and only surviving work is "The Evidence against and Refutation of what is falsely called the Gnosis." The first men to write against the Gnostics are always very careful to designate them as the so-called or self-styled Gnostics and their teachings as the *false* gnosis.[2] This is very important to note because it shows that there was or had been a real *gnosis* which those people were imitating. "They took utterly false ways," wrote Eusebius, "and announced themselves as the bearers of what they falsely called the *gnosis*."[3] In contrast to them, Origen and Clement of Alexandria describe themselves as *true* Gnostics.[4]

Since the *gnosis* has given rise to more research and speculation than any other aspect of Christian doctrine, one would expect scholars to be most grateful for the genuine definition of the true *gnosis* which Eusebius has handed down to us from very early Christian times, and to make it the point of departure for all their studies. Strangely enough, they never mention it. And yet it is the key to the whole business. Eusebius thus quotes Clement: "To James the Just and to John and Peter after the resurrection of the Lord conveyed the *gnosis*, these handed it on to the rest of the Apostles and in turn to the Seventy."[5] So we have a true *gnosis*, a certain knowledge, entrusted to the general authorities of the church after the resurrection and, as far as we know, to no one else.

This was precisely the knowledge which the Gnostics so-called later claimed to have. From the titles and contents of recently found Gnostic writings it is plain that their special boast was to possess "What Christ taught to the Apostles after the Resurrection."[6] Eusebius has preserved an account from Hegesippus, one of the earliest Christian writers, describing the emergence of these pretenders.

"Up until those times [says Hegesippus] the church had remained a pure and uncorrupted virgin, while any that were inclined to pervert the sound doctrine of the saving Gospel were still sulking as it were in dark corners. But when the holy quorum (*choros*) of the Apostles had ended their lives in various ways, and that generation passed away of those who had heard the divine wisdom with their own ears, at that moment the conspiracy (*systasis*) of godless error took its rise through the deception of false teachers who, as soon as the last Apostle had departed [or, 'since there were no longer any Apostles left'], first came out openly and henceforward undertook to match the teaching of the truth with what they falsely styled *Gnosis*."[7] Note it well: as long as there were living Apostles these impostors had been kept in their place by apostolic authority. As long as people were still alive who had actually heard the preaching of the Lord, these deceivers could not claim to have it but lurked in dark corners biding their time. And that time came! As soon as the apostolic generation passed away the barriers of apostolic authority were removed; the deceivers had nothing to fear; and overnight the church swarmed with them, says Eusebius elsewhere; they sprang up like mushrooms, says Irenaeus, and operated with complete impunity and immunity.[8] Where, then, were the successors of the Apostles who should have kept them in their place and continued to wield the authority which had so long overawed them? That authority was not there, and the church found itself in a serious predicament, a predicament fully set forth by Irenaeus in his work on the Gnostics.

"Many," he says in his introduction, "are bringing in false doctrines, making convincing noises . . . taking liberties with the *logia* [that is, the written sayings] of the Lord, having become bad interpreters of the good and correct word. And they turn many aside, persuading them that they have the *Gnosis* from Him who planned all things and ordered them, and so are able to teach higher and greater things of God who made the heavens, the earth and all that in them is. They argue very convincingly because of their training with words, . . . making truth and falsehood indistinguishable." He describes them as working inside the church as regular members, wolves all but indistinguishable from the sheep, "making what they say appear truer than truth itself." From this it is evident that the Gnostic teaching was not particularly strange and exotic; that it was so Christian as to fool the most orthodox; that it dealt with the mysteries of the universe; and that it purported to come from Christ himself.

Nearly all studies of Gnosticism in the past have sought the key to its origin and nature in the original sources of various Gnostic doctrines. Thus some scholars have maintained that Gnosticism is simply the adoption by the church of Greek philosophy; others say it is a typically Jewish production; others have claimed to find its origin in Egypt, Asia Minor, Babylon, Samaria, Persia, and India. Opinions differ as widely today as ever.[9] It is as if various parties called upon to describe the nature of a bucket were to submit careful chemical analyses of all substances carried in buckets: there would be a milk school, a water school, a bran school, etc., each defining *buckets* in terms of a particular content. The important thing about the Gnostics is not that they adopted doctrines and practices from Iran or from Alexandria, but that they showed a desperate eagerness to latch on to anything that looked promising no matter where it came from. Irenaeus' survey of those practices and doctrines easily explains this urgency: the Gnostics had caused an immense sensation and gained a huge and growing following by the electrifying announcement that they had the *gnosis*, revealed knowledge, the wonderful things that the Lord taught to Peter, James, and John after the resurrection. Having made the claim, they were, so to speak, "on the spot." They had to deliver—they had to come through with something wonderful, supernatural, which at the same time would correspond in some degree to widespread rumors and traditions in the church as to what the *gnosis* really was.

And so they welcomed any teaching or practice that combined an air of mystery and superior knowledge with a cosmic sweep and scope. For them, God was something beyond the grasp of ordinary Christians; they gave secret lessons and charged money for them; they built up elaborate philosophical systems based on abstract and personified concepts; they practiced ordinary magic and specialized in trick miracles such as changing wine into blood (all this according to Irenaeus); they tried to produce supernatural experiences by the use of drugs and stimulants; they cultivated a large vocabulary of fancy technical words to impress the public; they made a big thing of numerology; they brought forth libraries of faked apocryphal writings to cause a sensation; they parodied celestial marriage and baptism, while teaching that water baptism was not necessary since the spirit is everything; they said it was impossible for the body, since it is made of earth, to participate in salvation; they condemned marriage; they practiced extreme unction; they taught transmigration of souls; they venerated holy images, in particular a portrait of Christ.

These are a few of the things charged against them by Irenaeus. What a hodgepodge! But it all has one obvious purpose—to give the impression that the powers and gifts and knowledge of the ancient Apostles were still on the earth, for that is what they claimed to have, but did not have. "This much is known for sure about the Gnosis," writes Quispel, the present-day leader of Gnostic studies, "that we may say with confidence, that the proportion of nincompoops and crackpots [*stoethaspels en warhoofden*] was greater among them than elsewhere."[10] And yet what a lot of stuff introduced by them was preserved by conventional Christianity—a most suspicious circumstance!

The Gnostic experiment proved a number of important things. First, that the gifts of the Spirit cannot be faked. The Gnostics made desperate and determined efforts to display the powers that the Apostles had once enjoyed, but after the passing of the talented and enthusiastic first generation—the school of Simon Magus (who, you will recall, once tried to buy the power of the priesthood from Peter)—they fell back on the safe and conventional supports of philosophy and mysticism which were deep and recondite enough to satisfy the church. Eusebius has preserved from a number of sources the pathetic attempt of Montanists to keep alive the gift of prophecy, a project which was finally given up in despair after the death of the Lady Maximilla.[11]

In the second place, the Gnostic affair of the second century showed how terrribly hungry the Christian world was for the spiritual gifts. They yearned for prophecies, tongues, and the marvelous *gnosis*, and they never stopped yearning even after the Gnostics had been reabsorbed into the main church. A number of recent studies have shown the tendency of Gnosticism to pop up in every century, only to be discredited when the claims put forward were found to be unsubstantiated,[12] for the third and most significant point proved by the Gnostic experience was that the main church was not able to satisfy the demand for spiritual gifts. Irenaeus himself can make fun of all the silly pretentions of the Gnostics, but he is every bit as pitiful and frustrated a figure as they when *he* tries to come forward with a positive program.

The false *gnosis* wouldn't have stood a chance against the true one, which was conspicuously not there to set up against it. As Neander pointed out long ago, to meet the *gnosis*-so-called, the church had to invent another *gnosis*, which *it* then claimed to be the ancient one.[13] But it was much too late to regain or claim ancient gifts that one had already denied, and it is not surprising that in setting up its counter-*gnosis*, the main church imitated her rival all down the line. They end up resembling each other exactly. "It is by no means a paradox," says Harnack in concluding his study of the subject, "when one maintains that in Catholicism Gnosticism . . . won half a victory."[14] The only trouble with Gnosticism, Harnack explains, is that it was ahead of its time, and the problem of the Gnostics was solved when the rest of the church finally caught up with them and adopted their way of thinking.[15]

Certainly it is a remarkable thing that there never was a formal condemnation of Gnosticism, as in the case of other heresies and as there certainly would have been if any Apostle or the equivalent in authority had been alive. There was no general council held to consider this greatest and most dangerous of all heresies—because there was nobody to call one. Self-appointed defenders of orthodoxy, such as Irenaeus describes himself to be,[16] could only oppose the Gnostic doctrine with a new doctrine of their own, and the teachings of Irenaeus himself differ from those of the Gnostics he refutes only in the matter of terminology. Their Propator is his God by another name; their Pleroma is his Cosmos; what they call the Logos of God, he says, is Jesus Christ, no more nor less—so he falls in with nearly all their arguments, beliefs, and concepts, and the only real argument is about words.

The rise, prosperity, and absorption of the Gnostics is one of the most significant commentaries on the loss to the church and to the world of the gift of prophecy.

9

The Schools and the Prophets

The declining years of antique civilization saw an unparalleled boom in the education business. Everybody went to school, says St. Augustine, because it was the thing to do.[1] Education in a sick world became a fetish, and leading educators enjoyed (and thoroughly enjoyed) unlimited authority and prestige. The curriculum was highly standardized everywhere, and nonconformists were quickly dealt with in a field in which nonconformists are rare enough at any time. Strictly speaking there were not schools, but only *the* school, the one authorized institution following the one official curriculum.[2] One can easily imagine that this overwhelming predominance of an accepted institution of learning led from the very first to conflicts with the church. It was the schoolmen, the "scribes," who furnished the earliest and steadiest opposition to the preaching of the Master and the Apostles. It was the young fellows from the school who started heckling Barnabas in the earliest description of a street meeting that we have after the New Testament, and the questions they shouted on that occasion were the questions which the schools continued to ask until the church itself came around to their way of thinking.

The early Christians were understandably suspicious of the schools, on which philosophy had put its intellectual stamp, for as we have often noted in these talks, the ancient saints were, to put it mildly, cool towards philosophy. Even so, it is surprising to learn that the Christians had no schools

of their own until well into the third century. Justin introduced the first regular school earlier, but it was not carried
on after him, and there is no evidence that it had any status
among the Christians. Certainly the many schools that flourished in the second half of the second century all found
themselves outside the general communion.[3]

But about the year 200 the schools start to take over
everywhere in Christian society. In Asia Minor, Palestine,
Edessa, and the West, important schools suddenly come into
being and a strongly intellectual orientation becomes evident
in the church. Incomparably the most important of these
new schools was the catechetical school of Alexandria, the
true home of conventional Christian theology, whose foundations were laid by the famous Clement of Alexandria and
his more famous pupil, Origen. Both these men are typical
schoolmen, brought up from infancy in the four walls of an
institution from whose authority they can never free themselves.

It was Clement's project to put the intellectual superiority of Greek philosophy at the disposal of the church. The
knowledge of *scientiae humaniores*, he maintains, is indispensable to the correct understanding of the scriptures; "Why,
then, should it not be necessary for one who desires to share
the power of God to do so by the philosophical contemplation of intelligible objects?"[4] Clement generously offered to
make Christianity intellectually respectable. For him, says
Harnack (upon whom we shall lean heavily in this talk for
the sake of safety), "Greek religious philosophy . . . was the
means of achieving and explaining for the first time the highest and inmost meaning of Christianity."[5] He was all for the
church; he was going to give it a break by lending to it the
advantages of his training and intellect. Very patronizing,
one must admit, but one can imagine how that would have
gone down with the Apostles. Such a point of view, really
quite naive, was only possible, says Harnack, because Clement missed the whole point of what Christianity was all about,

"because for him the heritage of the Church in its totality and in every particular—with the exception of some utterances in the Gospels—*was something foreign."*[6] The university was his world, and his offer of assistance to the church had dangerous strings attached to it: "He submitted to its authority," writes Harnack, "but could only adapt himself to it after a specific and philosophic re-working (*Bearbeitung*)."[7] He would embrace the teachings of the church, but only on *his* terms. He would take the literal Christianity and "spiritualize" it. Photius says Clement cannot possibly have believed in a real incarnation, for example.[8] As a member of the church in good standing and as one careful to quote the scriptures somewhere in all his arguments—a very easy thing to do—he saw no reason why he should not go all the way in giving the Christian message a new intellectual stature that would recommend it to the more educated classes. His slogan was "All truth belongs to the Gospel,"[9] which he took as a franchise not to accept the gospel as the guide to his studies, but to use his studies to establish for the first time the really deep and inner meaning of the gospel. Firmly convinced that what he had learned in school was *the* truth, and that *all* knowledge is revelation (following Plato), he proceeded to re-edit the gospel to something nearer to his heart's desire: "The total revamping (recoining, *Umprägung*) of the Christian heritage into a Hellenic religious philosophy on a historical foundation cannot be denied," says our authority Harnack. And what remained of Christianity after that, aside from some of its practical and sentimental appeal? he asks, and gives an almost shocking answer: *"Ein Phlegma*—a sediment, a scum—that can under no possible circumstances be called Christian."[10] Yet Clement was a moral and an earnest man, the first great teacher of the Catechetical School of Alexandria, the school that was to have more influence on the making of Christian doctrine than all the rest put together.

Now Clement of Alexandria with his training and his eager project of helping the church out of its morass of old-fashioned ideas and childish literalism was not a new phenomenon in the church. It was just his kind that the Apostolic Fathers had opposed with all their energy. Paul had known them very well in his day—these over-clever men who wanted to "turn the truth of God into a fable," who denied the literal resurrection, who claimed that they and they alone knew the real Christ ("lo, here is Christ, and lo there!"), and who falsely claimed to possess the *gnosis*. Clement was actually one of these: he emphatically *does* claim to have the true *gnosis*, and he defines the substance of that *gnosis* not as revelation but simply as Greek religious philosophy, which for him *is* revelation. [11] All students of Clement have recognized strong Gnostic elements in his writings. In him Gnosticism wins half a victory. The doctrine which Clement thought an improved Christianity was, to use Harnack's expression, at least half an enemy of the church. How, then, was it possible for him to "get away" with so much? We explained that in the last lecture: In the earlier days of the church he could not have gotten away with it because of the presence of the Apostles and their disciples in the church. These men actually had the fulness of the gospel, and everybody knew it. The church was their doing. To put forward a feeble imitation as the original teaching entrusted by the Lord to the Apostles while those Apostles were still alive was obviously out of the question. The same liberty that allowed the Gnostics so-called to come out openly with their monstrous pretentions "upon the death of the last Apostle" allowed men like Clement—semi-Gnostics at best—to operate with complete immunity. And so it is that the prosperity of the Gnostics is matched by the sudden blossoming of the schools everywhere, and especially that of Alexandria. "Alexandria," wrote Baur, "the fatherland of the Gnosis, is also the birthplace of Christian theology, which in its earliest form was meant to be nothing but a Christian Gnosis." [12]

Clement is completely overshadowed by his pupil Origen,
next to St. Augustine alone the most influential thinker of
the Christian church. "Origen created the doctrinal theology
of the Church," writes Harnack.[13] Not Christ, not the Apostles, but Origen. "Among the ancient Greek writers of the
Church," writes Delarue in the *Patrologia*, "there is possibly
none who has left to posterity such a reputation for learning
as Origen." Jerome notes that his reputation was as great
among the pagans as among the Christians.[14] In his time, he
was indisputably the foremost authority in the church on
doctrine; the greatest bishops eagerly sought his counsel and
instruction; his voice was the deciding one in grave disputes;
requests for information poured in on him at such a rate that
we are told he kept seven secretaries, shorthand experts, busy
night and day taking down the answers he dictated to all
parts of the world.[15]

Like his teacher, Origen betrays strong Neoplatonic and
Gnostic leanings. Like Irenaeus he ends up using the arguments and language of those he attempts to refute, and like
all the schoolmen of the time he is more than a little embarrassed and ashamed at the unsophisticated and unphilosoph-
ical nature of the faith of his simpler brethren. I think this
embarrassment is best expressed by Origen's contemporary
Minucius Felix, whose Christian apologist, Octavius, goes to
considerable pains to make clear to his educated pagan opponents that they have really misunderstood Christianity by
judging it from the behavior and beliefs of the ordinary members and officers of the church. All Christians are not like
that, he explains. Cultivated Christians really think just like
cultivated heathens, so that "anyone would think either that
present-day Christians are philosophers or that the philosophers of yore were Christians." There is no real difference
between them, and just as the ignorant pagan masses tell
childish and superstitious tales and believe them, so do the
common run of Christians. The real difference after all is not
between Christian and pagan but between the educated and

the uneducated. [16] The story of Moses seeing God is for Origen
simply "one of those old wives' tales," and if you take it seriously, he says, you "run into the absurdity of saying that
God is corporeal," [17] a thing which any pagan philosopher
could tell you is just too silly for words. Harnack has an
interesting reflection on this "spiritualizing" of Christian teachings by Origen: "No one can deny," he says, "that this kind
of flight from the world and possessing of God contains in
itself a specific secularization [Verweltlichung, lowering to
worldly standards] of Christianity." [18] Most people have always
been taught that the opposite is the case; that to move from
realms of literalism to those of spiritual abstraction is a sign
of higher thought and purer doctrine. But to those who know
Christian and pagan thought as Harnack does, it is painfully
clear that the spiritual abstractions were the daily bread of
the pagan schools and had been for more than 500 years,
while the real and the literal was the very thing that gave
Christianity its peculiar stamp and its unique appeal. Spiritual abstractions were a dime a dozen in the world of late
antiquity; the rolling of eyes, plucking of breasts, and heav-
ing of sighs are pagan gestures of piety; and the incurable
appetite for allegory, abstraction, and symbolism was a disease which by Origen's time had seriously crippled pagan
thought. The fact that these things were not Christian does
not condemn them, but we cannot insist too emphatically
that the early Christians had known all about these things
and had firmly rejected them. We have the gospel, was their
argument; all this other stuff is nothing to us. Then why did
the church finally break down and accept it? And why did
Origen go for it? The answer is clearly set forth in the prologue of his work significantly entitled On the First Principles.

   This is not a work against the pagans but an attempt to
find the right track for the Christians themselves to follow
since, he says, "there are many who profess to believe in
Christ who disagree among themselves not only in small and

minor matters, but rather about the great and the greatest matters."[19] It is the very first principles of the gospel, the foundations of the Christian faith, for which Origen seeks, as he says, to lay down a clear and definite rule on each point. On certain of these things, he notes, all Christians agree: that there is one God, that Jesus Christ was the first-born of the Father, and that the Holy Ghost comes next in honor. "But it is *not* stated clearly whether the Holy Ghost was begotten or not—that we must find out from the Scripture." The scripture does not tell us in so many words, and so the answer must be carefully worked out "to the best of our ability by sagacious investigation [*sagaci per-quisitione*]." Again, all Christians agree "that the devil and his angels exist, but why or how or what they are, the church has not made sufficiently clear—*non satis clare exposuit*." All agree that the world was created, "but what came before or comes after it is not evident in the teachings of the Church." Even the nature of God's person "is not clearly set forth in our preaching." We know that there are angels, but what, how, when, etc., "is not made adequately manifest and so must be worked out by us by the aid of reason following manifest and necessary conclusions."[20]

Note well, it is the *first principles of the gospel* on which Origen seeks light, not trivial and minor matters. He says plainly and repeatedly that the church itself lacks satisfactory answers; he does not know the answers, and what is more he knows of no one else in the church who does know them. Now it should be plain enough why the Gnostic schoolmen met no serious rebuff—they could and they had to bring forth faked answers to the great questions of the gospel because there was no one left alive who knew the real answers. Origen's solution of the great questions is enough in itself to prove that. He started out with confidence that his method and his learning, both acquired in the schools, would be equal to providing the missing answers. But he very soon discovered that they were not, and being both a good and an honest man, he is frank to admit it. Let us quote a few of his final conclusions. "I suppose the Spirit of God is the Holy Ghost, as far as I can understand, not historically or literally, but in the sense of spiritual intelligence."[21] As to the possibility of bodies, resurrected or otherwise, being eternal, he concludes that if anyone can work out a better explanation of things from the scripture, he is welcome to do so. [22] "There may be other worlds but what their nature and number may be I confess I do not know. If anyone can show me I would gladly learn. . . . We have done our best: let every reader decide for himself what is right."[23] On the incarnation of Christ he says, "On this head we shall present our suspicions rather than any manifest affirmations." And having done so he says, "If anyone can find out anything better, or confirm by more evident proofs the assertions he makes concerning the Holy Scriptures, let such conclusions be accepted in preference to these."[24] Regarding the nature of the souls he says, "The ideas put forth by us are not to be regarded as dogma, but more in the nature of speculation and inquiry." And on the Spirit of God: "And if it is allowed us to dare to say any more on the subject, it is possible perhaps that the Spirit of God is to be understood as his only-begotten Son."[25]

On all these points and many more, Origen, the foremost doctrinal authority in the church, has no certitude and claims no authority—and this on themes which lie according to his own assertion at the very heart of doctrine, the first principles of the gospel. Origen does not know the answers and, what is far more significant, he knows of no one who does, though he has visited every important churchman in Christendom, including the bishops of Jerusalem, Alexandria, and Rome. There never was, indeed it is hard to imagine how there could be, a more zealous, devout, single-minded student than Origen, nicknamed *Adamantinos*, "the unshakable." Born and reared in a school, he was convinced that all knowledge of the gospel could be acquired by study alone and only ended up proving to the world that where there is no revelation there is no certitude.

10

St. Augustine and the Great Transition

Catholic and Protestant authorities vie in proclaiming their incalculable debt to St. Augustine, the man "who laid the foundation of Western culture" (Seeberg), "who stands between the ancient world and the Middle Ages as the first great constructive thinker of the Western Church, and the father of medieval Catholicism" (Raby), "dominating like a pyramid antiquity and succeeding ages—among theologians he is undeniably the first, and such has been his influence that none of the Fathers, Scholastics or Reformers has surpassed it" (Schaff), "the greatest doctor of the Church" (Lot), "the true creator of Western theology" (Grabmann), "in whom, in a very real sense . . . medieval thought begins and ends" (Coulton). "His philosophic-historical work remains one of the most imposing creations of all time; it posits a capacity and originality of mind which none other possessed either in his own day or for a thousand years after," wrote Eduard Norden.

Far be it from us to pass judgment on such a man or his works: we shall consider not how St. Augustine acquitted himself in his great task, but only what that task was. From what we have already quoted, it would seem that St. Augustine's great significance lies in the final fixing of a new orientation for the Church. "It was to him more than to any other single man," says McGiffert, "that the spirit of classical antiquity gave way to the spirit of the Middle Ages."[1] "The Christian theology and philosophy of the Middle Ages," according to Grabmann, perhaps the foremost authority on that subject, "is in form and content almost exclusively Augustinian until late in the 13th century," and even then "the world-historical achievement of St. Thomas was the synthesis of Augustine and Aristotle."[2] For the medievalist Coulton, Augustine is "the man who closes ancient thought and begins medieval thought."[3] "It is he," writes Ferdinand Lot, "who set the Church irresistibly on the course which she has followed to the modern era."[4] "Upon Augustine, Petrarch and the great masters of the Renascence [sic] formed themselves," says Harnack, "and without him Luther is not to be understood. Augustine, the founder of Roman Catholicism, is at the same time the only Father of the Church from whom Luther received any effective teaching, or whom the humanists honoured as a hero."[5] Many have called St. Augustine the first man of the modern world; the historian Troeltsch calls him the last man of the ancient.

Apparently Augustine is to be respected before all things as that rarest of all humans, a founder and creator. Grabmann says he was "the true creator of the theology of the West, just as Origen was the founder of the speculative theology of the Orient."[6] Troeltsch also describes Augustine as continuing the work that Clement of Alexandria and Origen had undertaken two centuries before.[7] The names of Origen and Augustine are often linked together, and with good reason. For each devoted his life to the same project, namely, the working out of a Christian theology which he personally could accept. We have already talked about Origen's allegiance to the schools and how it conditioned and inspired his whole effort to develop a theology that would be intellectually respectable. St. Augustine was, if anything, even more a child of the schools than Origen, who was a far more austere and independent character. For twenty years Augustine absolutely refused to accept the Christianity learned at his mother's knee, however powerful his sentimental attachments to it, because, as he explains at great length in the *Confessions*, it simply could not stand up to the arguments of the schoolmen. He tells us how in his youth, after reading Cicero, he would laugh at the prophets,[8] and how from the very first the pagan schools had taught him to abhor any suggestion that God might have a body—it was instruction like that, he says, that convinced him that the Christians could not possibly be right.[9] And this is the significant point: Augustine never changed the ideas and attitudes he acquired in the schools. He did not turn away from them back to Christianity; rather he built them firmly and finally into the structure of Christianity before he would accept it. He never came around to accepting on the one hand the naive beliefs with which he charged the Christians, nor on the other hand did he ever swerve in his allegiance to the Platonists. According to Professor Grabmann, the whole explanation of Augustine's "tremendous influence on the scholasticism and mysticism of the Middle Ages" lay in the single fact of his being "the greatest Christian Neoplatonist," whose life's work was "the christianizing of Neoplatonism."[10]

Augustine has described as few others could the tension and agony of a twenty-year deadlock, "a struggle within his breast," Grabmann calls it, between the teachings of the schools and the teachings of the Christians. In the end something had to give way—and it was the church. It was Augustine, in Lot's words, who "set the Church irresistibly on the course" which she was to follow for the future: it was *not* the Church that drew Augustine into her orbit. Or rather let us say this is the classic problem of three bodies, in which the orbit of each alters and is altered by each and both of the others. Augustine, as our experts have declared, brought forth a new Christian theology when he solved the problem of which should prevail, the prophets or the philosophers, by deferring to *both*—uniting them into a new and wonderful synthesis which has been the object of endless scholarly panegyrics. "Augustine," wrote Reinhold Seeberg, "laid the foundation of Western culture when he fused Antique civilization and Christianity together once for all in a single mighty mold."[11] Reitzenstein declares that Augustine's life-work was "the program of a reconciliation of Antique civilization and Christianity, whose synthesis still determines our culture."[12]

This fusion of the classical and Christian heritages was the culmination of a long process. "All the Christian writers from Justin to Gregory of Nazianzus and from Minucius Felix to Jerome used the classics to explain, to enrich, and to defend Christianity," wrote Father Combès in his valuable study of Augustine's education, and this fusion of classic and Christian "attained its perfection in the work of St. Augustine."[13] Note that the trend begins with Justin and Minucius Felix, Christian converts who had been thoroughly indoctrinated by the schools before ever joining the Church, and who remained fiercely and unshakably loyal to the schools to the end of their lives, regarding themselves as the real or esoteric Christians and pooh-poohing the others as an uneducated and uncritical rabble. We have noted already how these men thought their fine heathen educations would be a great boon to the Church. This is the group to which Augustine belongs; Father Eggersdorfer has shown how he remained up to the end of his life completely a child of the schools.[14] Augustine himself calls the adoption of pagan education "spoiling the Egyptians," and in his famous *de doctrina Christiana*, written at the end of his life, he presents his program for sending the Church to school with the rhetoricians and philosophers.

In making his perfect fusion of Christian and classic knowledge to produce a doctrinal system which he and his intellectual friends could accept, Augustine, to quote Combès, "uses the ancient theodicy, metaphysics, morality, and politics. . . . He often seems to reproach himself for doing this, to be sure; but the protests of his heart are silenced before the implacable dictates of his intellect. It is his desire to endow the Church with a doctrine so solidly constructed that she will never again have anything to fear from her enemies."[15] That

is a remarkably revealing statement which deserves some
examination. From the first quotation of Combès we learned
that the idea of reconciling Christian with pagan ideas was
one that had been current among the intellectuals of the
Church for a long time—it was anything but the blinding
flash of inspiration that some would make it out to be: it
was in fact a creeping sickness in the Church. The idea of a
super-synthesis had become an obsession in the schools, where
work on encyclopedic *summas* of all knowledge had long
since brought all original research to a complete halt. In his
pre-Christian days Augustine had displayed a passion for
this kind of activity, and it never left him. Next we learn
from Combès that Augustine was not at all happy about
what he was doing to the Church: "He *often* seems to
reproach himself for this." Why should he reproach himself
unless he knew there was something fundamentally wrong
about his program?

Monsignor Duchesne opens the third volume of his *Early
History of the Christian Church* with the remark: "In uniting
itself closely to the State, the Church under Theodosius was
not making a good match: it was wedding a sick man, soon
to become a dying one."[16] We might paraphrase the sentence
to read: "In uniting itself closely to the learning of the state
schools, the Church under Augustine was not making a good
match: it was wedding a sick man, soon to become a dying
one." The two "weddings" are actually phases of the same
movement, for Theodosius' work of consolidation and
Augustine's were going on at exactly the same time. Classical learning was a very sick man in Augustine's day, and he
knew it. Many authorities have remarked how the saint constantly denounces the arts of the schools while constantly
practicing them.[17] This fatal inconsistency has been immor-
talized in the story of St. Jerome, St. Augustine's great contemporary (they died but ten years apart), who in a dream
was chastised by an angel with the awful accusation, "You
are not a Christian, but a Ciceronian!" And after he awoke,

Jerome went right on being a good Ciceronian, as did Augustine to the end of his days. In a recent study Marrou has shown Augustine's own education to be that of a decadent age, and has pointed out that the only change St. Augustine made in introducing pagan education into the church officially was to make the courses even more simple, superficial, and streamlined than they had been, thus contributing to "that lowering of the general level of civilization which already, all around Augustine, announces the coming age of the barbarians."[18]

Well might Augustine reproach himself for what he was doing; but he had no choice: "The protests of his heart are silenced before the implacable dictates of his intellect." What are the implacable dictates that thus override desire? Combès continues, "to endow the Church with a doctrine so solidly constructed that she will never again have anything to fear from her enemies." Never again? To be sure: in the past the philosophers could pick Christian doctrine to pieces—they could show you in black and white that God could *never* have a son, or that, since he was "the totally other," nothing could possibly be in his image, etc. As Peter remarks in the *Clementine Recognitions*, Simon Magus could always give him a bad time and usually win the argument—but that didn't worry him. The ancient saints were not impressed by the pompous schoolmen, because they had their testimonies. It was because revelation had ceased that Augustine was driven to come to an understanding with the philosophers, who were now feared and respected as possessing the only available key to knowledge. Whence this new attitude, yielding to "the implacable dictates of the intellect"?

The world of St. Augustine's day was willing enough to become Christian, since the emperor's approval and compulsion had made such a course both safe and popular. But the new Christian world community was *not* willing to fulfill the conditions necessary to receiving revelation—not by a long

shot. We can best describe the situation by another quotation from Monsignor Duchesne: "Long distances separated
them [the Christians of St. Augustine's time] from the spiritual enthusiasm of the early Church. . . . Now everyone was
Christian, or nearly everyone; and this implied that the profession involved but little sacrifice. . . . The mass of the community was Christian in the only way in which the mass
could be, superficially and in name; the water of baptism
had touched it, but the spirit of the Gospel had not pene-
trated its heart. Upon their entry into the Church, the faithful invariably renounced the pomps of Satan; but neither the
theatres nor the games were deserted: it was a subject on
which preachers uttered their most eloquent protests, and all
to no purpose [Augustine himself has much to say on this
theme]. . . . Was it really the Church which was overcoming
the world? Was it not rather the world which was overcoming the Church?"[19] Whoever was winning, in Augustine's
day the people of the church no longer had testimonies: from
now on they insisted that the gospel be proved to them by
intellectual arguments and clever demonstrations. Augustine
himself says he wanted to be as sure of its truth as he was
sure that four and three make seven; like Origen, he wanted
to put the doctrine of the Church on an intellectual basis,
which was the nearest thing to certainty that he could ever
get. He was, says Arnold Lunn, the well-known English Catholic, "the first of the Fathers to realise fully the necessity for
a rational foundation of the faith."[20] And Professor Grabmann
reminds us that in his theological explorations, Augustine
"had almost no predecessors, and for the most part was the
very first man to experience the intellectual difficulties of
these questions."[21] For four hundred years, during which the
philosophers constantly made fun of them, the Christians
had failed to realize that their faith should be founded on
reason and speak the language of philosophy! Whence this
astounding oversight? Why must Augustine be the *first* to
see the light? Obviously, as we have often pointed out on

other evidence, the early Christians had a revealed faith and were not interested in things reasoned out by man.

Augustine wanted to endow the church with a solidly constructed doctrine, says Father Combès. Hadn't Christ and the Apostles already done that? It was certainly not their intention to work out a system that would please the schoolmen. Just before he was put to death, the Lord told his disciples not to be afraid, because he had overcome the world. That was as far as the ancient saints would go: they made no attempt to win popularity with those who would not accept the gospel as it stood. The Apostles were instructed when the people would not accept their teachings, simply to depart and go to others—*not* to change those teachings under any circumstances into something the world *would* accept. But that is precisely what St. Augustine did. He, and not the Lord or the Apostles, is, in Grabmann's words, "the true creator of the theology of the West."

What a comedown from the days of revelation! Let us summarize what Father Combès has told us: (1) Augustine found the Church without a solid doctrinal foundation; (2) he took it upon *himself* to steady the ark—but who gave him the necessary knowledge or authority to do it? Where did he go for his information? Combès tells us that (3) he went to the pagan schools—he took *their* theodicy, metaphysics, moral teachings, and politics and worked them into his system. Is that the proper source for Christian doctrine? (4) That question worried Augustine too, but (5) he had to go ahead with his project because the times required it urgently. And what was the world clamoring for? A theology that would appeal on rational grounds alone to a Christian world which was, as Duchesne puts it, Christian in name only, and which had forgotten the meaning of a testimony. The wedding of the sickly philosophy of the fourth century to Christian doctrine could take place only after Christianity had been once for all definitely divorced from the gift of prophecy and revelation. St. Augustine fully deserves his title of the man who changed the whole course of world history and of church history. He found himself in an intolerable situation, and he made the best of it. It is the situation, not the man, that teaches us what hard necessity and fateful decisions faced the Church once the gifts of revelation and prophecy were withdrawn.

11

A Substitute for Revelation

St. Augustine's program was to endow the church once for all with a solid doctrine that all rational people could accept. We have cited various authorities, all of whom agreed that it was St. Augustine who put Christianity on a new foundation, the shift being to a new emphasis on philosophy, made necessary by the new and sudden growth of the Christian community to a world church. Christ had said that his sheep hear his voice—and no others.[1] But now the church, following the emperor's example rather than the Lord's, would speak with a voice that all the world could hear.

We have said that Origen's case proved that "where there is no revelation there is no certitude." But we have also noted that Augustine's problem is the same as Origen's: to achieve certitude without revelation. We are aware of various degrees of transport in Augustine's writings—but they are not really revelation. Many have pointed out that when Augustine's logical quest bogs down he leaps the gap by a kind of inspiration. He anticipates his answers, says Grabmann, "with a purely spiritual far-sightedness"[2] so that he does not really have to work them out; where his logic fails, according to Professor Coulton, Augustine wins through by sheer force of character.[3] Call it what you want, it is not revelation. The most ecstatic period of Augustine's life were the weeks he spent at Cassiciacum, culminating in what many consider to be his final conversion; yet of that period Combès writes: "He prays, he meditates, he idles, but especially he chats; and these conversations, minutely recorded by stenographers, [show that] the ideas of Cicero, Plato, and Plotinus . . . still occupy even in his spirit the foremost position, leaving only a little corner . . . for Christian ideas."[4] We must not forget that various types of ecstasy were carefully cultivated in the schools of rhetoric in which Augustine had been raised, and we meet them all in his writings. Take this description of a "manifestation," for example. He says that as a result of reading certain books of the Platonists it was made manifest to him that things could be both good and corrupted; this leads him to another logical conclusion and this to another and so on: "therefore whatever is deprived of all good ceases to be; therefore things that are, are good; therefore whatever is, is good; . . . therefore evil is not any substance," etc., and so after some eighteen "therefores" or the equivalent, he triumphantly announces: "I perceived therefore, and it was manifested unto me that Thou madest all things good."[5] This is what the schoolmen would call a manifestation. "Slowness and sinuosity" are the characteristics of Augustine's reasoning, according to Gilson,[6] but swiftness and directness are the hallmarks of revelation.

The formal ecstasies and intellectual insights of the schoolmen are not real revelation, and Augustine knew it. In all fairness to him we must report that he would infinitely have preferred revelation to philosophy. Not only did he feel guilty about what he was doing, but it was only after long years of agonizing struggle and indecision that he at last, painfully and with heartbreaking reluctance, closed the book on revelation or recognized that he could not open it. What a difference there is, he cries in the *City of God*, between the ambiguities of the academicians and the certainty of the Christian faith![7] And yet it is the Academy that he brings into the church, and without Plato, he informs us, his own conversion would never have taken place.[8] The *Confessions* is the story of a man who all his life hungered for revelation—"Here are my ears, God speak to them!"—but in the end had to settle for a second best. He tells us of the founder of the state religion of heathen Rome, the great and good Numa, who though he did his best, had for inspiration to resort to hydromancy and the arts of divination. He was *compelled (compulsus)* to do this, says Augustine, because the poor man "had no prophet of God, nor any holy angel sent to him."[9] Divination was a poor substitute for prophecy, yet Numa had no other choice. And was that not Augustine's position? In his quest for certainty, he tells us, he consulted the astrologers and soothsayers with a determination that moved even his superstitious friends to merriment, and he continued to seek out the astrologers even after he was a catechumen, a candidate for baptism, in his thirties.[10] All his life he snatched at straws, condoning such practices as the use of *sortes* (divination by the random opening of the scriptures) and the visiting of oracles as being, if not desirable, at least better than nothing.[11]

The yearning of Augustine for real revelation and the inadequacy of all substitutes is beautifully brought out in his last conversation with his mother. Here these two saintly people bare their souls, and what they both wish for above all else is a real revelation: what is it like when God really speaks, they ask each other, when he alone speaks, not by any intermediary "but by himself, that we may hear his word *not* through any tongue of flesh nor angel's voice, nor in the sound of thunder, nor in the dark riddle of the similitude; . . . but we might hear the very One whom we only love in these other things, that we might hear his very self *without* these, . . . and if this thing could be continued on . . . so that life might be forever like that one moment of understanding for which we now sighed—would not that be 'entering into thy Master's joy?' And when shall that ever be?"[12] In this moment of frank self-revelation Augustine admits that what he really wants is not revelation that comes by the preaching of men or even of angels, nor that comes through his laborious intellectual demonstrations, nor is the manifestation of God in nature—the voice of thunder—nor even the

mystic flash of insight which both he and his mother experienced in their last conversation together, for even then they
still "sighed after" the real thing and wondered what it was
like.

In the 270 letters of Augustine that have survived, we see
the man at work trying to answer the great questions of doctrine and administration that should have been answered by
the head of the church. Letters pour in to him from all over
the Christian world, and he answers them as best he can: He
never refers the questioners to any higher authority, even
though the cases are sometimes very serious and have nothing at all to do with his diocese; nor does he personally ever
appeal to any higher authority, either in administrational or
in doctrinal matters, however important they may be. This is
not surprising if one knows the situation. "If there had been,
in the Church of the 4th century, a central authority recognized and active, it would have offered a means of solution.
But it was not so." Thus wrote Monsignor Duchesne, speaking of the administrative solution.[13] But it goes just as well
for the doctrinal. "There was not there a guiding power,"
says Duchesne, "an effective expression of Christian unity.
The Papacy, such as the West knew it later on, was still to be
born. In the place which it did not yet occupy, the State
installed itself without hesitation. The Christian religion
became the religion of the emperor, not only in the sense of
being professed by him, but in the sense of being directed by
him."[14] Many of Augustine's letters illustrate this point admi-
rably, but we cannot go into them. Let us consider briefly
the doctrinal perplexity and the complete lack of leadership
and direction in the church that is apparent in the *Confessions*.

For twenty years at least, Augustine was never able to
find out just what the Christian church believed. He tells
how he went to school as a boy and made fun of the things
his mother believed, how he joined a strange Christian sect,
the Manichaeans, which enjoyed enormous popularity at the

time, and for once in his life thought he knew certainty; when he left the Manichaeans, he says the bottom of his world fell out, and he spent the ensuing years in black despair; he joined a group calling themselves the *sancti*, large numbers of whom were living secretly in Rome; and all the time his mother kept after him to return to the church of his birth, but this he could not do because their arguments could not stand up to those of the Manichaeans, from whom in a vague way he still hoped for light; when he finally became a catechumen upon the urging of his mother and St. Ambrose, easily the most important leader in the church of the time, he still did not know what to believe but was "doubting everything, tossed back and forth in it all." In listening to Ambrose, he says, he gradually came to the conviction that "*if* the Catholic Church did not teach the truth, at least it did not teach the *kind* of error I formerly attributed to it."[15] Ambrose was another man with a thoroughly non-Christian education who had joined the church by compulsion late in life; it was he, says Augustine, who "drew aside the mystic veil, laying open spiritually those things which if taken literally seemed to teach perversity."[16] Perversity to whom?—to Augustine and his fellow sceptics in the schools. Ambrose taught them that it was not necessary to believe all that childish literal-minded stuff in order to be a Christian. But why had he not known that from the first? He was born and reared a Christian by a singularly devout parent; now he was over thirty years old and had studied Christianity all his life—he was anything but stupid: why then had he been so thoroughly convinced that the church accepted the scriptures literally, as he and the other intellectuals never could? Simply because the Christians did accept them that way. Augustine says he could never accept the Bible until he realized that it was a double book, "so it might receive all in its open bosom, and through narrow passages waft over to thee some few."[17]

After this discovery, he tells us, a great hope began to dawn on him, namely, that the church did not teach as he

had always thought it did, "that God is bounded by the figure of a human body."[18] But why was he so convinced all
those years that that *was* the teaching of the church? What
had his earnest Christian parents and teachers been telling
him about God all through his youth and adolescence if at
the age of thirty he is still absolutely convinced that the
Christians believe God has a body? "Since my earliest study
of *sapientia* [that is, the learning of the schools]," he explains,
"I had always fled [from the idea that God had a body]."[19] It
was the schools that taught him to do that; the Platonic God
was the foundation of the current pagan instruction, and
from it Augustine never freed himself. What he did free himself from was the beliefs of his mother—and I cannot doubt
that the things which he thought his mother believed, after
he had had constant and careful instruction from her from
infancy to manhood, were what she and her church really
did believe.

After describing the immense relief that came to him
when he finally realized that he might become a Christian
without giving up any of his philosophical ideas, Augustine
says that he still did not have the vaguest idea how he *should*
think about God![20] Couldn't the church tell him? Didn't
Ambrose know? To make a very long story very short, he
finally got his answer only when God procured for him, as
he puts it, certain books of the Platonists. But he still thought
that Christ as a man "had a human soul and mind," while
Alypius, his inseparable friend, "thought the Catholics had a
different idea about Christ; . . . that no human mind was to
be ascribed to him." Many other people believed as Alypius
did, he says, and many didn't.[21] Where is the leadership of
the church? Who could really tell him about God? Like
Origen, he searched hard but found no one: in the end he
had to work out the solution all for himself—from the ground
up, and the church was only too glad to accept *his* solution.

"Augustine," says Thomasius, "is the true founder of the
speculative theology of the Trinity,"[22] which was to remain

the most active branch of philosophy and theology for fifteen centuries. Convinced that the highest blessedness
depended on a true and complete grasp of this mystery,
Augustine exerted prodigies of energy and genius in trying
to achieve it. For fifteen years he labored away at his thesis
on the trinity, "without," says Thomasius, "ever reaching a
satisfactory conclusion."[23] Beginning with axiom No. 1 of
the schools, the absolute oneness and immateriality of God,
he tries to work a threeness out of it by a series of elaborate
analogies with the human mind, only to reach the final conclusion that if such a procedure furnishes an inadequate
answer, it is at least an answer: *Impar imago, sed tamen
imago!*[24] The Father and the Son "cannot be really different
persons, yet neither can they be entirely the same"; and "since
the Father *has* a Son, *he* cannot very well be the Father."
Again, Augustine *wants* the Holy Ghost to be a person, but
his philosophical training will not allow it. Here certainly is
a place where revelation would be helpful; its intellectual
substitutes break down at every point. We say there are
three persons, Augustine sums it up, not because there are
three, but because we must say something. (*Non ut illud
diceretur, sed ne taceretur*).[25] "Thus," Thomasius concludes,
"this attempt, carried out with such labor and perspicacity
by the great teacher of the Church, is only a proof that the
Trinity is not to be proven in such a way."[26] This is the same
conclusion we reached regarding Origen, and a confession
of Augustine to a friend in a letter reads exactly like Origen's
frequent admission in the *First Principles*: The friend had
asked why, since the trinity are in all things inseparable,
Christ alone took on a human body? "This is such a supremely
difficult question," the saint replies, "and such a very important matter that it cannot here be settled by a *sententia*, nor
can we be sure of solving it by any investigation. I make so
bold, therefore, in writing to you, to indicate what I have in
mind rather than giving an explanation, that you might judge
the thing according to your own best understanding."[27]

"Augustine," says Grabmann, "confronted face to face the hardest questions of Christian doctrine; those which have presented the greatest challenge to the human mind; and for years and for decades he worked away trying to solve them." That authority then lists the most important of these as unsolved, and says, "In these questions and others he has largely failed to work through to full clarity of understanding, and if dark and difficult passages on those themes are found in many places in his writings, he at least showed the way for all later theology."[28] Wilhelm Christ, in the best-known "standard" history of Greek literature, writes that in the fourth century, Hellenism *forced* Christianity to go to its schools; "Christianity was squeezed into a system congenial to pagan-Greek-rationalist thought, and in that safe protective suit of armor was able to face up to the world, but in the process it had to sacrifice its noblest moral and spiritual forces."[29] How aptly this recalls Father Combès' declaration that Augustine wanted to give the church a doctrine so strong that she would never again have anything to fear from her enemies. The armor was provided—and at what a price!

As to the administrative problems with which Augustine wrestled, we can do no better than quote from a recent study by the learned Jesuit, Father Bligh: "St. Augustine provides the perplexing spectacle of an extremely wise and holy man who began by condemning the use of force against heretics, but changed his mind after observing the good effects of coercive measures taken without his approval. . . . Reverence for Augustine," he concludes, "forbids me to say that his justification of persecution was wrong; but its fruits were evil in the centuries which followed, and we may suspect that, if he had had as much experience to reflect on as we have, Augustine would have reverted to his first opinion."[30]

Here two able Catholic scholars have described St. Augustine, the one as toiling away for whole decades trying to work out the basic problems of doctrine and failing to come out with a clear solution, and the other as doing his best in the light of his limited experience to work out a basic policy of church government—with unfortunate results. The Latter-day Saints have always maintained that guidance both in doctrinal and administrational matters can come to the church only by revelation. We couldn't ask for a better case to prove it than that of St. Augustine, precisely because he is such a good and great man. The better man he is, the better he illustrates the point, which is that *no* man, no matter how good, wise, hard-working, devoted, and well-educated he may be, can give us certainty without revelation. In Father Bligh's opinion, time has not vindicated Augustine's opinions. It has shown that we can trust only the prophets.

12

Prophets and Mystics

So far, from the tenor of these discussions one might suppose that the only access men have ever claimed to higher knowledge has been either through prophecy or philosophy. Such is far from the case: Many types and degrees of inspiration have been claimed by men through the ages, and it is time to discuss one of the most important of these, namely mysticism. Authorities on mysticism are agreed that the thing is extremely difficult if not impossible to define; yet there is a common ground upon which the experts all seem willing to stand, namely that mysticism is "an intuitive and ecstatic union with the deity obtained by means of contemplation and other mental exercises." That is the definition of Eduard Lehmann, the great Swedish scholar of comparative religions, who finds the mystic experience to be present among people in all ages and in all parts of the world, even among the most savage.[1] In the words of another authority, mysticism "under various aspects appears among all races and in all periods whenever religion and the relation of the soul to the unseen powerfully occupy the attention of men."[2] The universality of the mystic experience is matched by its remarkable uniformity in certain aspects. When a tenth-century Persian, a thirteenth-century French lady, a seventeenth-century Englishman, and a modern Hindu all report certain peculiar and unusual sensations in almost identical words we must grant that there is something behind what they say; for while any

collusion between them is impossible, yet they tell a remarkably uniform story. There certainly is something to mysticism. Is it the same thing that animated the prophets of old?
Is mysticism a form of revelation? Historically and psycho-
logically the answer is a definite negative. Consider the historical aspect of the thing.

The very universality of mysticism shows that it is not
peculiarly Christian or Jewish; it is the peculiar property of
no nation, race, society, or church. Only by a determination
to see mysticism in everything can one detect it in the Old
and New Testaments, which, as scholars are constantly discovering, are remarkably free of mystic elements. We will
recall that it never occurred to Augustine that one might
view the Bible as a mystic book until Ambrose "drew aside
the mystic veil" and showed him the hidden meaning of things
which if taken literally appeared to him simply as "perversity."
Taken as it stands, the Bible is anything but a mystic document.

How then did mysticism get into the Christian church?
In the same way it invaded the Jewish—through the schools.
It is a remarkable thing that specialists in describing the
mystic practices of various religions—Hindu, Buddhist, Sha-
manistic, Taoistic, Sufistic, etc.—always refer to Neoplatonism as supplying the best illustration. In Neoplatonism we
have the classic meeting ground of the intellectual and the
"spiritual" quests for God. "The theology of Judaism was
studied side by side with the works of Plato and Aristotle,
and thus was produced that curious blend of Jewish and
Greek thought," whose classic representation was Philo of
Alexandria, the fountainhead of Jewish and later of Christian mysticism. It may seem strange that the intellectual and
the mystical should run thus side by side in the search for
God, but it is really quite natural. "Aristotle's 'active reason,'"
as Abelson further points out in this connection, "possesses
a decidedly mystical turn."[3] And why not? Positivism is
constantly bumping into brick walls, and the mind can only

continue its course by repeated recognition of its limitations: these recognitions are momentary surrenders to mysticism, expedient admissions that the mind might move forward even where logic breaks down. Whenever Augustine finds himself in a logical deadlock, he releases the tension by the ecstatic declaration: "Still, I will cling to God!" after which he can return to his intellectual quest refreshed and relaxed. According to Jones, "The fundamental metaphysics in which the doctrine of Christian mysticism is grounded is Greek rationalistic metaphysics, formulated by Socrates and his great successors, Plato, Aristotle, and Plotinus."[4] According to Chapman, a Catholic writer, "Clement of Alexandria is the first Christian writer on mystical theology," having taken over from Philo the idea "that God is to be sought, as Moses sought Him, in the darkness."[5] Next comes Origen, to whom the cynical Celsus points out, referring to the mystical parts of his writings, that no real Christian would know what Origen was talking about. To this Origen's reply was what might be expected: that all true Christians are mystic. They close their physical eyes, he says, to see only with the spiritual,[6] just as he had declared earlier that all true Christians would, if they could, do nothing but study philosophy. We seem to be telling the same story about mysticism that we did about philosophy: The same men are introducing it into the church and using the same arguments. Why? Because they all have the same Neoplatonic background. We quoted Grabmann as attributing Augustine's great influence to the fact that he was "the greatest Christian Neoplatonist," and along with that his *Confessions* have been described as the purest mysticism. Anyone who mingled Neoplatonism with Christianity would necessarily have to bring in the mystical as well as the intellectual element, for the wedding of the two is the essence of Neoplatonism.

The founder of Neoplatonism was Ammonius Saccus. Porphyry reports that this remarkable man was born of Christian parents but left the church and returned to the religious practices of the pagan Greeks, opening a school in Alexandria, where he laid the foundations of a new interpretation of Plato: hence *Neo*platonic—the new departure from the old teaching of Plato being the doctrine that God is unknowable to the mind and must therefore be sought in the mystic darkness.[7] It is a significant fact, and one diligently bypassed by church historians, that the founder of that school of thought which was completely to remake Christian doctrine was himself an apostate from the church. Just as he was not satisfied with what he found there, so those who introduced his teachings later into the church were likewise unsatisfied with what they found—St. Augustine being the best but by no means the only example: Neoplatonism whenever it appears in Christian theology is an attempt to improve upon the gospel.

The essentially unchristian nature of mysticism is apparent from the surprisingly late date at which it was introduced into the church. It was not until Maximus the Confessor in the seventh century that "mysticism and dialectics were fused together in their authoritative form," and "Pseudodionysius and Neoplatonism were officially adopted by the Church."[8] The Pseudodionysius, the cornerstone of Christian mysticism, was produced by an unknown writer, probably a Syrian, at the end of the fifth century. From the sixth century on and for more than a thousand years, the whole church firmly believed that it was the work of that Dionysius who had been a disciple of the Apostle Paul, and "thus," writes Harnack, "Neoplatonism and mystic cult practices were accepted as classic Christian," i.e., as part of the genuine apostolic heritage![9] The writer of the pseudo-Dionysius "is influenced," according to a Catholic authority, "mainly by the Neo-Platonist Proclus. . . . He asserts the transcendence of God with extreme expressions, exaggerated from the Platonic."[10] In the opening lines of the pseudo-Dionysius we read: "Leave behind both thy senses and thine intellectual operations, and all things known by sense and intelligence, and all things which are not and which are, and set thyself, as far as may be, to unite thyself in unknowing with Him who is above all being and knowledge; for by being purely free and absolute, out of self and of all things, thou shalt be led up to the ray of the divine darkness, stripped of all and loosed from all."[11] This is the typical language of mysticism.

The Neoplatonic origin of Christian mysticism and its late introduction into the Church along with the philosophic substitute for revelation show plainly enough that we are not dealing with the prophetic gifts of the early church but a substitute for them. That mysticism is something totally different from the ancient "gifts of the Spirit" will appear if we consider its salient and universally recognized characteristics.

The foremost present-day Protestant student of mysticism writes: "From the nature of the case this experience of ecstasy and absorption is something unutterable and incommunicable. . . . It is not *like* anything else, consequently there are no terms of description for it." The mystic, having found God, "cannot hint to human ears any descriptive circumstances about the actual character of God."[12] Of the four marks of mysticism, according to William James, the first is its *ineffability*.[13] There is nothing in the mystic experience that can be conveyed to others. According to the Catholic definition, "mystical theology" originally meant "the direct, secret, and *incommunicable* knowledge of God received in contemplation."[14] As against this, the whole calling of a prophet is to communicate the will of God to men; he is a mouthpiece and a witness, and he tells what he has seen and heard; he is a man with a message. The mystic, on the other hand, has no such message: Mr. Rufus Jones becomes positively indignant at the thought of contaminating mystic purity with anything as crass and tangible as a message. Mystics, he says, "have not had secret messages from sociable angels. They have not been granted special communications as favored ambassadors to the heavenly court. They have been men and women like the rest of us," and their mystical experience is

rather an enrichment of the individual mind, an increase of
its range and depth, an enlarged outlook on life, a heighten-
ing of personality. It is much like what happens with the
refinement and culture of artistic taste, or with the appreciation of beauty in any field. [15] In other words, the visions of
mystics are not like those of prophets at all. What they convey is not knowledge, says Jones, but rather an "increase of
serenity." [16]

Even when mystics do come forth with concrete revelations, according to Jones, these "prove always, when they are
examined, to have an historical background." The greatest
mystics are bound in their mystic experiences by their social
conditioning. Thus we are told that "some of the many con-
fusions and apparent contradictions in St. Theresa's writings
may be explained by her having subordinated her own views
to the dicta of some of her confessors." [17] Can one imagine a
prophet changing his visions to suit instructions? "While they
were persecuting me, reviling me, and speaking all manner
of evil against me falsely for so saying," wrote the Prophet
Joseph of his first vision, "I was led to say in my heart: Why
persecute me for telling the truth? I have actually seen a
vision, and who am I that I can withstand God, or why does
the world think to make me deny what I have actually seen?"
Mystics are a more flexible sort. "It seems," writes Lord Raglan, "that mystics are always persons who have been brought
up in an intensely religious atmosphere. . . . The actual type
of mystic experience is always strictly conditioned. The experiences of mystics, however strange they may seem, are never
new. . . . Savage mystics and visionaries always have the
experiences which they are expected to have. . . . The experiences of mystics are never original." [18] These generaliza-
tions of Raglan's show the glaring contrast between the socially
conditioned mystic and the socially obnoxious prophet. The

dependence of mysticism on the social milieu is further illustrated by the fact that there are fads and fashions in mysticism. The mysticism of the thirteenth century was very different from that of the post-scholastic mysticism in which a
great number of inspired ladies had revelations. In the seven-
teenth century, mysticism went completely out of favor with
the churchmen; in the eighteenth, it took forms of extreme
self-dramatization and became a spectacle in literature and
art; in the nineteenth century, it almost died out entirely or
took the form of transcendentalism; in the fifth century, it
was monastic; most recently "nature-mysticism" has been in
favor. The mystics invariably follow the fashion of the hour,
both as to whether they should be mystics at all and what
form their mystical discipline should take. No such choices
are open to the prophet.

While the mystic experience itself is ineffable and incommunicable, the means by which it is arrived at comprise a set
and established discipline which the aspiring mystic must
always learn from a teacher. Dean Inge gives as the first of
his four characteristics of mysticism its esoteric nature, which
can be learned only in silence and subordination at the feet
of an expert.[19] The great bulk of mystic writings, Christian
and non-Christian, is taken up with discussions of the course
of study and action to be followed by any person who would
achieve the mystic experience. Elaborate systems of discipline are carefully worked out; mental techniques must be
acquired; above all, clearly marked steps of progress, usually three—(in St. Theresa's system seven)—are set before
the student. This disciplinary procedure, the way of illumination, is the chief mark of mysticism throughout the world.
Thus in theory the Buddhists deny any but rational and scientific knowledge, yet "where such practices [concentration,
trances, ecstasies, etc.] are found, there is 'mysticism.'"[20]
Recall that Lehmann defined mysticism as a "union with
deity *obtained* by means of contemplation and other mental
exercises." This is a totally different thing from the "good

works" by which the saints become deserving of revelations. They do what God prescribes for their good, and in return he gives them what he wants to and in the way and the time he wants to. The mystic, on the other hand, works his way forward to an expected objective; he knows what he wants, and he knows there is a way to get it; a tried and tested procedure has been handed down from mystic to mystic through the ages.

Earlier we quoted from the *Didaché* the true test of a prophet, namely that if he attempts to teach his gift to another he is not a true prophet. The mystic gift, on the other hand, *must* be taught. It is an interesting thing that the Montanists, though they practiced true mystic techniques, were *false* prophets. They tried to use the steps of the mystic discipline to arrive at the gift of prophecy and of course failed. Though one person can tell another exactly how to have an opium or marijuana dream, he can never tell the other what the dream is like—he can only wallow in vague superlatives. It is so with mysticism. The great mystics tell us what we must do to have a mystical experience, but the experience itself is ineffable. With the prophets it is the very opposite. The mystic has his experience as the dreamer has his dream—all to himself. The mystic, according to Jones, finds "in a consciousness transcending images, ideas or states of any kind, a junction of soul-centre with Absolute Reality—'a flight of the alone to the Alone.'"[21] Since we know that the mystic experience must be induced, usually by long years of dedicated practice and determination, and since it is wholly the experience of the Alone by the alone, how can we deny that it is *self-induced?* "Introspective" is Dean Inge's word for it. The mystic deliberately works himself into a state. This is what impresses students in the extremely unmystical nature of supernatural experiences in the New Testament. On Pentecost a large group shared a common experience, saw certain sights, and heard certain sounds; so it was at the baptism of Christ, on the Mount of Transfiguration, at the Ascension—always there was a *plurality* of witnesses; always they are surprised by what happens; always definite things are seen and heard, and definite knowledge is imparted to the human race. There was nothing self-induced and nothing expected in these experiences. The Way of Light in the ancient Christian Doctrine of the Two Ways is not the Mystic Way of Illumination: we are told fully and explicitly what it was, namely the keeping of the Lord's commandments, the reward being not the sudden flash of mystic illumination nor involvement in the Cloud of Unknowing, but a strong and steady testimony of the gospel.

Not only are the mystics wholly alone in their private and incommunicable inner clouds of darkness, but also when they compare notes, we can never find out where they stand. Of the post-scholastic mystics we are told that "the accounts given by these various seers are impossible to reconcile with each other," and that "the value of all these revelations varies according to the intellectual power of the recipient. . . . Delusions," furthermore, "are always exceedingly common in such cases, even in real mystics of holy life, and may occur in the case of saints who have insisted that all their words came from God." We must not deny that they are real, holy revelations, according to our Catholic authority, "simply because they are mistaken or even absurd."[22] But if that is so, what have we got? The Dominicans, Benedictines, Carmelites, and Jesuits all hold radically different opinions as to who, if anyone, has beheld the beatific vision; St. John of the Cross, one of the greatest mystics, will have nothing to do with visions and locutions, which he ascribes to bodily weakness, while other doctors of the soul urge such experience upon their disciples as the culmination of the Mystic Way. Such mystic revelations, we are reliably informed, "are commoner in women than in men, and are more frequent in persons of feeble intellect."[23] Finally there is the confession so often met with in the great mystics, that, in the words of Gregory the Great, "it is impossible in this life to see God as

He is—that is reserved for Heaven."[24] What you get instead is such vague expressions as those which Rufus Jones has reverently collected: one mystic feels "an overbrimming sense of presence," another is "inclosed in a warm lucent bubble of livingness," another "hires sunshine for leaden hours," and so forth.[25] Plainly the mystics are in a class by themselves, with their big, vague, inexpressible, self-induced, hotly pursued moments of indefinable and incommunicable union with something whose nature totally escapes them. They are a bona fide historical phenomenon, but not necessarily a Christian one. They are a fascinating society, but as unlike the prophets, ancient and modern, as humans can be.

When revelation ceased from the church, an intellectual substitute was ready to hand in the culture and learning of the schools; the same schools also came forward with a "spiritual" offering which the church gladly accepted. That was mysticism. Few if any scholars will deny that Neoplatonism is the source of Christian mystic theology, Catholic and Protestant, and none will deny that it is a key representative of a universal pagan world mysticism. The gospel lies wholly outside this historical current. It has been restored in these latter days by direct revelation, and has flourished in the earth for over one hundred years, without ever having to draw upon the dubious resources of mysticism. One alone among all the churches in the world since the days of the ancient Apostles has been able to resist the blandishments and dispense with even the occasional services of this useful but highly unreliable discipline. Here we have another most convincing test and vindication of the prophets.

13

Rhetoric and Revelation

No less significant than the invasion of the church by philosophy and mysticism was the victory of rhetoric in the preaching of the word. Again we must turn to the schools if we would find the culprit. By the time the church was ready to adopt the teachings of the schools, they were no longer following the way of philosophy but had become wholly rhetorical. It was rhetoric that conquered and destroyed ancient education.[1] In St. Augustine's day rhetoric had won complete control of all education. When the emperor established the great state University of Constantinople in 425, just when Augustine's work of introducing secular education into the church was at its height, he provided for one chair in philosophy, two in law, and twenty-eight in grammar and rhetoric.[2] Augustine himself we are told "studied it [rhetoric] for ten years, taught it for fifteen, and practiced it all his life."[3]

What was rhetoric? Aristotle defines it as the "art of persuasion," the technical skill by which one convinces people —convinces, that is, everybody of anything for a fee, according to Clement of Alexandria. It is the training and skill by which one can make unimportant things seem important, according to Plato, or, to quote Clement again, "make false opinions seem true by means of words."[4] With the rise of the so-called second sophistic movement in the middle of the second century B.C., an army of brilliant and high-powered talkers, having caught the public fancy as traveling virtuosi, opened schools which in short order got a monopoly of public and private education. Their method of procedure in talking everyone else out of the picture followed a well-defined pattern. The first step was to choose some object of science or art upon which society placed a value and for which it was willing to pay in cash and glory. The subject chosen was immaterial, the teacher of rhetoric boasted, since rhetoric is equal to anything. Having chosen his "field" the student was then introduced to the broad and general aspect of the thing—the *skopos*; detailed knowledge was not the object but only a good grasp of the main idea, the *prothesis*. In a very short time, a matter of weeks, the student would find himself in the happy position of being able to meet the public with a plausible imitation of real knowledge which if it was lacking depth and solidity enjoyed certain added features that more than made up for the obvious defects in his learning. These added features, which were guaranteed to make the imitation product more appealing than the genuine, were simplicity, brevity, and glamor.[5] Clement of Alexandria, following Aristotle, says that rhetoric "abstracts in a specious manner the whole business of wisdom, and professes a wisdom which it has not studied."[6] But that sort of thing paid: Boethus of Tarsus, who advertised that he could speak extemporaneously for any length of time on any subject in the world, became the most powerful man in his city and one of the richest in the Empire. Rhetoric, "the queen of the world," was simply super-salesmanship; and the rhetorician sought in the end to sell not goods but himself, in the words of Seneca, who repeatedly advises the youth of the land to study nothing but rhetoric since it alone holds the key to success. If you can impress people, rhetoric taught, the world is yours.[7]

The ancients attributed the founding of this wonderful *techne* to Empedocles. After he had reached the conclusion that life is too short to be seeking truth the hard way, that brilliant impostor, in his hunger for quick and sensational success, saw his way clear: Wealth, fame, and even divinity, he discovered, are the gift if not of heaven, certainly of the general public for the man who knows how to talk it out of them. Empedocles' pupil Gorgias, like himself a born showman, enjoyed a sensationally successful career teaching rhetoric, which he frankly describes as the secret of winning success by cultivating appearances. In the dialogue named after him, Gorgias is flatly charged by Socrates with propagating a mock philosophy whose aim is not knowledge but the appearance of knowledge. Socrates also foresees that honest study has no more chance of competing with this sort of thing than a conscientious doctor would have of keeping his child patient, in competition with a pastry cook who prescribed nothing but dessert. As if to prove this point, old Strepsiades in Aristophanes' delightful comedy the *Clouds* leaves Socrates' "Thinkatorium" in disgust when instead of being taught how to get rich by "out-talking every other man in Athens by ten stades" he is put to work on the problems of Ionian science. What he was looking for was education for success, the very thing that the rhetoricians guaranteed to supply. Lucian tells us that the public simply laughed at the hard courses of the philosophers and went across the street to the rhetorical schools that advertised the *same* knowledge available in quick and effortless courses with positive assurance of a good job and big pay. Rhetorical education eliminated from its curriculum everything that the student would not put to direct use in the social situation. Lucian illustrates this with the story of a youth who came to consult the foremost flutist of the day, Harmonides, about taking lessons. A serious preliminary discourse by the master on the work, sacrifice, and hardship entailed in mastering his difficult instrument was interrupted by the young man, who hastened to explain that he was not interested in being a *good* flute player, but only in becoming a *successful* one. [8] The flute was not his passion, but a career was, to which the flute was merely a tool to aid him.

As their courses became ever simpler, shorter, and spic-
ier (by the time of the Neoplatonists Proclus and Iamblichus
little remains but a violent spicing), the rhetoricians supplanted content with glamor, which they cultivated with great
skill. Psychologists by avocation, they saw that if the lost,
witless world of declining antiquity hungered for intellectual
and spiritual guidance, it was simply mad for entertainment.
So with their wonderful art the Sophists, the great traveling
orators, supplied everything at once. Performing foxes, a tight-
rope artist, a fifteen-minute domestic skit, a couple of clowns
telling dirty jokes, and a famous traveling rhetor would make
up an afternoon in the theater. In the schools they were sensational. No ambitious youth would think of studying in
their time with anyone but Polemon or Stilpo. Topnotch
rhetors amassed immense fortunes by fabulous gifts and fees;
their sons and daughters married into the imperial family;
they ruled their communities like little tyrants, while great
cities eagerly bade for their services, and the whole world
zealously followed every detail of their private lives.[9] Never
had an educational project succeeded so well as theirs once
the resistance of philosophy had been broken by their imitation philosophy. Their schools became the state schools, and
all private instruction was officially prohibited. Every town
in the empire kept its own staff of high salaried grammarians
and Sophists, and boasted of being a little Athens in its own
right. And it was all just show: the deliberate cultivation of
appearances as the surest road to money and success. "It is
astounding," writes Professor Schanz, "with what silly stuff
the public was fed." But the public asked for no better, and
the rule of rhetoric was: Give people what they want, and
you have them where you want them.[10]

Why have we dwelt at length on this unhappy theme?
Because this rhetoric as we have been describing it was adopted
lock, stock, and barrel by the church at the same time it
embraced philosophy and mysticism. To become a world
church, according to Raby, the Christians had to come to

terms with the public schools, with the result that "the influence of the schools of grammar and rhetoric is apparent in every page of Tertullian, of Jerome, and of Augustine," and he cites Norden on how "Augustine could pile rime upon rime in an array of parallel phrases, and use all the resources of rhetoric in tasteless profusion."[11] In the early church, according to Zellinger in his study of Christian rhetoric, rhetoric was avoided like the plague; "content was everything while its verbal presentation counted for nothing." But when the church became the Imperial Church, then the "pampered ear demanded of the preacher the same language which it was used to hearing in the lawcourts and from the rostrum. And the church gave in, in spite of all theoretical insistence on preserving the old simplicity of the gospel."[12] In the fourth century, says this authority, "the simple language of the primitive Christian sermon had to compromise with the idiom of the sophistic rhetoric." The process began, according to him, with our old friend Origen, and reached its full development under the great Christian orators of the fourth century. The first and foremost qualification for the office of bishop from then on was *eloquentia*. "In the middle of the fourth century a complete revolution took place in the language of the Christian sermon," he writes. "The earliest Church had preached in exceedingly plain and simple language, and . . . scrupulously avoided any contact with the ill-reputed rhetoric of the imperial age." But all this was suddenly taken over by the church, and, says Zellinger, "along with hellenistic rhetoric and its ear-tickling refinements there were smuggled into the churches the established techniques of applause. Approval was expressed by noisy shouts, hand-clapping, stamping of feet on the floor, jumping up and down, and the waving of handkerchiefs. The sermons were interrupted by resounding shouts of 'True Believer!' 'Teacher of the Universe!' 'Thirteenth Apostle!' 'Anathema to whoever disagrees!'" and so forth.[13]

Augustine's plays on words, says Norden, the foremost authority on the subject of ancient rhetoric, were eaten up by the general public, and those sermons of his that seem "tasteless and contrived to us . . . enchanted the congregation"; [14] by the middle of the fifth century, he says, Christian rhetoric had reached a permanent state of "absolute inanity." Augustine and all the great orating fathers knew that what they were doing was wrong, and often confessed it, but it was what the public expected, and no rhetorician ever denied the public that. "The age of preachers had begun," writes Raby; the speech-hungry crowds everywhere "waited in tense excitement for the pointed epigram or for the rimed periods which were worthy of their applause." [15] The Christian preachers adjusted their style to their audience, like true salesmen, or true rhetoricians. [16] The classic charge brought against the rhetoricians throughout antiquity—one that Socrates never tires of repeating—was that their whole search is not for truth but for success: their trade was fundamentally dishonest. Of the orating bishops, the glory of the fourth century, Gibbon says, "the true size and color of every object is falsified by the exaggerations of their corrupt eloquence," [17] a verdict fully confirmed and illustrated by the works of Zellinger, Norden, Rhode, Raby, and others.

The bequest of pagan rhetoric was part of the permanent Christian heritage. "The education of Augustine was," according to Marrou, "that of a lettered man of the decadence, formed by the *grammaticus* and the rhetor, with dialectic thrown in. Grammar and dialectic! But these are actually the foundations of scholasticism!" [18] Rhetoric was in to stay; and in two ways the rhetorical school fatally undermined the Christian society that embraced it. The first was by its strong note of unveracity, the second by the tyranny of numbers. As to the unveracity, even the great Cicero had announced that *facultas* and *copia* must take precedence over *veritatis forma* in rhetoric, [19] and Augustine says rhetoric is the more praiseworthy the more fraudulent it is. [20] This falseness was, as Rhode has pointed out, inevitable. One was trained to give speeches on great occasions, and to be proficient one had to practice. The rhetorical philosophy of education took to heart the admonition of Aristotle in the eighth Book of the Metaphysics that "we learn to do by doing." Accordingly, month after month and year after year in the schoolroom and in their field trips to the forums and lawcourts, armies of students addressed imaginary nations on the brink of legendary wars or shed real tears for a mythical Hecuba.[21] Augustine recalls that his first assignment in school was to declaim the words that Juno would have spoken when she realized her failure to keep Aeneas away from Italy—to put real feeling into a totally unreal situation, to pour out his soul in a fictive and artificial crisis.[22] And in such exercises the secret of success was before all else to convince one's hearers that one was "sincere." Drilled endlessly in this sort of thing, the rhetorical mind becomes incurably trivial; it takes the wrong things seriously; a neat manipulation of words passes as thought; hackneyed and extravagant declamation goes for feeling. Because of rhetoric, says Dio, words have lost their meaning and all things are thrown into confusion.[23]

Equally dangerous and equally persistent in the heritage of the rhetorical school is its second gift to civilization: the tyranny of numbers. During those same childish speeches in which he feigned the whole gamut of emotions, the youthful Augustine was, he tells us, in a very real panic of anxiety, knowing the slightest slip on his part might well mean the ruin of his whole career. For the rhetorician the bottom of the world falls out and everything goes black when an utterance fails to "go over." A mortal fear of failing to please; a morbid dread of being out of line; an anxious, hair-trigger attention (so often betrayed by Cicero) to the exact volume and direction of applause are the ingrained product of such training. By definition the success of the rhetor is directly

proportional to the applause he receives: the greater the cheer-
ing, the greater the authority and glory of the one cheered.
This goes even for God, described by Augustine as the Great
Orator, whose glory is defective as long as a single voice
fails to acclaim him. [24]

This idea of *gloria* saturates the world of late antiquity,
which was to an astonishing extent preoccupied with theatrical demonstrations designed to proclaim the power and
perfection of some earthly or heavenly leader. It receives its
fullest expression in the panegyric orations of the fourth and
fifth centuries in the grandiose, monumental architecture of
the period, both of which were adopted whole-cloth by the
church. And why? Why was this ruinous thing which wrecks
all values and confounds reason, which is constantly
denounced as a snare and a delusion by the very fathers that
use it most, so completely triumphant in the church? "Those
modest orators," wrote Gibbon with his usual touch of irony,
"acknowledged that, as they were destitute of the gift of miracles, they endeavored to acquire the arts of eloquence." [25]
That is the answer: like philosophy and mysticism, rhetoric
was a substitute. The synthetic glory of the panegyrist is, St.
Augustine declares, most welcome to the church, which needs
a spice and vigor in its doctrine that only rhetoric could
give[26]—so far had the church come from the day of Pentecost! For St. Augustine the Christian orators, properly trained
in the schools, speak with the voice of God; they are angels
mediating between heaven and earth; they are the tongue of
Christ, the doctors of the soul, the mountain of refuge, shel-
tering clouds, nurses of the church, the feet of the Lord;
they, in short, are henceforth what the prophets and Apostles once were to the church. [27] To speak in tongues, says
Chrysostom (whose own title means Golden-mouth), is not
as great as to prophesy, since prophecy is the interpretation
of tongues; but a greater thing than prophecy even is to be
able to give a good oration! [28] This was in answer to people
who kept asking Chrysostom why the church no longer had

the gift of prophecy: The answer is an enlightening one, namely that the church now has rhetoric, which is better than prophecy. John's own sermons, of which, fortunately, a great number have survived, clearly proclaim his intention of making rhetoric do the work of prophecy and revelation. The clarion voice, the waving arms, the flashing eye, the studied poses and sweet modulations, and ear- and mouth-filling words that thrilled the hearers like the clash of cymbals and had just as little meaning, the sweeping robes, the musical background (a very important adjunct of church-rhetoric)—what spells could they not weave? What multitude could resist them? St. Augustine himself reports that he listened spellbound to the electrifying sermons of the immortal Ambrose without paying the slightest attention to what the man was saying; carried away by his words; as he puts it, he remained indifferent or even contemptuous of their content. [29]

Since the fourth century the Christian church has talked with strange voices, the voices of philosophy, mysticism, and rhetoric, coming to us from the decadent schools of late antiquity. The third of these voices, that of rhetoric, was designed for the manipulation of the masses, and has been the guiding voice of the churches throughout the centuries. Like the others, it is a substitute for the voice of prophecy. But even more conspicuously than they, its artificial vocabulary and studied delivery, not to mention its fully documented history, proclaim its true origin and its sad inadequacy. If the cerebrations of the philosophers and the fervid sighs of the mystics fall pitifully short of anything resembling true revelation, the careful sound- and stage-effects of the rhetorician are the ultimate declaration of bankruptcy. After attending the discourses of the greatest Christian orators, we can only repeat what we have said before: there is no substitute for revelation.

14

Prophets and Reformers

Our text for this discussion is Hebrews 6:4-5: "It is impossible for those who were once enlightened, and have tasted of the heavenly gift, and were made partakers of the Holy Ghost, and have tasted the good word of God, and the powers of the world to come"— At this point we pause and ask the church historians just what is impossible regarding those people who have been blessed with every gift and power that God gives to men on earth? To our question we receive the unanimous and reassuring answer that it is impossible for people once so mightily endowed ever wholly to lose the gospel; God has not given his greatest gifts to men, we are assured, simply to have them turn their backs on him. Is it possible or even conceivable, the churchmen have asked in every century, that after giving such great blessings and signs and wonders to the church, God should ever remove his Spirit from it or rather remove his church from the earth? Here is the answer of the Apostle (and the Apostolic Fathers later confirm it with passion): it *is* possible, entirely possible, for those who have received the greatest promises and blessings that heaven bestows to lose everything; the words of the author of Hebrews are meant as a warning against just that. What is *not* possible is that men who have once lost those blessings should ever regain them again by any efforts of their own: "It is impossible . . . if they shall fall away, to renew them again unto repentance" (Hebrews 6:6). Our author then compares such people to ground which has become overgrown with thorns and briers. Other land, he says, can drink rain from heaven and bring forth vegetation when the time of refreshment comes, but for that land that was once rich in goodly herbs and then turned to weeds there is no such hope: "But that which beareth thorns and briers is rejected, and is nigh unto cursing; whose end is to be burned" (Hebrews 6:8). The *Pastor of Hermas* reminds the church again and again that after a certain day soon to come it will no longer be possible for Christians to repent or reform though repentance will continue to remain open to the heathen. There is, we are informed in this wonderful writing, a point of no return for the church beyond which reform will be impossible.

Perhaps the foremost living authority on the history of Christianity, the German Lutheran scholar Heinrich Bornkamm, has stated in a recent book that there are just two periods in church history; the first, he says, is that of "Hellenization, that is, the absorption of antique sacramental religion into the early Catholic and Medieval Church," and the second is the period of "the purging of the Church of these foreign elements following the Reformation, that is, the epoch of recapturing the prophetic religiosity of Primitive Christianity."[1] Read in the light of conventional church histories of the past, this statement is really quite an astonishing admission: first of the extent to which alien and unchristian things came to displace the real gospel; and second of the fact that any return to the pure religion of Christ must necessarily be a return to *prophetic* religion. Can such a return be achieved by reformation? It cannot. For one thing, Bornkamm speaks as if the pagan elements in Christianity were a single concrete intrusion of a foreign body into the organism, a hard, unassimilated lump which needed simply to be rejected in one piece to restore perfect health to the ailing system. Yet no one knows or describes better than Bornkamm how long and thorough the process of assimilation has been. The teachings of the schools and the practices of the world have become an integral part of the organism; they have transformed it completely; we have already quoted scholars of various faiths who all marvel at the perfect organic union of the Christian and classical traditions into a new and perfectly integrated whole. Could the church suddenly and easily slough off what had been completely assimilated into its very being for over a thousand years, to return again to what she had been before the great compromise with the world? Can one reconvert a petrified organism that has been transmuted from one substance to another through the centuries, molecule by molecule? Or, to use the figure employed by the Lord himself, when salt has lost its savor there is only one thing to do with it—throw it out (Matthew 5:13). To corrupt the gospel is to lose it; the plan of salvation and the Church of Jesus Christ may not be changed without being lost and when lost may not be regained by any process of reformation. This is not narrowness or pedantry; we see it in all our basic institutions.

When a language is changed, whether for better or for worse, that language is lost, and the only way we can find it again is to discover ancient and undefiled sources—all the zeal in the world can never reform us back to early English. A French scholar has recently asked, can we revive classical studies by reproducing "the miracle of the Renaissance?" The Renaissance was not actually a revival of ancient learning, however, but a wholly new type of learning based on the study of the ancients, and what brought it about was not the work of reformers but the accidental discovery of ancient texts preserved in some purity by centuries of complete neglect. Consider the gospel in this light: When the covenants were broken and the ordinances changed, and the churches taught for doctrines the commandments of men, the old gospel was simply no longer there. Today church historians, Protestant and Catholic alike, agree that this was so, and they easily reconcile themselves to the situation by insisting that what took the place of the old church was really something much better, something far more fit for survival in a wicked world, much more available to the grasp and amenable to the taste

of the average man. The early church, they explain, was
something hopelessly impractical and of extremely limited
popular appeal; therefore, it had to go; it was merely a tiny
acorn from which a mighty oak was to grow, etc. Well,
what interests us here is not their explanation and justification of what happened, but the admission that it did happen.
The primitive church was changed, and thereby the primitive church was lost. And to this we add the thesis that such
loss was an irreversible process. Reformation could no more
bring it back than it could bring back Old English, eighteenth-
century monarchy, or the thinking of the Scipionic Circle.

In the earliest Christian writings we often come across
the prediction regarding the future of the church that the
sheep would turn to wolves. What would they be in that
case—a new breed of sheep? Not a bit of it: the sheep as
such would cease to exist, however loudly the wolves might
continue to call themselves sheep and parade their Christian
background and tradition and name. The Lord and the Apostles use the examples of the salt that is spoiled, the tares that
destroy the wheatfield until they can be burned, the wolves
that destroy the flock, and the sheep that turn into wolves,
precisely because weeds and wolves, briers, and salt that has
lost its savor are things that can never be reformed: they are
beyond saving. "In the days of old," writes Duchesne, "Christians had cursed the Babylon of the Seven Hills; now they
were conquering her and were going to convert her. What
triumph could be more desirable?"[2] That was the fourth century view, but, as Duchesne knows, for the true Christians
Babylon was never going to be converted or reformed.
Babylon, like the tares and the brambles, had but one fate in
store for it—it was reserved for the burning. It was common
for the earliest Christian writers to speak of the church as a
virgin. "Up to that time," wrote Hegesippus, speaking of the
end of the apostolic age, "the Church had remained a pure
and uncorrupted virgin."[3] Can that status when lost—and
Hegesippus says it *was* lost—ever be acquired again? What

about repentance, you ask; wasn't Israel, though her sins were as scarlet, to be washed white as snow? (Isaiah 1:18). Yes, but never by reformation—always by restoration. If Israel is ever renewed, it must be by a new covenant and a new Jerusalem—and such can never be worked out by men here below; they must always come from above.

Such a renewal came in the time of Christ. He restored the gospel to the earth; he did not attempt to reform the doctrines and institutions he found there. As a reformer he would have been welcomed by the Jewish and Hellenic worlds, as we have noted before; reform was in the air, and the early Christians greatly offended by refusing to join in the ecumenical movements of the times.[4] Christ brought the true teachings of Moses, Abraham, and the prophets; but he did not obtain them by antiquarian researches; he made no attempt to establish an historical continuity with them, as all the Christian churches do. What he brought to men he brought directly from the presence of the Father; that is why it was identical with what the other prophets had received—not because he got it from them, but because they too had received direct revelation from on high. As Eusebius tells us, in every dispensation the eternal gospel is brought to the earth as something *new*. We have talked on this before; what we want to emphasize now is that the Lord never renews his work on earth by reforming old things. The gospel is not built on old traditions. When God sets up his work in any age of the world he chooses his own instruments, and they are bright and shining ones, clean and undefiled, whether institutions or men and women. He does not leave them to guess and wonder, as the great reformers, Protestant and Catholic, do through decades of perplexity and doubt, but calls them directly from heaven, often as children—as David, Samuel, Nephi, and Joseph Smith were called—before they have any knowledge of the world at all. The reformer takes his cue from the world about him—the prophet never does. The sad state of the world may lead one to call upon God, and as a result God may speak to one directly, but the mere recognition that this is a wicked world and that the divine order is sorely needed in it does not constitute a call from God to establish that order. The Lord chose his Apostles from among men who showed no signs of wishing to reform the world, each being apparently resigned to his position in life; Paul was actually a reactionary seeking to defend the status quo when the Lord called him.

A reformer is one keenly aware of the abuses in the world about him, who wants to do all he can to remedy things. Any honest and alert person can discover on every side much need for reform in this dark and dreary world; and God expects us all to engage in such activities on our own initiative, as did the Good Samaritan. But God's work is not founded on the wickedness of men. There is nothing negative about it. Who does not know that men are foolish and unkind? "It needs no ghost come from the dead, my lord, to tell us that." If the purpose of man's existence were but to remedy evil, he would be a dependent of the devil. "If the gentiles have not charity," said the Lord to Moroni, "it mattereth not unto thee." There is nothing negative in the gospel. If we have said a great deal about the falling away and the loss of the true gospel to mankind in ancient times, let us make it clear here and now that such a teaching is *not* a part of the gospel at all; it is not found in the Articles of Faith; it has no bearing at all upon the plan of life and salvation; Joseph Smith almost never referred to it. We only mention the great apostasy because it is an historical point on which we are constantly being challenged: "How can you say," we are asked every day, "that the gospel of Jesus Christ has been restored to the earth if the Christian church has never ceased to be here?"

One answer to that question is found in the activities of the reformers. Let us make it clear that the attempt to reform the Christian church to its lost state of pristine purity did not begin with Luther. In *every century* since the Apostles men have made determined attempts to reform the church, and they have always run into the same problem that Luther did, namely the question: Who has the right to inaugurate reform? We know who can amend the Constitution, as we know who established it. But with the church it is an entirely different thing. It was established by Jesus Christ personally. If any amendments, changes, or reforms are in order, they should be his doing, but how can that be unless he speaks to men by revelation? Bornkamm says the Reformation was a return to the "prophetic religiosity of Primitive Christianity." The word *prophetic* is significant: Bornkamm realizes that to return to the primitive church is to return to a church led by prophets. That was what the Reformation should have been and tried to be. The first enthusiasts of the Reformation, as of many earlier reformations, wanted before everything to get right back to the prophets—not just to reading them, but to enjoying the actual gift of prophecy itself. And so we have such determined and enthusiastic men as Thomas Münzer, Andreas Karlstadt, and Sebastian Frank, against whom in 1525 Luther wrote his work entitled *Wider die himmlischen Propheten,*—Against the Heavenly Prophets. His objection was not that there should be no prophets, but simply that these men were not prophets; with characteristic honesty he saw that the mere recognition of the fact that prophets are necessary does not authorize one to be a prophet. Luther himself was very cautious on this head; he "did not want a schism in the Church," writes Bornkamm, "but the renewal of the Church of Christ. . . . He deliberately put off giving new orders to the renewed churches, and he *never* felt that he himself was called to give such orders." He actually waited twenty years "before he admitted in the important writing, *Concerning Councils and Churches* (1539), that the movement which he had inaugurated was not a provisional thing pending the general reform of the Church, for which he hoped, but was itself that reform."[5] Luther hoped for action by a general council. But what is the authority of such? In the introduction to his famous work on the councils, von Hefele, the Catholic Bishop of Regensburg, shows that the question of whether even an ecumenical council is under the direction of the Holy Ghost has never been definitely settled. Luther's reform was promptly followed by a thoroughgoing reform of the Catholic Church itself—and that again was the work of a council, one of the most famous of all councils, the Tridentinum, at which the French and Spanish clergymen were alarmed and incensed over the claims to authority put forth by the Italians—even there the issue of authority was not clear.

Today it is admitted throughout the whole Christian world, and moreso every day, that "a plurality of churches contradicts the fundamental nature of a religion that claims that absolute truth which alone is commensurate with the character of a revealed religion."[6] The true revealed church can only be one; but reformers take many directions, and there is not a single church in the Christian world which is not the product of many reforms—and the largest of these churches has undergone the most numerous and the most thorough reforms of all. And now a new reform is proposed by which the many should become one: all the Protestants should amalgamate on the one hand, and on the other the Eastern and Western churches should again become one. This illustrates the impossibility of restoring a divinely established system to its state of pristine divinity once men have spoiled it, for the oneness of the church is original to it, and essential; it is not a thing contrived or achieved by ecumenical movements and fusions. It is not a unity that men work out in recognition of its logical necessity. It is a thing which is given to men with the church itself, by divine direction. If "a plurality of churches contradicts . . . that absolute truth which alone is commensurate with the character of a revealed religion," such a plurality is none the less implicit in the proposition that reformers as such have the authority to act in the name of the Lord, for if the recognition of evils, the urge to correct them, and the guidance of the Bible can authorize one man to step forth and change the church, they can also authorize another, and there is no end to the doctrines and factions that result. The Church of Jesus Christ of Latter-day Saints is not the product, as are all the other churches in Christendom, of reformation or of counter-reformation; it is the product of direct revelation only. Changes there must be, but they can come in only one way—through a prophet of God.

15

The Prophets
and the Open Mind

Being expert neither in the field of science nor of religion, we are relieved of the responsibility of discussing a theme whose treatment has suffered from everything but neglect. It is possible, however, to treat the well-worn problem of science versus religion in all its familiar aspects purely as history and without ever leaving the ancient world, for not only were the people of late antiquity even more modern and sophisticated than those of our own world, but they thought of themselves as being very scientific, and they were. Long before and after Lucretius, the intellectuals insisted on a religious belief that would square exactly with everyday experience, a thoroughly common-sense and practical religion, a scientific religion in which there was no place for any nonsense about the supernatural, that is, for anything that lay beyond their own immediate experience. The fashionable religion of the educated classes was a sort of social gospel; its attitude to the universe that of *nil admirari*—"don't get worked up about anything." The only problems worth troubling about were the social problem of getting along together and the individual problem of making money and enjoying life as much as possible—all the rest was "Old Wives' Tales."

Such a philosophy of life may be very well in its way, but let us not call it religion. Not long ago there flourished a Soviet poet, Vadim Shershenevich, who demanded "in the name of modernity, or futurity, the liberation of words from the burden of meaning. 'Free the words from their sense and

contents [he cried], which have stuck like chewed paper about
the word's pure image. . . . There is not, and should not be,
any sense or contents in art.' "[1] To attribute meaning to
words is a stuffy, quaint, narrow, old-fashioned, bourgeois
prejudice; yet poor Shershenevich himself could not preach
his doctrine of liberating all words from any meaning except
by using words that still had meaning. Just so there are ministers who would give us religion freed from the burden of
the supernatural, liberated from any old-fashioned involve-
ments with anything beyond our everyday experience, but
this doctrine of religion, with religion left out, they can convey only by using a religious vocabulary which taken in the
denatured sense in which they want it to be taken would
have no meaning at all. Like Shershenevich, they appeal for
the abandonment of the only thing that gives their appeal
any force. Nothing has been more often defined than religion, and after all the philosophy, ethics, aesthetics, and sen-
timentality are accounted for and claimed by their proper
practitioners, the irreducible religious element of religion
remains— the concern with things which are not of this
world.[2]

The Barthian school, according to Mr. Rufus Jones,
"insist[s] that God must be 'an absolute Other.' We belittle
Him and drag Him down from His true being, they say,
when we say anything about Him in terms of our poor, thin,
finite selves. There is nothing in us or about us through
which He can be interpreted. No piling up of our empty
zeros will even start on the road to infinity. Earth had no
clue to offer, history had no word to say that gives any light
on the exalted theme of God. We belong in the order of
'nature' and He is utterly supernatural." Now no one will
accuse Mr. Jones of being stuffy or fundamentalist—none of
your supernatural religions for him! Yet this attitude of the
Barthians is too much even for him to take; it might all be
perfectly true, he tells us, but true or not, it cannot possibly
be called Christian or religion: "If nothing of the divine nature

can be expressed in the human," he retorts, "then the incarnation of God in Christ has no real meaning or significance, and nothing that we say about God is anything more than a *flatus vocis*, an empty breath of sound. Religion once more withdraws from earth and becomes an irrationality—a mere surd—and is therefore to be left behind."[3] Jones sees the folly of the whole thing—when it is carried to its logical conclusions. But has he any right to take Barth to task simply for taking his own liberal dogma farther than he himself is willing to go? Barth has put God out of the reckoning; in the name of the Bible and religion we cannot do that, says Jones. Yet he and the whole liberal school have long since struck the prophets and the miracles and the devil from the record and made of the resurrection a mere *flatus vocis*, though the Bible insists on them just as emphatically as it does on the incarnation. Mr. Jones wants to keep an open mind—up to a point. He chuckles and chides at those quaint reactionaries who won't carry open-mindedness as far as he thinks it should be carried, but rolls a scandalized eye and clucks a warning tongue at those foolish radicals who carry it farther than that. The whole question turns out to be not whether one is going to be open-minded or not—Jones himself is not open-minded in the matter of the incarnation, and the Barthians have their minds completely made up on the unsearchability of God—but at what point one chooses to draw the line. And even in the case of these two extreme liberals one cannot help noting that where each man is strong and positive is precisely in the area in which he has made up his mind, i.e., where he is *not* open-minded.

Is an open mind, then, a negative thing—an empty mind? It is, unless it is a searching mind. An oyster has few prejudices—in the field of astronomy it has, we may safely say, absolutely none. Are we then to congratulate the oyster for its open-mindedness? A first-rate and very broad-minded scientist, J. B. S. Haldane, defines prejudice as "an opinion held without examining the evidence."[4] Prejudice does not

consist in having made up one's mind—in defending an opinion with fervor and determination—as too many liberals seem
to think; it consists in forming an opinion before all the evidence has been considered. This means that freedom from
prejudice whether in the field of science or any other field
requires a tremendous lot of work—one cannot be unpreju-
diced without constant and laborious study of evidence; the
open mind must be a searching mind. The person who claims
allegiance to science in his thinking or who is an advocate of
the open mind has let himself in for endless toil and trouble.

But what has happened? Those who have called themselves liberals in religion have accepted science with open
arms precisely because they believe that excuses them from
any toil at all. For them to have an open mind means to
accept without question, and without any personal examination of evidence, whatever the prevailing opinions of the
experts may prescribe. This is what Haldane calls prejudice.
Evolution was hailed as the new gospel not because it raised
new questions or spurred some men to new searches, but
because for the man in the street and the lazy student, as
well as for the people who wrote books for them, it meant
the end of all searching and the end of all doubt. Here was
the answer to everything, and no open-minded nonsense about
it. I recently reviewed a two-volume work on ancient history
in which the author had obviously not bothered to read
more than a fraction of his sources. Why should he bother?
By the evolutionary rule-of-thumb he could reconstruct the
whole broad course of history with confidence and ease,
oblivious to the disquieting fact that the documents, had he
taken the trouble to read them, would have told him a very
different story. Evolution was the conclusion on which he
based his facts. The doctrine, however useful in other fields,
has had a crippling, even a paralyzing effect on humanistic
studies, where its ready-made answers to everything have
spared students the pains and denied them the experience of
finding out for themselves what the texts actually say.

In the field of religion especially, the actual study of evidence constantly rebuffs the evolutionary prejudices of the scholars, who feel they cannot do without this precious time-and-thought-saver. It is a "well-known law of the history of liturgy," for example, "that the development . . . has led from pluriformity to uniformity, and not the reverse."[5] Again, scholars have searched long and in vain for an *Urtext*, a pure, simple original, to the Septuagint, unaware, Paul Kahle points out, that "a standard text of a translation is always found at the *end* of the development, never at the beginning," where one would expect it.[6] Any college student can tell you that the organization of the Christian church must have passed from primitive, loosely coordinated beginnings to an increasingly integrated and effective system. If the evidence makes the mistake of proving the opposite, the evidence must be dealt with; accordingly, to quote Schermann, "every letter of Paul in which such a fixed organization [of the church] is implied is, in spite of its linguistic affinity to other letters which are recognized as genuine, and in spite of the close identity of its content and thought with theirs, condemned without mercy and overwhelmed with charges of interpolation."[7] This is not a rare but a typical example of the way the school of "scientific" scholarship operates. As another example, the unfolding pattern of history requires that the idea of the Messiah shall have first arisen in Israel after the Exile. But there are some significant preexilic passages in the Old Testament that refer to the Messiah. What do the scholars do with these? They simply declare them to be interpolations, and then remove the offensive things from the text: The result is a reformed text which brilliantly confirms the theory on which it was reformed. They produce a new text that is carefully tailored to their theory, and then point to that text as proof that the theory is correct![8] Incredible as it may seem, this cheap and easy circular method became the standard procedure and the indispensable tool of the higher critics, who operated on the principle that, while to ignore evidence is a sign of prejudice, to alter and adjust it to fit one's preconceptions is a mark of brilliance and ingenuity.

This may be the result of trying to apply the scientific method in an area where judgment must always remain largely subjective. And yet one wonders when one contemplates the behavior of the scientists themselves. In 1953 at a meeting of the Geological Society of London, the famous Piltdown Man was shown to be a hoax. It was not only a hoax, we are now told, but it was such an extremely clumsy hoax that it is hard to see how it ever fooled anybody. Only one thing can explain the solemn acceptance and high honors accorded this battered skull by the highest authorities for over half a century, and that is an overpowering desire, a fierce determination to accept as genuine whatever looked promising in an area where evidence was badly needed. The news has now leaked out that the November meeting "broke up into a series of fist fights, so strong was the feeling on both sides of the question. The fracas resulted in the expulsion of several members of the dignified scientific body."[9] "Strong feeling," says the news dispatch. It was wishful thinking that saw priceless evidence in the Piltdown skull and then defended it with a passion that did not draw the line at bloody noses and black eyes. Where is the cool, impartial, objective detachment which we have been taught is the badge and authority of science? Well, there is nothing wrong with behaving as average human beings—unless, of course, one claims, as these men do, to have risen above that sort of thing. I recall to mind certain professors of natural science who could not give a lecture without taking potshots at foolish and gullible people who accepted things on faith. These men with monotonous persistence fire millions of rounds at the opposition, but when the opposition proposes to present a few of their duds for our inspection, they instantly appeal to our humanity and insist that it is not sporting to advertise the chinks in *their* armor.

Modern liberalism, like modern education, goes on the theory that the scientific attitude can become the possession of every man, woman, and child in the democracy. Nothing can be farther from the truth. The only way you can get the scientific attitude is to be a scientist. The only way one can know what mathematics is about, according to Courant and Robbins, is actually to work problems—lots of hard problems—in mathematics. One cannot acquire the attitudes of a painter or a teacher or a musician or a zoologist or a tap dancer without doing actual work in those fields. A really scientific attitude cannot be imparted by lectures about it or pocket books or popular articles that glamorize it or survey courses that play with it; the masses can embrace science only as many people embrace religion—in name only. The real enemy of true science is the glib and superficial lip service to science that goes under the name of liberalism. And the same holds true for religion. There is no substance to the easy and sentimental "religion of man" by which the human race was expected to lift itself to infinite heights by a gentle tugging on its own boot-straps. The mathematician Gödel has demonstrated, or at least has proposed to demonstrate, that "no logical system can ever prove that it itself is a perfect system in the sense that it may not contain concealed self-contradictions. . . . This means that the human intelligence can never be sure of itself; it is not . . . capable of unlimited perfectibility, as is so often fondly imagined."[10] What is more, even that ultimate rock of refuge, common sense, has become a rapidly melting ice floe. "The sort of phenomena with which quantum theory is concerned," writes Professor Bridgman, "teach[es] the same lesson as relativity theory, namely, that the world is not constructed according to the principles of common sense." Actually, he reminds us, "we acquire our perceptual abilities only by arduous practice. Yet we take our space and time with deadly seriousness. . . . Perhaps when we learn to take them less seriously we will not be so bedeviled by the logical contradictions . . .

about the beginning or end of time or the boundaries of space."[11]

It is time we came to the moral of our discussion—the religious part of it. Schoolmen—ancient, medieval, and modern—have persisted in proclaiming to the world that there is aside and apart from that knowledge which has come to the human race by revelation and which is an object of religious faith, another type of knowledge—real, tangible, solid, absolute, perfectly provable knowledge—the knowledge (according to the prevailing taste of the century) of philosophy, science, or common sense. The exponents of this knowledge, we are told, are impartial and detached in their searches and their conclusions. I have met many students who have been convinced that anyone who experiences any doubt regarding the scriptures has only to remove his troubled mind from old legends and dubious reports to realms of clear light and absolute certainty where doubt does not exist. Significantly enough, this gospel of hope is almost never preached by scientists but enjoys its greatest vogue in departments of humanities and social science. What the true scientists of our day are telling us, as they have told us before, is that no such realm, no such intellectual Hesperides, is known to them. One never knows which of our most cherished and established scientific beliefs may be next to go by the board.[12] A brief illustration may be in order.

If there is anything at all on which the overwhelming consensus of New Testament scholarship claims to have reached the highest certitude, it is the nature of the gospel of John, a relatively late production that shows clear and unmistakable marks of Hellenistic influence. Professor Albright reminds us that the term *rabbi* used by John was seen to be a hopeless anachronism, that the personal names in the gospel were obviously "fictitious and had been chosen for specific purposes," and that John's inaccurate topography showed his ignorance of the local setting of the time of Christ. Yet the discoveries of the last few years, Albright observes, have shown that the experts were completely wrong on all these points. [13] Most recently, the study of the Dead Sea Scrolls shows us that "John, far from being the creation of Hellenistic Christianity, has exceedingly close ties with sectarian Judaism, and may prove to be the most 'Jewish' of the Gospels." [14] Let us not be hard on the specialists. How could they be expected to know what lay hidden in the sand? But that is just another way of asking, how could they be expected ever to know the answers? Until the final returns are in, no one is in a position to make final pronouncements, and as long as science continues to progress, the final returns will remain at the other end of a future of wonders and surprises. In the world of things, we must forever keep an open mind, because we simply don't know the answers. But we are not claiming that because science does not have the ultimate answers, religion does have them. What we do claim is that the words of the prophets cannot be held to the tentative and defective tests that men have devised for them. Science, philosophy, and common sense all have a right to their day in court. But the last word does not lie with them. Every time men in their wisdom have come forth with the last word, other words have promptly followed. The last word is a testimony of the gospel that comes only by direct revelation. Our Father in heaven speaks it, and if it were in perfect agreement with the science of today, it would surely be out of line with the science of tomorrow. Let us not, therefore, seek to hold God to the learned opinions of the moment when he speaks the language of eternity.

16

Prophets and Miracles

From its very beginning the church of Christ ran into trouble in the world, where it was everywhere regarded as an intruder on the rights and prerogatives of established and going concerns. Its doctrine collided with philosophy; its offices and priesthood aroused the suspicion of governors and politicians; its divine gifts and powers scandalized the schoolmen, Jewish and Greek alike; the inspired preaching of the word had to settle a score with rhetoric as its revelation did with a great heritage of mysticism. We have touched upon all these things in preceding chapters, but there is one important phase of the story which we have not mentioned. God is a God of miracles. Everything he does is marvelous and in the end surpasses the understanding of men. As the gospel with all its gifts and powers was introduced into a world of philosophy, mysticism, and rhetoric—all of which were hostile to it—so too it was introduced into a world of miracles. And just as it is important to distinguish between the gospel and philosophy, the spirit and rhetoric, revelation and mysticism, so it is necessary to distinguish sharply between the *kind* of miracles that were found among the saints and the kind that enjoyed currency and popularity in the outside world; for here too we have a sure key to the presence of God's church and his prophets in the world.

Among the early Christians, miracles were a common and a useful thing. It is no contradiction of terms, as later Christians claimed, to speak of common miracles. In the restored Church the sick are healed every day, but for all its

frequency, that occurrence loses none of its miraculous quality that fills the beholder with joy and thanksgiving. We are
told in emphatic terms in the scriptures that the Lord and the
Apostles performed very many miracles during their short
ministries on earth; in their day miracles were a daily event.
More than forty specific miracles are attributed to Christ
alone in the New Testament, and on one occasion we are
told (Luke 6:17, 19) that "a great multitude of people out of
all Judaea and Jerusalem, and from the sea coast of Tyre and
Sidon . . . came to hear him, and to be healed of their diseases. . . . And the whole multitude sought to touch him:
for there went virtue out of him, and healed them all." Here
was no concern lest the spectacle value of miracles be diminished by making them over-common, for the ancient saints
did not value miracles for their spectacular qualities at all.
For them, miracles were a supremely useful gift of God to
those who believed, and emphatically not a means of impress-
ing the opposition. "And these signs shall *follow* them that
believe," says the Lord at the end of the gospel of Mark
(16:17-18); "in my name shall they cast out devils; they shall
speak with new tongues; They shall take up serpents; and if
they drink any deadly thing, it shall not hurt them: they
shall lay hands on the sick, and they shall recover." And in
the very last verse (20) of this gospel we read, "And they
went forth, and preached every where, the Lord working
with them, and confirming the word with signs *following*."
The signs follow the word; they do not precede it. And note
just what these signs are: they are the intervention of the
power of God in situations in which men need help very
badly and cannot help themselves, when they are possessed,
poisoned, and sick. In the days when the church had to bear
witness within a short time to very many people, the language barrier was an insurmountable one: so the Lord gave
them power to "speak with new tongues," as is plainly seen
in the day of Pentecost, when every man heard the gospel
preached in his own tongue, and Paul tells us (1 Corinthians

14:22) that this particular gift is specifically "for a sign . . . to them that believe not."

But what about the other signs? They are *not* for unbelievers. The pagan world of the time was, as we have said, a world of miracles and miracle-lovers. Those popular miracles were of the type calculated to excite awe in all beholders and stir up general public interest. Of this type of miracle the Lord strongly disapproved. Not only did he repeatedly instruct those who had been the beneficiaries of his miraculous powers not to spread the news abroad, but in every instance where he was asked for a sign, he rebuked the askers and quickly withdrew from the scene. Father Garrigou-Lagrange in his recent treatment of the subject, defending the thesis that the purpose of miracles was to prove the divine origin of the Christian religion "by most certain signs accommodated to the intelligence of all," cites the instances in Matthew 11:4-6 and Luke 7:18-23 where the Lord answered John the Baptist's question as to whether he was the Messiah by referring him to the miracles he had done.[1] But a personal message to his friend and relative John, a righteous man and a believer all his days, can hardly be construed as a policy for converting the heathen; and here John does *not* ask for a sign—he is ready to take the Lord's word for it. The powerful rebukes administered by the Lord to those who sought signs, Lagrange explains as applying only to the Pharisees, "who were always seeking new signs after they had had other signs." Yet we also read (Luke 11:29): "And when the people were gathered thick together, he began to say, This is an evil generation: they seek a sign." Speaking to the whole multitude, he condemns the whole sign-seeking generation. The Lord says those who seek a sign will receive a sign—but it is *not* the sign they want, it is the sign of Jonah. When the Pharisees asked him for a sign, "he sighed deeply in his spirit, and saith, Why doth this generation seek after a sign? verily I say unto you, There shall no sign be given unto this generation. And he left them" (Mark 8:12-13). And yet

there were signs all around them, but only those who
believed could see them—the signs only *follow* them that
believe: "O ye hypocrites," said the Lord to the Pharisees
and Sadducees asking him for a sign from heaven, "ye can
discern the face of the sky; but can ye not discern the signs
of the times? A wicked and adulterous generation *seeketh*
after a sign; and there shall no sign be given unto it, but the
sign of the prophet Jonas. And he left them, and departed"
(Matthew 16:3-4; italics added).

Whenever people asked the Lord for a sign, he walked
out on them, telling them that to those who ask for a sign,
no sign shall be given save one they don't want. (Cf. Luke
21:11-28.) When the Jews pinned him down with the request
for a specific demonstration, asking him, "What sign shewest
thou unto us, seeing that thou doest these things?" he evaded
them neatly with the challenge, "Destroy this temple, and in
three days I will raise it up" (John 2:18-19), that being a
thing he knew they would never do—they brought this against
him later as a serious charge, and of course missed the real
significance of the remark. In the other passages cited by
Lagrange we read (Acts 5:14-15): "And believers were the
more added to the Lord. . . . Insomuch that they brought
forth the sick into the streets" to be healed, etc. Here they
bring out their sick inasmuch as they believe: They *believe*
first; the miracles follow. Does not the Lord in preparation
for a miracle often ask the recipient whether he or she believes,
this being a prerequisite to the miracle? In his own native
district the Lord "did not many mighty works there because
of their unbelief" (Matthew 13:58). If the purpose of miracles
was to convince the unbelieving, this should have been the
very place where the Lord would perform his greatest ones,
but the rule is very clear—no belief, no miracles: "Ye receive
no witness until after the trial of your faith" (Ether 12:6-30).
Lagrange again cites the case of Simon, who "wondered,
beholding the miracles and signs which were done" (Acts
4:30; 8:13), but that was only *after* he had believed and was

baptized. He was not converted as a result of those miracles, but they followed his belief. In the King James Bible, the twelfth chapter of 2 Corinthians is headed Paul's Visions Are Apostolic Credentials. Yet he never reveals the content of those visions, least of all to unbelievers; what he does in this chapter is to remind the Corinthians, "Truly the signs of an apostle were wrought among you . . . in signs, and wonders, and mighty deeds" (2 Corinthians 12:12). The Corinthians had been treated to this *after* their conversion as Christians, not as pagans, but even these signs did not guarantee a lasting conversion, for Paul goes on to describe how these same Corinthians are falling away.

Credentials must be infallible, as the word of the Lord is infallible, but miracles employed for purposes of demonstration never can be, for miracles are not exclusively Christian: one need only recall the vast miracle literature of the Mohammedans. When the question was brought up at an early council in Antioch, "How does it happen that heretics often perform miracles?" the answer was, "It is not proper to enquire into such a matter."[2] The question could not be answered by men who believed that miracles were sure credentials. Like philosophy and mysticism, miracles—real miracles—are found throughout the whole world and are used by practitioners of religion everywhere to bedizen, amaze, and convince the doubters. "There shall arise false Christs," says the Lord, "and false prophets, and shall shew *great signs* and wonders; insomuch that, if it were possible, they shall deceive the very elect." In this passage (Matthew 24:24) Christ further explains that a time is coming when many shall claim that Christ is with them, but none, not a single one of them, should be believed, because they would try to convert by signs and wonders. In Mark 13:21 it reads, "And then if *any* man shall say to you, Lo, here is Christ; or, lo, he is there; believe him not: For false Christs and false prophets shall rise, and shall shew signs and wonders, to seduce, if it were possible, even the elect." Here we see plainly enough who it is who employs signs and wonders to convert the unbelieving, "whose coming," says Paul, "is after the working of Satan with all power and signs and lying wonders" (2 Thessalonians 2:9).

What should people seek, then? The word of life. After declaring that "an evil and adulterous generation seeketh after a sign" (Matthew 12:39), the Lord explains that the people of Nineveh would condemn such a generation in the judgment, because the preaching of the prophet had been enough to convince them; and that the Queen of Sheba would judge them likewise, since she was satisfied not with a sign but with the wise words of Solomon (Matthew 12:40-42). In the last verse of Mark (16:20) we read that "they went forth, and preached . . . confirming the *word* with signs following." To prove that miracles were meant to convert, Lagrange cites John 2:11: "This beginning of miracles did Jesus in Cana of Galilee, and manifested forth his glory; and his disciples believed on him."[3] His disciples—not the whole multitude. "Many other signs truly did Jesus in the presence of his disciples," says John, speaking of the time after the resurrection (John 20:30). If the purpose of miracles is to convert, then Jesus wasted his miracles all on believers. Next Lagrange cites John 10:25-27: "The works that I do in my Father's name, they bear witness of me. But *ye* believe *not*, because ye are not of my sheep. . . . My sheep *hear* my *voice*, and I know them, and they follow me."[4] Father Lagrange could not have picked a better passage to demonstrate that miracles do *not* convert the unbelievers—"but ye believe not"; well, who does believe? Those, says the Lord, who *hear* his *voice*, for whom his words are enough. When the Lord "granted signs and wonders to be done" by the hands of the Apostles in Iconium, the result was that they got kicked out of town (Acts 14:3-6). The miracles did not break down opposition.

Then there is the famous case of Nicodemus, who came to the Lord by night and said, "We know that thou art a teacher come from God: for no man can do these miracles that thou doest, except God be with him" (John 3:2). But this was not the way the Lord wanted Nicodemus converted, for in answer he did not praise those who believed his miracles, but rebuked those who would not believe his *words*: "Verily, verily, I say unto thee, We speak that we do know, and testify that we have seen; and ye receive not our witness. If I have told you earthly things, and ye believe not, how shall ye believe, if I tell you of heavenly things?" (John 3:2, 11-12.) To impress people with miracles is one thing; to give them a testimony of the gospel another. As the experience of the Apostles showed, if people will not accept the gospel by the word without miracles, they will not accept it with miracles: "If they *hear* not Moses and the prophets, neither will they be persuaded, though one rose from the dead" (Luke 16:31).

After the first century, miracles ceased entirely from the church. This has been a much-discussed phenomenon. We have touched on it in these talks, and quoted Bishop John of Bristol's statement: "I perceive in the language of the Fathers, who lived in the middle and end of the second century . . . , if not a conviction, at least a suspicion, that the power of working miracles was withdrawn, combined with an anxiety to keep up a belief of its continuance in the Church."[5] This can be illustrated by the instance of the Thundering Legion. When a Roman army was delivered from death by thirst by a timely shower of rain during an expedition in Germany, everybody rushed to claim the miracle for his church: Devotees of Isis claimed that the rain was sent in answer to the prayers of the Egyptian priest Arnuphius who was with the army; on the Antonine column we still see the miracle cited in support of the Roman state religion and attributed to the intervention of Jupiter Pluvius from whose outspread arms the shower pours down; Tertullian, however, attributes the miracle to the prayers of the Christians who were with the army. For Bishop John this eager exploitation by Tertullian of a mere coincidence shows how hard up the church was for real miracles, for in all his extensive writings Tertullian, like other Christian contemporaries, is at a loss to produce a single case of a good contemporary miracle. But more significant than this is the fact that this upright Christian is now competing with the pagan religionists for a miracle to prove his religion: He is speaking *their* language.

The total absence of miracles in the church in the second century—at the very time when the apologists were looking most eagerly for them—is usually explained as the laying aside of credentials that were no longer necessary. The arguments against this are only too obvious. Why didn't the Christians themselves ever give that explanation? Why did they stubbornly insist on clinging to every old or new miracle they could find? When did the missionary work of the church ever reach completion or come to a halt so that the alleged credentials would no longer be necessary? When did the Christians ever cease to need help against evil spirits or become immune to the effects of poison, snakebite, or disease? The church proceeded to remedy the fatal defect exactly as she made up for the loss of doctrine and authority—by substitution. As might be expected, the substitution followed two lines: the esoteric and the vulgar. Left to human providence, religious things, as has often been pointed out, tend to gravitate to two opposite poles—a purely intellectual on the one hand, and a vulgar and superstitious on the other. So among the intellectuals, Quadratus of Athens was the last man in the second century to insist on the literal nature of the miracles of Jesus;[6] those who followed him, Aristides, Justin, Tatian, Athenagoras, and Theophilus—though they could not deny the miracles, being among the most fundamental things in Christianity—gave them a more sophisticated appraisal[7] and, moving as fatally to a Neoplatonic "spiritual" explanation as a needle to the pole, took the position illustrated by Irenaeus who, when asked "why the Lord rained down manna on the people in the days of the fathers, but now does so no more?" replied: "If you only knew it, he

still rains down manna upon his servants—every day, . . .
even the perfect bread of heaven, the body born of the Virgin, [etc.] But there is also a spiritual manna, that is the
downpouring of spiritual wisdom."[8]

Later on, John Chrysostom, Augustine, and especially
St. Ambrose have a great deal to say about how much superior these mystic and spiritual miracles are to the crass physical article of the primitive Christians. For a while, as we
have told before, the Gnostics tried to fake miracles of the
old kind, but that was a strenuous program: A far richer
source of substitute material lay near to hand in the fullblown cult of miracles that flourished throughout the ancient
world. A great deal of research has been done on the adoption of local and general cults, legends, liturgies, vestments,
rites, etc., by the Christian church. The local hero cults, the
trips to healing shrines, the lovely old legends, the brisk cult
of relics, such things were firmly rooted in popular devotion;
they were thousands of years old and commanded the unshakable devotion of the masses. This is no time to explore this
fruitful and colorful field, but we might refer our listeners to
Franz Josef Dölger's study of the adoption by the church of
the ancient and wide-spread pagan practice of throwing coins
into holy fountains in hopes of getting a blessing. Dölger has
produced many stout volumes packed with evidence to illustrate this transition from popular pagan to Christian miracles.[9] Such well-known classics as Livy, Dio, Virgil,
Pausanias, Hyginus, etc., provide plenty of description of
the kind of popular miracles that were taken over by the
Christians. Heavenly visitations and manifestations are common among them, but one thing they all have in common:
they have no real message to convey; they have nothing to
say; they are essentially just "eye-wash." The Seven Sleepers
of Ephesus arose from their century-long sleep, praised God,
and promptly fell dead again. We talked once about letters

from heaven and the tremendous impact they had on medieval society—what was wrong with them? They had nothing to say.

The gifts and miracles all go together in the true Church and are taken as a matter of course. Where you have the one you have the others, for they are really but manifestations of the same power—the power that made and sustains the world. We see that miraculous power at work all around us, and the Lord has told us that he is displeased with those who fail to see his hand in *all* things. That power is operated directly through the priesthood; and where you have the priesthood, as Tertullian long ago observed, you must necessarily have the powers and the miracles that go with it. "He that believeth on me," said the Lord to Philip (John 14:12), "the works that I do shall he do also; and greater works than these shall he do; because I go unto my Father." The Lord then continues with the promise of the Holy Ghost, whom the world cannot receive, who will teach the saints all things. These things are not for the world, they are promised to the saints and them alone. And the greatest of all these things promised is the Holy Ghost. Now it is a significant thing that the Christian world loudly proclaims the gift of the Holy Ghost, but just as loudly denies the presence of any of the lesser gifts that accompany it. If one has the Holy Ghost, the other things are there as a matter of course—it does not supplant them; here it is explicitly promised along with them. To deny literal miracles, as one part of the Christian world does today, or to look for faith in rare, theatrical, stunning, and sensational displays—in a word, to seek after signs—as the rest do, is to miss the whole point of miracles. They *belong* to the church; they are a useful, natural, necessary part of it. They are not something to be handled in the abstract with the precious affections of the academicians; nor are they something to be spread abroad in hushed and excited whispers or written up in popular magazines for their publicity value. Since we say we know that God can do these things, it is a poor demonstration of faith when he actually does them to act as if he were a magician trying to make our eyes pop out. Where you find the true Church, there you will find true prophets and the priesthood in all its authority; and where you have that, all the signs and wonders will follow as a matter of course.

17

Prophets and Ritual

A visitor to the earth from another planet would discover in his wanderings that our whole inhabited globe is sprinkled with buildings more beautiful and costly for the most part than any other buildings and totally different from them in purpose and design. What would seem most surprising to the visitor upon investigation is the fact that these imposing structures seem to serve no practical purpose whatever. While they plainly represent a tremendous output of talent and energy, from the point of view of common sense these mighty works are really quite unnecessary. One really does not need a golden dome or a Gothic spire to keep out the rain or the heat of the sun. Further research would lead the investigator to the discovery that these weirdly impractical buildings were but one of the products of an intense and ceaseless activity, all of which from the point of view of survival and comfort seems perfectly pointless. The church, in a word, is not a practical institution. Its charitable activities, by the very fact that they do have a practical purpose, are not peculiarly religious in nature and are by no means reserved to churches or to religiously inclined people. What sets off religious activity as such from all other expenditure of effort is the very fact that it does not need to be done in the normal course of existence.

Take the present-day activities of Latter-day Saints, for example. Genealogical research is not essential or even helpful to making a living. One can get along in the world without attending innumerable meetings, partaking of the sacrament, going to the temple, paying tithes, keeping the Word of Wisdom, and all that. In all these things we put ourselves out unnecessarily. Even sexual morality is not a prerequisite to survival and success in this world—a surprising number of people dispense with it. Why do we do all these things that don't need to be done?

The usual explanation of religionists is that man has a natural urge to do such things as are required by religion. But if the urge were natural, as Lord Raglan points out, everyone would have it, which is far from the case. It is a cultivated thing and as such is much stronger at some times and places than at others. Great civilizations in the past have made religious activity the principal concern of all their people, whereas today men are taught that they are fulfilling the measure of their existence if they are diligent in producing and consuming goods, with the accumulation of wealth as a work of supererogation to add character and status to mere survival. But among many objections to the natural theory of religion, perhaps the most instructive is the fact that the impractical things men do in the name of religion through the ages of time and in every corner of the earth do *not* present an endless and bewildering variety of nonsense as they would if men simply created their ritual activities spontaneously everywhere. While there is no limit to the number of impractical and senseless activities and rituals one might devise in response to the simple urge to do solemn and mysterious acts, the number of ritual acts in which human beings actually do engage from Oceania to Iceland is surprisingly limited, and they can all be embraced in a few well-marked but peculiar ritual patterns. This suggests that the religious rituals of men have not been invented locally but have been inherited from a few main sources, perhaps to be traced ultimately to a single one.

When the folklorists and comparative religionists in the last century first noticed amazing parallels among the rituals and legends of people as widely scattered as Central Europe and Celebes, they naturally assumed that this strange uniformity was produced by a natural urge common to all men to express their deepest desires and experiences in a few basic ritual patterns. The patterns, however, were altogether too elaborate, too peculiar, and too far removed from the dictates of any practical necessity to be explained in terms of a spontaneous and untutored invention, and when subsequent studies began to tie up what had looked like isolated (in many cases even primitive) instances to larger cultural traditions, it became increasingly apparent that the almost monotonous repetition of the same basic ritual patterns in Europe, Asia, Africa, and America was actually to be attributed to a common origin. For all that the religious rituals of the vast bulk of mankind *might* have been spontaneous and local in origin, the established fact is that they have *not* been. With this discovery most of the armchair speculation about the primitive origins of religion has gone by the board, but we cannot discuss this now; here it suffices to point out that the common theory that man engages in impractical and difficult religious activities simply because he has an urge to do so has been seriously challenged, for wherever men are found engaging in those activities there is an historical tradition at hand to compel them, and if asked why they do these odd things, they will invariably reply that it is because their fathers did so before them.[1]

Divinely instituted rites and ordinances have to do in the first instance with things which men do for no other reason than that God has commanded them. They are, first of all, acts of faith and are meritorious as such. They must be hard enough and demanding enough not to become mere acts of dull, automatic repetition, and their immediate practical value may not be so obviously apparent that there is no room left in their performance for a real test of faith. When one goes to train with a master, not merely with the object of serving time for a certificate as in our modern "character factories," but in order to learn all the master has to teach and to become as far as possible perfect in an art, a science, or a craft, the first and all-important step is to establish a condition of complete trust between the master and the disciple. The candidate must by sure tests show his implicit faith and unhesitating obedience to every command in every situation. Soon enough he will understand *why* he must take a seemingly absurd position or perform some apparently meaningless operation; but unless and until he does the thing and does it entirely on faith and does it with a will, he will never come to that understanding, worlds without end.

There are many things that can only be explained after they are done, and then the explanation of what seemed so arbitrary and mysterious usually turns out to be extremely obvious and natural. We are required, for example, to use oil in some of the ordinances of the Church, and water in others. If you ask me why, I will answer, "I know not, save that the Lord hath commanded" (Moses 5:6). That is reason enough. It does not follow that these things have no real purpose aside from the symbolic and disciplinary: A small child uses soap on faith—a mere act of obedience, we might say, with the soap as a symbol of cleanliness, but actually it goes much further than that; the soap performs a real function which the child does not understand. I doubt not that when we know the reason for some of the things we do now on faith, the practical value of the actions will be so plain that we will wonder how we could have missed it, and then we shall be heartily glad that we did what we were told to do. Meantime the Lord advises us in these things, and it is up to us to trust his judgment. If the primary purpose of our being on earth is to be tested, and the first thing to be tested is our faith and obedience, it is foolish to ask for a full explanation before we will move a muscle. There are many operations in mathematics and the arts that can only be understood *after* they have been carried out.

The human race lives as it were a double life; it pursues a double economy: a practical one and a religious one. The conflict between these two, the treasures of earth and the treasures in heaven, is frequently mentioned in the New Testament. Of these two lives, the religious one is obviously the real one; otherwise it would have been given up long ago. In every serious crisis, in every life-and-death situation when men are brought face to face with reality, the so-called practical life is pushed completely out of the picture, and religion springs to the fore as the only reality after all. We have seen this happen time and again. As the philosophers have always told us, the everyday things we see about us, far from representing the real world represent the very opposite—a shadow existence, a toy world, the most trivial and transitory aspects of our existence. As to the things we are told to do in our religious observances, they *should* seem strange to us by the very fact that they are not of this world of *things*. Here we are concerned first and last with the preservation of our physical plant: we are essentially animals; Adam was condemned to an economy of sweat and dirt. All things necessary for that economy—the building of bridges, the processing of food, the selling of insurance, etc.—are temporary in nature. They are but a means to an end, they are not—as we are being constantly told and as we are constantly forgetting—an end in themselves. They are as temporary as our temporary life here below; they belong strictly to the corruptible order of things, and they will all pass away, nay, they are passing away at this moment. It is to them that we as individuals and as a society are wholly conditioned, adapted, reconciled, and abandoned. They represent for our age the whole life of man. Would you expect the eternal ordinances of the gospel to fit naturally and practically into such a setting? Are you surprised that they seem strange and out of place to us?

In nothing does the uniqueness of the Latter-day Saints stand out more clearly than in matters of rites and ordinances. In the first place the restored Church of Jesus Christ presents the astonishing spectacle of the entire religious community engaged in the performance of rites and duties of a sacred nature. Much of the world believes that the primary purpose of all ritual and liturgy is to glorify God by more or less theatrical demonstrations and that it makes no difference, accordingly, how many engage in the performance as long as the thing takes place. Everywhere throughout the world men have delegated their own religious duties to full-time professionals, so that they could be free to go about their everyday tasks unhampered by annoying religious obligations. If they participate at all in religious rituals, it is as spectators at a show, and one can easily demonstrate the steps by which rites originally established, we are told, for the express benefit and direct participation of all the covenant people—not just the priests—have become more and more a show put on by way of pleasing and mollifying God. Thus with the passing of time, the ordinances given to the fathers have lost their effectiveness and their meaning.

One of the most remarkable features of Latter-day Saint ordinances is that they are, or claim to be, pristine. They are the same ordinances that were given in the beginning. That is the way God wants it, and that is the way it must be. The whole validity of such ordinances depends on their having been revealed directly from heaven. No effort is made to give practical or rational explanation of these ordinances; they are not interpreted symbolically, nor are they justified by their aesthetic appeal, which is extremely limited. We do these things on faith for no other reason save that the Lord has commanded us to do them. The importance of a living prophet in such a ritual scheme of things will be at once apparent. Granted that the real business of life is to do what God wants us to, the whole problem is then to determine what that is. Only a prophet can tell us.

Now the religious rituals of men wherever we find them are very obviously the product of a thorough working-over by men aimed at adapting them to the economy of this earth.

To document this point as briefly and authoritatively as possible, I shall confine myself to a few quotations from the latest official work on the *Liturgy of the Roman Rite*, Lechner and Eisenhofer's book published in 1953 in Freiburg. The Roman Catholic liturgy, we are told, has a twofold foundation, (1) in human nature, and (2) in history. While on the one hand the spiritual, physical, and social nature of man find expression in this ritual, its historical foundations consist of *pre*-Christian and *non*-Christian elements, three in particular. First, there is the Jewish element, of which our authorities write: "The Christian cult took from the Jewish . . . not only a rich treasure of prayers, readings and forms, but also the entire external structure of the Eucharistic [communal] service, the basic structure of the Church year and many hints for the development of the same." Second, the Hellenistic-Roman pagan world "through which the Church had to pass," as our authors significantly put it, contributed to her ritual heritage "along with a high evaluation of cult-practice as such, special elements of cult and cult-forms that were significant for future developments." Third, the Germanic world, from which "the Church enriched her liturgy through manifold inspirations for festivals and devotions, through the building up of established rites by the German delight in symbolism, and even through the creation of new forms which it became necessary to develop as a result of the ties between the Church and the German culture (*Germanentum*)," e.g., the Imperial coronation rite. But that is not all. "It is by no means out of the question," write Eisenhofer and Lechner, "that in the future other cultural and ethnological areas may not introduce new elements into our Liturgy, that older forms shall disappear, so that the cult practices of the Church may some day be adapted to other nations and concepts as they once were to those of the Western world."[2]

Note that the rites of the church are to be adapted to the established practices and concepts of men; the tastes and the institutions of *this* world, in a word, are to be the determining factor in the formation of rites in the future as they have been in the past. This is not the heavenly order, this pursuit of the practical, the popular, the aesthetically appealing. At the very least we have here an admitted compromise with these things which the ancient saints were taught to avoid, "for all these things do the nations of the world seek after." On the other hand, the great Reformers, having rejected these things, found themselves greatly embarrassed in matters of ritual. They had to do something, but what would it be? Both Catholics and Protestants have of recent years made diligent and determined attempts to discover a real foundation for their liturgical activities in a zealous study of Christian archaeology.[3] The quest is a pathetic one; the sight of men digging in the dust and mud of decomposition to discover what God wants them to do now is a strong reminder that where the rites and ordinances of the church are concerned neither scripture nor tradition will suffice, but only the direct word of God.

The rites and ordinances of the Latter-day Saints fall into a totally different category from those of any other people. Their sacredness does not reside in their age, their appeal does not reside in their beauty, their effectiveness does not reside in their symbolism. They are revealed ordinances, and their faithful observance often leads to revelation and always to great blessings.

18

Easter and the Prophets

We have suggested that Latter-day Saints might be said to accept certain traditions common to the whole Christian world more wholeheartedly and with less reservation than most Christians do inasmuch as they take as literal what the rest of the world accepts in a rather vague, symbolic, or sentimental sense. Easter furnishes as good an illustration as any of what we mean by this.

There are two aspects of Easter—a formal and a literal or, one might say, a ritual and a doctrinal. The formal aspect is that which everybody knows so well and to which we all subscribe. We all *do* certain things at Easter whatever we may *think*. The uncritical acceptance of ancient customs has precious little to do with any particular doctrine. The bands and fireworks at a political rally are *not* an expression of the multitude's irrepressible enthusiasm for the party's principles; they are rather the means employed to create a popular enthusiasm with the hopes of transferring some of that emotion to the cause of the party. In the same spirit, the Christian church, long after the Apostles, adopted the myriad Easter practices now found throughout the world. At the end of the sixth century, missionaries to Britain were impressed and disturbed by the great spring festival of the heathen natives of the island; they asked Gregory the Great what they should do about it, and in a famous letter he replied that they should let the people keep their darling festivities while turning the whole thing into a Christian celebration. Let them continue to slaughter their oxen and build their

booths of green boughs, is Gregory's advice, only let it now
be done not for the devil but in praise of God, "for," he
writes, "it is absolutely certain that it is quite impossible to
uproot everything at once from stubborn minds, since . . . it
is necessary for them to aspire by degrees or steps, and not
by leaps and bounds."[1] Long before, Constantine the Great
had followed the same policy in the East.

The equinoctial rites of the rebirth of nature have been
celebrated throughout the world from the remotest antiquity.
The rabbits, eggs, lights, and flowers of Easter were no more
Christian in origin than Christmas trees and Yule logs. Yet in
most parts of the world, these things were retained by Christians because of their extreme popularity and because they
actually do express man's hope for a new and better life. The
danger of embracing non-Christian practices was a real one,
however, and did not go unnoticed.[2] Clement of Alexandria
warned the Christians against the marbles and paintings of
heathen temples, not, he explained, because they were bad in
themselves, but because to the minds of most people they
were sure to appear so imposing as to be treasured for their
own sakes, living as it were a life of their own and completely eclipsing the things of the spirit.[3] When in the fourth
century the church started taking over these things, St. Jerome
expressed grave concern at what was happening.[4] Since the
Christmas and Easter rites of the Christians are the most
imposing of all artistic and ritual complexes, it would be
strange indeed if they did not quite overshadow the doctrinal
concepts which first justified their introduction into the
churches. Gregory's hope, as he clearly stated it, was that by
making large concession to the popular will, the people might
be swung gradually over into the Christian orbit. Yet, bearing in mind that the old customs were being retained precisely because the people were too stubborn to give them up,
there certainly was great danger that the opposite would
take place, and the established customs of a thousand years

would prove of greater mass and charge than the new Christian teaching which, accordingly, would be sucked into the older orbit. This was exactly what happened.

Constantine considered as one of his greatest triumphs the christianizing of the great international festival of Mamre in Palestine. He retained the festival, but he christianized it thoroughly.[5] Yet a pious Christian lady who visited the celebration a generation later reported that while the wonderful rites were in full swing, the Christian veneer had worn off, and the whole show had reverted to its primal paganism.[6] At the same time, almost in the same year that this observation was made, John Chrysostom, the bishop of what claimed to be the oldest and greatest church in Christendom, that of Antioch, complained that everybody came to church at Easter and at Easter only, simply because it was the thing to do. For the rest of the year, he spoke to empty walls.[7] Even at this early date, the formal aspect of Easter had completely overcome the doctrinal.

The only real justification for the Christian Easter is the proposition that the resurrection of Christ actually took place —not as a symbol, a myth, a hope, a tradition, or a dream, but as a real event. The Lord himself after the resurrection took the greatest care to impress the literalness of the event on the minds of all his followers. Having risen from the dead, Christ came to his disciples and found them confused, perplexed, incredulous. He "upbraided them with their unbelief and hardness of heart, because they believed not them which had seen him after he was risen" (Mark 16:14), and showed them in detail how the ancient prophets had actually predicted what had happened. He ordered them to feel him and see for themselves that he was not a spirit, but that the *flesh* had been resurrected; he ordered food to be brought and ate it in their presence, inviting them to dine with him. He told them that whenever they met after his departure they should continue to eat real bread and drink real wine to remind them that he had been with them in the flesh.

There was need to make this lesson perfectly clear, for men have always been reluctant to believe it. Matthew concludes his gospel with the report that "when they saw him, they worshipped him: but some doubted" (Matthew 28:17). The Apostles had to rebuke members of the church who simply would not believe in the resurrection, and John noted with alarm that "many deceivers are entered into the world, who confess not that Jesus Christ is come in the flesh" (2 John 7). "Now if Christ be preached that he rose from the dead," writes Paul to the Corinthians, "how say some among you that there is no resurrection of the dead?" (1 Corinthians 15:12.)

Next, the writings of the so-called Apostolic Fathers, the oldest texts to survive after the time of the Apostles, show the spreading and deepening of the anti-resurrection trend in the church. Two charges are constantly brought against church members by the Apostolic Fathers: 1) that they are ashamed of the crucifixion, and 2) that they deny the resurrection. "I *know* that Christ had a body after the resurrection," cried Ignatius to the Smyrnaeans, "and I believe that he still has."[8] (We may note in passing that there is no thought here of a "mystic" body.) Ignatius pleads with the Trallians to believe that Christ "really and truly was born, and he ate and drank, and he was really and actually sentenced under Pontius Pilate, and was actually crucified and died. . . . And that he really and truly was raised from the dead. . . . But if as certain atheists, that is, non-believers, say, he only *appeared* to have suffered . . . why am I going to fight beasts?"[9] In the longer version Ignatius rebukes those who do not believe in the resurrection; others that say God cannot be known; others that think Christ was unbegotten; others who claim that the Holy Ghost is not a reality; and others who say that the Father, Son, and Holy Ghost are the same.[10]

The sorrows and alarms of the Apostolic Fathers were followed by the perplexities of the doctors. Most of the early

doctors of the church were ardent Hellenists or Neoplatonists, and there was no place in such schools of thought for a
God who contaminates himself by contact with the physical
or limits himself by taking the form of a man. "We are
stunned with the greatest amazement," wrote Origen, perhaps the most influential of all Christian philosophers next
to Augustine himself, "that this the most eminent of all natures,
putting off its state of majesty, should become a man. . . . It
is utterly beyond human comprehension that the Word of
the Father . . . should be thought of as confined within that
man who appeared in Judea. But that the Wisdom of God
should have entered the womb of a woman, and been born a
baby, and cried and wailed just like other crying babies, and
then suffered death and said that his soul was sorrowful unto
death, and been led off to the most undignified of all deaths
. . . seeing such things the human intellect is stopped in its
tracks, so stunned with amazement that it knows not where
to turn. . . . It is far beyond our powers to explain. I suppose it even goes beyond the capacity of the holy Apostles;
nay, it is quite possible that the explanation of this sacrament is beyond the powers of all the celestial beings." Not
only does Origen not know what to *think* about the Lord's
physical presence on earth; he does not even know what to
believe about it, and in his explanations is careful to specify
that he is presenting only his "suspicions rather than any
manifest affirmations."[11] And so he speculates on the resurrection of the flesh: only the Father, Son, and Holy Ghost
can live without bodies, he tells us, "because it is right and
proper to think of the Trinity alone as existing incorporeally."
But then he considers that if one thing can live without a
body, others can too, and if others, why not all? "That being
the case, bodies will be dispensed with in eternity, there
being no need for them. . . . To be subject to Christ is to be
subject to God, and to be subject to God is to have no need
of a body."[12] Commenting on this, St. Jerome writes a century and a half later: "If all things, as this order of reasoning

compels us to believe, shall live without body, the whole universe of corporeal things shall be consumed, and return again to that nothing out of which it was created."[13]

Note the vanity of the schoolmen in Origen's remarks: What *he* cannot conceive of because of his limited experience must necessarily be beyond the grasp of Apostles, angels, and all celestial beings! It is this sublime confidence in the adequacy of one's own knowledge and the finality of one's own experience that makes the resurrection of the flesh the principal thorn in the incorporeal minds of the schoolmen. According to St. Augustine, the resurrection of the flesh is the one thing that the pagans cannot take, it is the one thing with which the philosophers have no patience, and is above all the *one* thing that distinguishes a Christian from a non-Christian.[14] Since it is the one doctrine that makes Christians Christians, it is alarming to learn from St. Augustine that in his day "in nothing is there so much conflict and controversy among Christians themselves as on the subject of the resurrection of the flesh." "On no other matter," he writes, "do they disagree so vehemently, so obstinately, so resolutely, or so contentiously as on the subject of the resurrection of the flesh. For as far as the immortality of the soul is concerned many a pagan philosopher too has argued about that and bequeathed us vast heaps of writings to the effect that the soul is immortal. But when it comes to the resurrection of the flesh they won't argue, but dismiss it out of hand as impossible, and that on the grounds that it is impossible for this earthly flesh to aspire to heaven."[15]

I cannot resist noting here that the objection of the pagans to the resurrection is not a physical or a biological but a philosophical one, and it is the *very same* objection which the Christian world today makes against the Latter-day Saint conception of God: that there can be nothing of a bodily nature in the celestial. Yet the resurrected Christ was God. Is it any wonder that the Christians could never agree among themselves on this, the central doctrine of their religion? The doctors of the later church only touch lightly upon this theme, and with obvious embarrassment. St. Augustine had far more to say on the subject than any other father of the church; he speculates that the body *may* become spirit in the sense of acquiring unlimited mobility, but he is not sure; [16] he does not know exactly how to take the doctrine, very popular in his day, that the resurrection was a resurrection of the spirit (*anima*) only, [17] and again, he says he would like to know how he is to think of a "spiritual body" such as ours will be after the resurrection, but he does not know how, and would be glad to find someone who could teach him. [18] This was exactly the puzzled and hesitant attitude of Augustine's great eastern counterpart, Origen.

It was those teachings that were *not* common to the schools and *not* discoverable by the use of reason that set Christianity off from the rest of the world. As Clement says, if these things could have been discovered by human wit, there would have been no need for Christ to come to earth in person, and on the other hand, if human philosophy cannot discover them, then human philosophy has precious little to contribute to the study of the gospel. [19] The unique value of Christianity lies in those things which would never in a million years occur to men if left to themselves. Its moral and social teachings are by no means unique; as we have said before, the pagans laughed at idols as loudly as any Christian apologist; we have just quoted Augustine as saying that the pagan philosophers wrote reams on the immortality of the soul; the apologists love to point out at great length that the concept of one God, far from being a Christian contribution to knowledge, was clearly set forth in the writings of poets and sages who lived long before Christ.

It was Karl Holl who noted that an unanswerable argument for the historicity of Christ is to be found in the strangeness of his teachings. What he taught was not at all familiar doctrine but, to use Holl's own expression, "a slap in the face" to all the teachers of the time, Greek and Jew alike. [20]

The teaching that amazed and dumbfounded his own disciples could hardly have been familiar doctrine anywhere. From this emerge two obvious conclusions. The first is that Jesus actually lived—a man standing out in sharp relief against a totally hostile social environment, for without such a leader no group of men could have come together, formed a society, and propounded a doctrine that ran counter to all their own teaching, upbringing, and experience, both individual and collective. The second is that since Jesus was *not* a product of his time, is *not* to be explained in terms of his background, and cannot have got his ideas from a society to which they were utterly strange and obnoxious, he must have obtained his perfect conviction from personal experience. For the present, what can we do but accept his own version of the thing? He really had seen the Father; he really had seen Lucifer fall from heaven; he really did speak with Moses and Elias on the mount; he really did receive the ministrations of angels in the desert, and there he really did discourse with Satan; he really was before Abraham's day; and he was really resurrected.

The resurrection is the heart of the Christian teaching: "If Christ be not risen, then is our preaching vain, and your faith is also vain. . . . If in this life only we have hope in Christ, we are of all men most miserable" (1 Corinthians 15:14, 19).

There is nothing paradoxical about the resurrection. There is nothing paradoxical about a flying machine, once one has seen one in operation. But seeing the thing operate, over and above all theoretical considerations of whether it *should* operate or not, is the ultimate and only test. When falls of meteorites were reported in the eighteenth century, the learned members of the French Academy argued with perfect and unanswerable logic that such a thing simply could not be. In the spirit of the Enlightenment, Thomas Jefferson is reported to have said regarding a meteorite that fell in Connecticut in

1807, "I could more easily believe that two Yankee professors would lie than that stones would fall from heaven."[21] Logically, there was no answer to the natural philosophers. We *still* don't know where meteorites come from. But where the eighteenth-century scientists fell down was exactly where Origen failed. He was convinced that what *he* could not reason out was beyond reason; they were convinced that what their science had not officially noted simply did not exist, and that what could not be scientifically explained—by *them*—was necessarily impossible. But even with the fullest scientific information at hand such a conclusion is not warranted. Every scientist knows that the drawing board and the equation do *not* have the final word, no matter how accurate and exhaustive the work on them may be. There is only one way to know whether the thing will fly or not.

Once the fall of meteorites was proved by witnesses in 1803, the Academy promptly shifted from complete denial to complete acceptance, and all acted as if they had never questioned such a thing for a moment. So it was with the resurrection. In a moment, Thomas changed from doubt to assurance so perfect that he was astonished and humiliated at ever having doubted anything so obvious. No matter how wildly improbable or paradoxical or utterly impossible a thing may seem to the cleverest people on earth, only by witness and not by reason, theory, or speculation may its truth be ultimately established, whether the truth be scientific or religious. "This is the testimony . . . which we give of him: That he lives! For we saw him . . . and we heard the voice bearing record that he is the Only Begotten of the Father" (D&C 76:22-23). Compare this testimony of modern prophets with that of the ancients: "That which was from the beginning, which we have heard, which we have seen *with our eyes*, which we have looked upon, and our hands have handled, of the Word of life; . . . That which we have seen and heard declare we unto you." (1 John 1:1, 3.) After all, it is the testimony of the prophets that gives us the real Easter.

19

Two Ways to Remember the Dead

On Memorial Day we think of our dead and put flowers on their graves. Is there anything more we can do? Many like to think that the dead enjoy a kind of continued existence by living in our memories. That is a kindly sentiment but more depressing than exhilarating. It has the faint odor and faded colors of a Maeterlinck fantasy or a Russian novel (such as *Oblomov's Dream*), and it meets us often in the wistful and heartbreaking little epitaphs that have been found on the graves of pagan Greeks and Romans. To think constantly of the dead is morbid; to think of them occasionally is nice—but a poor sort of immortality. We have occasionally used the expression "earth-bound." Things of the spirit should not be earth-bound. What could be more depressing than the old-fashioned churchyard with its shadowy vaults; its seeping damp and odor of decay; its aged, mossy stones; its weeping willows and drooping plumes; in short, all those fixtures of the cult of the dead which seem like nothing so much as desperate devices to tie the dead to this world and keep them always within call.

This Gothic view of death, this obsession with the grisly remnants of the body, is not a healthy thing. The reaction from it in modern times has been a flight to another and equally unhealthy extreme, for the present age seems determined to leave death out of its calculations entirely, save for certain annoying details of a sanitary and legal nature. This has done much to make for shallowness and triviality in

modern life. We think and act as if death were not part of
the program at all, or as if it were a frightful piece of bun-
gling in the ordering of our lives, a terrible and senseless mistake. Death has disappeared from our serious thinking to
meet us in every drugstore and bus station as the leitmotif of
all our lighter reading. A strange and sordid business, this
preoccupation with the sensational, the sordid, and the bru-
tal aspects of death. The spectre which we drove out the
back door has returned by the front.

How then should one think of the dead? It is one of the
offices of true religion to teach us that. It was because philosophy could not answer the great questions of life, as we
have seen, that such men as Clement and Justin and Tertullian turned from it to Christianity. Speculation and tradition, then as now, gave dignified but quite unsatisfactory
answers, and the honest seeker saw clearly that if men were
ever to learn anything certain about the great mysteries of
the beyond, such information would have to come by revelation. That is true today as it was in ancient times. The
comfort of philosophy, the quiet resignation and calm acqui-
escence with fate are well enough in themselves, but they are
what in ancient times distinguished the pagan from the Christian, for the latter amazed the world by the robust and joyful
assurance with which he viewed things of the other world.
One of the most striking features of primitive Christianity
was its constant and hardheaded insistence on the nearness
and reality of the other side. A pagan critic of the early
Christians remarked with wonder and annoyance that "they
think nothing of present torments, but worry about what is
to happen hereafter; and while they dread perishing *after*
death, they don't fear dying here at all, so completely taken
in are they by the false hope of living hereafter."[1] In
Androcles and the Lion, George Bernard Shaw attempted to
depict the old and intriguing phenomenon of people who did
not fear death; he saw that the contrast of this point of view
with the normal one is so great as to create in itself hilarious

situations; he saw that without any irreverence, there was
something perfectly delightful in a religion which could view
the life to come without any of the sombre Mumbo Jumbo
of cult practices; and he also realized that in the primitive
Christian church he found a view of death that was unique
in history and totally unlike that of the later Christian
churches.

Now there is nothing unusual in a belief in an afterlife—
as St. Augustine observed, it was a view quite commonly
held by pagan philosophers. What set the early Christians
apart was that they were not at all vague about the business.
Just as for them the charismatic gifts—prophecy, tongues,
healings, etc.—were real, literal, and concrete, so the life to
come was not an abstraction or a rational necessity, but a
thing to be experienced. As long as we find living prophets
in the church, these things cannot be thought of as anything
but real; they are all part of the same picture and have the
same explanation—a living bond with the heavens, a continuous intercourse between this world and the other. And when
the gift of prophecy departs, we witness at the same time the
cessation of the other heavenly gifts, and with that the church
changes its views of the other world, becoming perplexed
and uncertain about things which it once knew so well.

A good deal has been written recently about the abrupt
and surprising reorientation of the Christian church in the
second century. At that time the attitude of the Christians to
this world and the next suddenly and completely changed.
So complete was this change of outlook and belief and so
different was the resulting church from the apostolic one that
the radical Dutch and German schools of church history
were able to maintain that the primitive Christian church
had never really existed, but was just an idealized reconstruc-
tion made in retrospect! One of the most instructive aspects
of that change is the attitude of the church writers toward
death. If we compare, say, Ignatius of Antioch with St. Basil
on this subject, we find that the two men have absolutely

nothing in common. Ignatius, who lived in the first and early second centuries, is straining every nerve to get to the other side. Any fame he might leave behind him as a saint or a martyr—any help he might give the church as its best-informed bishop—is no concern of his. As far as this world is concerned, he has lost all interest, every speck of it. Food and drink and the pleasure of life have ceased to exist for him: "I no longer wish to live after the manner of men," he writes to the Romans. "Believe me, I am sincere in this."[2] Though he is quite aware that no man on earth could do the church as much good as he by continuing to live, he is none-theless resolved not to linger here below for another moment if by any means short of suicide he can leave it. For Ignatius, the *only* reality is on the other side, and there is nothing metaphysical or abstract about it.

But consider St. Basil, the great theologian of the fourth century. Among his numerous surviving letters are a pair written to console friends of his for the loss of a child.[3] These consolations read exactly like those of the pagan clas-sical writers: The usual commonplaces about the inevitabil-ity of death and the shortness and misery of life do not attempt to hide the conviction that death is after all the supreme evil. But for a few scattered and conventional bib-lical terms, the letters might have all been written by Cicero, and some of them betray not the slightest trace of any Chris-tian influence. What had happened to the faith? I grant you the *consolatio* was a well-established literary genre in the schools, but Basil is writing to his dearest Christian friends to give them what comfort he can as a bishop—surely, if he had more to give them he would. When the great Boethius in the sixth century was condemned to die, it was not religion but Dame Philosophy who brought him consolation in the death cell, and the famous essay she dictated on that melan-choly occasion is not to be distinguished from the writings of a typical heathen philosopher in style, vocabulary, mood, or thought. Eventually the Christians ended up fearing death more anxiously than ever the pagans had. According to F. J. E. Raby, by the end of the Middle Ages "it now became a pious exercise to meditate on every ghastly detail which the imagination could add to the picture of the Passion," the individual identifying himself as much as possible with the suffering.[4] "For the medieval Christian," writes Raby, "the Day of Judgment was almost wholly a day of terror," and "this same sense of terror is expressed in the . . . Mass for the Dead. . . . The recurring refrain in this noble prose adds to the sense of fear and apprehension."[5] This Raby finds to be in complete contrast to "the joy and comfort of the early church."[6] And so we see, when revelation ceased, the Christians went back to thinking about death exactly as the pagans do. That is neither surprising nor reprehensible, but it does offer us a good test for a true and prophetic religion. For such a religion must surely be one in which the early rather than the later Christian view of death prevails, and such a view has always characterized the Latter-day Saints.

Now, I would like to point to one of the most wonderful and exciting aspects of the restored gospel, and that is the great work for the dead that is so peculiar to the Church of Jesus Christ. I do not specify "of Latter-day Saints," for this work was done by the primitive Christians as well. The knowledge of that all-important work was taken away at an early time, for after the third century the fathers of the church are much perplexed whenever it is mentioned, though all admit that the earliest Christians actually did perform certain ordinances for the salvation of the dead. Furthermore, there is ample evidence that the Christians of apostolic times placed great emphasis on this work, for among the very early fragments of Christian literature that have been discovered in recent years, the subject is referred to as a very special knowledge imparted by the Lord to the Apostles in secret conferences after the resurrection.[7] This is not surprising, in view of the evidence of the Clementine homilies that the earliest Christians baptized in secret places,[8] and the constant charges of secrecy that were being brought against them—charges which they did not deny.

What was the nature of this work for the dead? The early Christians were convinced, as modern Christians are, that no man can get into heaven without baptism. Now most of those early Christians were converts to the church, and that meant that their parents in most cases and their grandparents in all cases had died without ever having heard of the baptism of salvation. Would these loved ones be forever damned? One of the first things Clement asks Peter upon being introduced to him, in the *Clementine Recognitions*, is, "Shall those be wholly deprived of the kingdom of heaven who died before Christ's coming?" for he was thinking probably of his own forebears. Peter's answer is very significant: "You force me, Clement, to make public things that are not to be discussed. But I see no objection to telling you as much as we are allowed to. Christ, who always was from the beginning, has visited the righteous of every generation (albeit secretly), and especially those who have looked forward to his coming, to whom he often appeared. Still it was not yet time for the resurrection of bodies that perished then, . . . but those who pleased him and did his will were translated to paradise, to be preserved there for the kingdom, while those who were not able to fulfill the complete law of justice, but had certain traces of carnal weakness in their nature, when their bodies died went in the spirit to be retained in good and happy places, that at the resurrection of the dead each might be empowered to receive an eternal heritage for the good he had done."[9] This much Peter is willing to tell, but he will not divulge to the new investigator just how those who have never heard the gospel in life are to be saved.

Whatever one may think of this very old fragment, it certainly shows that there were some early Christians who knew about salvation for the dead as a doctrine not taught to the general public. Both the theory and practice were

remembered in the traditions of the church, where they provided no end of puzzlement and speculation to the commen-
tators. Typical is St. Bruno at the end of the twelfth century,
who still recalls, with routine disapproval, of course, that
certain of the early Christians in New Testament times "would
baptize themselves in the place of a dead parent who had
never heard the gospel, thereby securing the salvation of a
father or a mother in the resurrection."[10] It might be argued
that this work ceased in later times because after everybody
had belonged to the church for generations there would be
no unbaptized fathers and mothers. But one need only consider that in every age the church has been a missionary
organization—a believing minority determined to carry forth
the work of converting the heathen majority all of whose
parents and grandparents are without baptism—to realize
that work for the dead never should have ceased, since it is
necessary as long as outsiders continue to join the church.
When a Germanic king was converted to Christianity, for
example, he refused to accept baptism since that meant basely
leaving his noble ancestors to suffer in hell while he enjoyed
himself in heaven—that, in all conscience, he could not do.

From the earliest fragments, a good deal of the theory
and practice of baptism for the dead in the apostolic church
can be reconstructed. There were two main steps necessary
to achieving salvation for the dead—the *kerygma* and baptism. The *kerygma* is the preaching of the word to those who
are dead. It takes place, of course, in the other world, in a
place where the dead are retained, a place designated with
calculated vagueness—scrupulous avoidance of any attempt
to designate a particular locale. What is made perfectly clear
is that the dead who have not accepted the gospel on earth
for any reason are detained in a place which is by no means
disagreeable but is not heaven. To these (the ancient saints
taught) the Lord and, following his example, the Apostles
and other holy men of old went down and preached the
word.[11] No spirit was forced to accept the *kerygma*, but

such as did could leave their detention and advance in eternity just as soon as they had received the *seal*. The *seal* was what the early Christians called baptism in this connection. It was the seal of baptism that was put on the acceptance of the preaching on the other side. If it was accepted, the seal was effective, and what was sealed on earth was sealed in heaven. The seal was given by ministrants acting by proxy for the dead on this earth, for baptism could be given nowhere else, it was realized, and in no other way—"there is only one baptism," was the formula. In the *Pastor of Hermas* these earthly officiants are described as being the Apostles themselves, who while they were still alive baptized each other "for those who had fallen asleep before."[12]

Today, members of The Church of Jesus Christ of Latter-day Saints are everywhere engaged in the great work of searching out the records of their ancestors. Along with this the building and operation of our temples goes forward, for as in the ancient church, this work is not carried out in public. In these holy places the ordinances for the dead are performed by any worthy member of the Church who wishes to participate, from the age of eight years to extremely advanced ages when people are commonly thought to have passed their usefulness in most fields of work. Everything is done in a joyful and happy spirit. We love our kindred dead, and our own exaltation as well as theirs depends on the work we do for them. The New Revised Translation of the New Testament, recently greeted in many parts with considerable enthusiasm, gives an enlightening twist to the famous passage in 1 Corinthians 15:29 dealing with this work: "Else what shall they do which are baptized for the dead, if the dead rise not at all? why are they baptized for *their* dead?"

With the exception of the verse just cited, a few perplexed commentaries on it, and the unnoticed passage from the *Pastor of Hermas*, all our evidence for the practice of baptism for the dead in ancient times comes from fragments

recently discovered. The possession of this strange and wonderful thing by the restored Church of Jesus Christ for over a
hundred years would therefore seem to be an almost fool-
proof certificate of authenticity. The prophets of modern
times remember the dead exactly as did those prophets of
old, and in the growing evidence for the nature of that work
among the first Christians, time has vindicated the modern
prophets.

20

Prophets and Martyrs

This is the one hundred tenth anniversary of the martyrdom of the Prophet Joseph Smith and his brother Hyrum. That was a true martyrdom in the strictest and rarest sense of the word, recalling in every detail, as did so many events in the modern prophet's life, the trials, sufferings, and accomplishments of the prophets of old. This resemblance is by no means accidental, though certainly it was not contrived by the prophet himself. There is a deep significance in the events that culminated in the terrible crime of June 27, 1844, in which two prophets of God sealed their testimony with their blood.

As Peter, James, and John were descending the mountain with the Lord after they had had that wonderful manifestation in which the Father had personally introduced Jesus to them as his Son, they discussed together the subject of martyrdom. Having now a new knowledge of who the Master was, the Apostles naturally asked him whether Elias had come to announce him—for according to the ancient doctrine, the Lord does not come to this earth without an Elias to precede him and prepare the way. To this, Jesus replied that Elias would indeed come, as predicted, to restore all things, that is, in the fulness of times; but aside from that, he explained, Elias had already come as his forerunner. "Elias is come already, and they knew him not, but have done unto him whatsoever they listed. Likewise must also the Son of man suffer of them" (Matthew 17:12). The King James Version here says "shall suffer" as if a simple future were being used; but the word is *mellei* with the infinitive, and *mellei* regularly refers to a future event that *must be*, that is destined and unavoidable. This is actually a more emphatic statement than that which is rendered in Mark 9:12: "The Son of man . . . *must* suffer many things, and be set at nought." But the strongest possible expression is that which is translated from Luke 9:22: "The Son of man *must* [literally, *is bound to*] suffer many things, and be rejected of the elders and chief priests and scribes, and be slain." Now we know that it was necessary for the Son of Man to be put to death to accomplish the redemption of the human race. In that, he was unique—He trod the winepress alone. But in this matter of martyrdom—necessary martyrdom—his prediction does not stop with himself, for the Lord told the Apostles that they too must suffer the same fate as he. He even said that to follow him meant to take up a cross (Luke 9:23). The order he gave to all his followers was to endure to the end, and the early Christians had absolutely no doubt as to what that meant: "To endure to the end," Tertullian explains, "meant to suffer the end, to suffer death, no less."[1] The disciples of the Lord were firmly convinced of what their fate would be.

The Master having been rejected and slain, would the servants fare better? By no means: "If they have called the master of the house Beelzebub, how much more shall they call them of his household?" (Matthew 10:25.) "If *any* man will come after me, let him deny himself. . . . For whosoever will lose his life for my sake, the same shall save it" (Luke 9:23-24). This was no mere laying aside of a life of worldly desires, as the churchmen later rationalized it, but death in the literal, physical sense. "The servant is not greater than his Lord. If they have persecuted me, they will also persecute you. . . . They shall put you out of the synagogues: yea, the time cometh, that whosoever killeth you will think that he doeth God service. . . . These things have I told you, that when the time shall come, ye may remember that I told you of them" (John 15:20, 16:2, 4). "Then shall they deliver you up to be afflicted, and shall *kill* you: and ye shall be hated of *all* nations for my name's sake. . . . But he that shall endure unto the end, the same shall be saved. And this gospel of the kingdom shall be preached in all the world *for a witness* unto all nations; and than shall the *end* come" (Matthew 24:9, 13-14; italics added). When accordingly the time finally came when the doors of the synagogues were closed to the missionaries of the church and they were hated of all nations (remember how "all of Asia" turned against Paul after he had had his greatest success there), and they were in a very short time run down and exterminated—when this began to happen, Peter reminded the surprised and disheartened saints that this was exactly what had been predicted, and there was no need to lose faith because of it, though they could not expect to save their lives. "Beloved, think it not strange concerning the fiery trial which is to try you, as though some strange thing happened unto you: But rejoice, inasmuch as ye are partakers of Christ's sufferings" (1 Peter 4:12). In this letter he prepares the saints for death; he reassures them that our sojourn here is but a time of fear (1:17), that all flesh is as the grass anyway (1:24), that they are but "strangers and pilgrims" on this earth (2:11), where "the end of all things is at hand" (4:7). His great comfort for them is the thought that they are going to receive "an inheritance incorruptible, and undefiled, and that fadeth not away, reserved in heaven for you" (1:4).

It would seem from these and many like passages in the Bible, that to be the recipient of a special message from heaven disqualifies one for a place in the world of men. The *necessity* of martyrdom was a firmly established belief in the Christian church. For centuries Christians were absolutely convinced that to be a true follower of Christ one *had* to be a martyr. When the church became the world church, and it became impossible to get put to death simply for being a Christian, men felt that they were being cheated of their

glory which they still believed depended in a very real sense
on following the Lord to death. Men made determined
attempts to become martyrs at all cost, and the rationalizing
of men like Chrysostom—that to fight the lusts of the flesh
was just as heroic as fighting beasts in the arena—did not
prove very convincing. In the endless debates between Christian and pagan sects, between Christians and Jews, and especially between the numerous sects of Christians themselves,
the strongest argument that any side could bring forward to
its divine standing was that it had the most martyrs. The
idea that martyrdom was a *necessary* and indispensable part
of the picture is so deeply ingrained in Christian thinking
that it still persists, and people of all denominations are eager
to describe as Christian martyrdom any sufferings they
undergo.

But to be a martyr, it is not enough simply to be put to
death. In fact, it is not even necessary to be slain to be a
martyr. Most of the martyrs that Cyprian wrote about were
very much alive. The word *martyr* simply means "witness,"
not dead witness. The important thing is that the martyr is a
witness. Men have tried often and with great ingenuity and
determination to be martyrs and have sometimes got themselves killed, but that does not make them martyrs. After the
third century, the Christians were fond of comparing those
who died for the faith with the pagan heroes of antiquity
who gave their lives in this or that cause, and at an even
earlier time, Christians cite with admiration the example of
Socrates, who died for the truth. But none of these were
martyrs in the strict sense of the word. In every century and
every church there have been men and women who willingly
died for causes. Even the Saints who died crossing the plains
were not martyrs in the sense of actually being put to death
as witnesses. The missionary who loses his life while chop-
ping down a pagan idol or burning a heathen shrine is not a
witness either, for one of the most striking things about those
who are slain for bearing witness is that they have broken no

law of God or man. "Which of you convinceth me of sin?"
the Savior asked. "What evil has he done?" was Pilate's question to which there was no answer. A true martyr is put to
death for his testimony and that alone. We have already discussed "A Prophet's Reward" and pointed out that prophets
have been put to death not for their moral and ethical preach-
ings, however severely they may have castigated the manners
and practices of their time, but always for their insistence on
bearing witness to what they have seen and heard, and for
that alone.

This explains a peculiar circumstance of the restoration
of the gospel both in the Lord's day and in our own dispensation: namely, the fact that the Church was set up in the
most unfavorable, nay bitterly hostile, environment imagin-
able. From the appalling accounts of Josephus alone we see
what a dangerous, bloody, riotous, restless, treacherous, fanatical land Palestine was at the time of Christ—the last place in
the world to seek security for a new religious movement.
And from numerous letters, journals, newspapers, and
travelers' accounts, it is even easier to see what a dangerous,
bloody, riotous, and restless land was the frontier in which
the Lord called Joseph Smith to do his work. "Thirty-nine
times he was arrested," wrote John Henry Evans; "six months
he spent in filthy Missouri jails; on several occasions he was
mobbed, and once he was tarred and feathered and left for
dead; three times he and his people were driven from their
homes and from the state in which they lived; and in the end
he was murdered while awaiting trial on a false charge."[2]
Why were the prophets, ancient and modern, called to work
in such hopelessly hostile environments as frontier America
and frontier Palestine? Because only in those two lands could
a prophet ask, what evil have I done? what law have I broken? with the perfect assurance of being clear of all offense
to God and man.

When the Jews accused Jesus of treason and sedition,
they labored mightily to make their case stick with the

Romans, for it was only under *Roman* law that Jesus could be judged guilty of those crimes—under Jewish law there was no such crime. To come forward as a prophet or even as the Messiah was no crime; to proclaim the kingdom of God and even to be chosen king by the people was accepted procedure in Israel; if any of those crimes could have been charged against Jesus, then the Maccabees would have been the worst of offenders.[3] But under Roman or Greek or Persian law the Lord could have been charged with *lèse-majesté* and treason. It might be argued convincingly that Joseph Smith could have set up the Church in any country of the civilized world with only a fraction of the danger and persecution experienced in this land of the free. But to be free of any offense against the law is more important than to be free from persecution. Neither the ancient nor the modern saints were immune to attacks of the devil, but both had the satisfaction of knowing that under the free institutions of their forefathers, their testimony could never be a crime. The fault was all with their accusers.

"Partakers of Christ's sufferings . . . " (1 Peter 4:13.) The Lord told his Apostles that they would suffer death even as he. In their case, too, we find the usual cast of characters: the pathological mobs, the timid and dishonest government officials, the mob-inciting clergy, the corrupt and partial judges, the false witnesses, the wild gossip and planted rumors, the mass hysteria, the traitors within the church. Whatever the method of execution, the same individuals and interest groups are responsible, animated by the same motives. Consider for a moment the remarkable degree to which the Prophet's martyrdom resembled theirs.

He had had the vision of the Father and the Son, and from that day to the end he knew that as long as he persisted in the course of action to which he was called, every effort would be made to destroy him. He did not seek martyrdom any more than the ancient prophets did. The Lord advised his disciples to flee from place to place to carry on their

work; but one way out they could not and did not take, and
that was to save their lives by denying their testimony. Joseph
Smith never deviated from his course, not for a moment. In
the last week of his life, he prophesied his own death and
along with that uttered a number of most remarkable prophecies on the future of his people and his persecutors. The
immediate charge on which he was held was the same brought
against Jesus: treason and inciting to riot—both decided on
in secret meetings of the higher-ups.[4] Politically, Governor
Ford's position and powers corresponded exactly to those of
Pilate, and the man's character and behavior were precisely
the same. He recognized that Smith had broken no law, that
the charge of treason was preposterous. He tried desperately
to wash his hands of the whole business and in the end
skipped out, deliberately turning the Prophet over to the
ministrations of the mob, for a large, bloodthirsty, and fanatical mob made up the unfailing background to both these
terrible dramas. Joseph Smith was paraded before the mob-
militia to be greeted with savage taunts and demonstrations
which no one, including the vacillating and conniving governor, doubted presaged violent and deadly business. The
corrupt Sanhedrin was not wanting, with all its legal hypoc-
risy and flimflam, the Prophet's chief judge being the leader
of the very company of Carthage Grays most openly and
loudly sworn to have the blood of Joseph Smith. At the heart
of all the disturbance was a nucleus of conspirators, ambitious and jealous men whose machinations were urged and
hastened on by the bitterest men of all—those men who had
followed and betrayed the Prophet.

Since he was a child of fourteen, Joseph Smith had to
deal with desperate and determined men. They never let him
alone. To go through one week of what he had to go through
almost every week of his adult and adolescent life would
drive the average man out of his mind. The charges and the
threats never ceased; whether it was shots from ambush or
pompous blasts from the editors of the great metropolitan

papers, the Prophet was given no rest. No charge against him was too vile to be believed; no one asked for proof. God-fearing men felt it a public duty to call for Smith's extermination from the pulpit and the press; gangs of seasoned killers and professional thugs lived for the day when they could get Joe Smith. He had no private life, this kind, cheerful, home-loving man, whose name was made a synonym for baseness and depravity. And again and again he asks: What have I done? What man convinceth me of sin?

He had done nothing. The rabid Peter Cartwright, while hailing the murder of the Prophet with glee, gives everything away when he says, "An outraged and deeply-injured people took the law into their own hands, and killed him."[5] How, "deeply-injured"? In as bitter an anti-Mormon book as was ever published, Reed Peck is quoted as saying that the Mormons were driven out of Missouri "for causes too numerous to mention, though nothing of a criminal nature could be justly urged."[6] In a work of equal bitterness, one N. C. Lewis, while admitting that he could detect nothing wrong in Smith's behavior, was sure that he was nonetheless "an impostor, hypocrite and liar."[7] One is reminded of Dickens' statement: "What the Mormons *do* seems to be excellent; what they *say* is mostly nonsense." But if speaking nonsense were a capital offense, who would be left alive? The most quoted single commentator on Smith's early life, Pomeroy Tucker, straining every effort to pin some crime on his subject, must admit in the case of the only crime of which he can report, that it rests on hearsay of certain suspicions—forty years after, "though it is but common fairness to accompany this fact [the "fact" being the suspicion] . . . that it is not within remembrance of the writer . . . if the popular inferences in this matter were ever sustained by judicial investigation."[8] One cannot help recalling the famous passage in Tacitus (*Annals* XV, 44), where he tells us that though there was no evidence that the Christians ever set fire to Rome, still they

deserved to be punished for it in view of their general reputation and the utter depravity of their religion—an *exitiabilis
superstitio*.

There is another side to this. Did Joseph Smith want
fame, money, success, power? His biographers from the beginning to the present day make greed and ambition his ruling
passions. Take a couple of examples. Here is one from the
American Whig Review for June 1851. It tells us of Joseph
Smith that "great powers of reasoning were his natural gift
and . . . a deep vein of humor that ran through all he said
and did," he had "a retentive memory; a correct knowledge
of human nature, . . . a Herculean frame and a commanding appearance." Along with these formidable qualifications,
we are told, "he was one of the most avaricious of men. . . .
He had ambition that knew no scruple, and licentiousness
that scorned all bounds."[9] And here is another, from T. W.
T. Taylder in 1857: "In person Joseph Smith was a man of
commanding appearance, tall and well-proportioned. . . . The
skill with which he carried out his imposture and eluded
detection from the masses—his eloquence, rude but powerful—his letters, clever and sarcastic—the manifold character
and boldness that scorned all bounds of his designs—his
courage in enterprise—his perseverance despite great obsta-
cles—his conception and partial execution of the temple of
Nauvoo—these and other things mark him as a man of more
than ordinary calibre." But, says our informant, "that he
was a religious enthusiast we cannot grant. . . . One principle . . . actuated him through life, and that was—
selfishness."[10] This is a strange state of things! A man of
phenomenal ability for getting what he wants, combined with
boundless personal ambition, who somehow never places his
ability at the service of his ambition! Here was a national
figure of first importance, a man who received more publicity in the press at home and abroad than any other American of his day or, through the years, of any day. Everywhere
important people accord grudging admiration to his talents

or express pious regret that such genius could not have been expended in a better cause. Did this man need to risk his life every day and in the end go to certain death at the hands of the floating riffraff and professional desperadoes of the frontier? The public would not only have forgiven his past but praised and rewarded him the more for relieving it of the awful responsibility of having to answer to a prophet of God. Wealth, fame, and security could have been his at any time in the East, and he knew it.

Just so, Paul was recognized by Jews and Gentiles alike as a man of supreme ability. What a career he could have made for himself in the world! The Jews wanted to make Jesus their king and could have done so quite legally. Yet Jesus was accused of being an unscrupulous opportunist and a subversive. The world accuses the prophets of being career men and opportunists, and explains their death as a slip-up, as something going wrong with their plans; and all the time the prophets know, from the moment of their calling, what their end must be if they continue true and faithful. There is nothing accidental just as there is nothing devised in a martyr's end. He assumes the obligation to be a witness, knowing full well what that dangerous duty entails. The Prophet who was put to death 110 years ago was a true martyr and a true prophet in the strictest and holiest sense of the word.

21

The Ancient Law of Liberty

In his refutation of the Gnostics, Irenaeus in the middle of the second century set forth what he called the "Ancient Law of Liberty." Plainly, it does not originate with him. The law is illustrated, he says, by the scripture "How often would I have gathered thy children together, . . . and ye would not!" (Matthew 23:37.) God wants men to do right, but he does not coerce them to it. "For," says Irenaeus, "God made man free from the beginning. . . . For God never uses force. . . . He placed in man the power of election even as in the angels. . . . Glory and honor, he says, to all who do good, and it is due them because they could have done evil. . . . Now if God made some men good and some bad simply by nature, there would be nothing praiseworthy in their virtue or blameworthy in their vice, for that being their nature they could not do otherwise. But since to all is given equally the power of doing good or bad exactly as they choose, they are rightly praised or blamed for what they do. . . . That is why the prophets *appeal* to men to do good and eschew evil."[1] Irenaeus further explains that "God wants men to do good, but even the Gospel allows anyone who does not want to do good to do evil. To obey or disobey is in every man's power. . . . God forcing no man. . . . There is a godlike power of judgment in all men, making them envied by angels."[2] The ancient law of liberty is that God trusts men while on this earth to make their own choices, while they trust him alone to judge whether those choices have been good or bad.

This second aspect of the law—that God alone shall judge—is well brought out in Peter's apocryphal refutation of the arch-Gnostic Simon Magus, a valuable and ancient elucidation of Irenaeus' statement. Peter begins the discussion by invoking peace on the whole assembly and expressing the desire that everything be peaceably and amicably discussed. This is the signal for the self-righteous Simon Magus to explode with the indignant declaration that champions of truth don't ask for peace, since they are determined to "kick the stuffing" out of error and will only call it peace when the opposition lies helpless before them. It is weakness and cowardice in Peter, he says, to ask for peace for the wrong as well as for the right side. In reply Peter says we must imagine this world as a vast plain in which two cities strive for mastery, each claiming the whole land as its own. The king of one city sends to the other proposing a peaceful discussion in which the matter might be decided without killing anybody. In this he is not weak; he has no intention of giving the other king a single blade of grass that does not belong to him. Now the other king can think of no other course than to take what is his by force, and that, says Peter, shows that his cause is really a weak one.[3] Simon Magus then applies his argument against Peter to Peter's God, bringing out the favorite old chestnut of the schools: either God is vicious because he does not want to prevent evil or weak because he cannot. "Could not God have made us all good," he asks, "so that we could not be anything else but virtuous?" To which Peter replies with a statement of the ancient law of liberty: "A foolish question," he says, "for if he made us unchangeably and immovably inclined to good, we would not really be good at all, since we couldn't be anything else; and it would be no merit on our part that we were good, nor could we be given credit for doing what we did by necessity of nature. How can you call any act good that is not performed intentionally? For this reason the world has existed through the ages, so that the spirits destined to come here might fulfill

their number, and here make their choice between the upper
and the lower worlds, both of which are represented here, so
that when their bodies are resurrected the blessed might go
to eternal light and the unrighteous for their impure acts be
wrapped in a spiritual flame."[4] In this work, says Peter,
"every man is given a fair chance to show his real desires."
To the question put to him in a later discussion, "Did not the
Creator know that those he created would do evil?" Peter
replied, "Certainly, he considered all the evil that would be
among those whom he created; but as one who knew there
was no other way to achieve the purpose for which they
were created, he went ahead. He did not draw back or hesi-
tate, nor was he afraid of what would happen." Evil is forced
on no one, he explains, it is only there for those who want it.
No one comes under its sway "save he who of his own free
will deliberately subjects himself to it."[5]

At the end of the discussion with Simon Magus, according to this account, Peter's good faith in this law of liberty
was put to the test. Simon had lost control of himself; he had
started raving and antagonized and scandalized everyone
present. The people accordingly wanted to mob the arch-
enemy of the faith, but Peter vigorously opposed them: "We
must bear wicked men with patience, brethren," he cried,
"knowing that God who could easily wipe them out, suffers
them to carry on to the appointed day in which the deeds of
all shall be judged. Wherefore should we not then suffer
whom God suffers? Why do we not bear with fortitude of
spirit the wrongs they commit against us, when he who can
do all things does not avenge himself for the wrongs they do
him?"[6]

In our discussion of "The Prophets and the Plan of Life,"
we quote other early Christian writers who described this
world as a testing ground in which everyone was to be given
the choice between good *and* evil, the presence of evil and
the possiblity of a wrong choice being just as essential to the
plan as the presence of good. No teaching is more frequently

met with nor more emphatically brought home in the earliest
Christian literature than the famous doctrine of the "Two
Ways," which proclaims that there lie before every human
being and before the church itself two roads between which
a choice must be made. The one is the road of darkness, the
way of evil; the other, the way of light. Every man must
choose between the two every day of his life; that choosing
is the most important thing he does, and the two ways, good
and evil, are absolutely essential to God's plan.[7] There is
nothing weak or vicious in the arrangement, for every man
is clearly given to understand that as he chooses so he will be
judged. He will be judged by God in the proper time and
place. Meantime he must be free, perfectly free, to choose
his own way.

Now this is a thing which the kings of the world have
never been able to see. Trespasses against persons and property are things that can be and always have been settled
among men themselves by payment of one sort or another.
But the particular concern of despots in every age has been
to prevent and punish trespasses against God—those sins
which shake the very foundation of the universe, according
to the established dogma. Sin is wrong; therefore all possible
means should be taken to prevent men from sinning. What
could be more logical? From the earliest to the latest times
kings have claimed to be what the Roman emperor called
himself, the *virtutum rector* of the world, the *magnus parens
mundi*, whose mission was to force all men to be virtuous.[8]
For a man to set himself up as judge and parent of the
human race is to usurp divine authority, but the kings of old
always had an answer to that: "We are God's representatives
on earth," they said, "and whatever we do is, after all, in the
name of virtue; we *want* everyone to be virtuous, and it is
our business to see to it that everybody is virtuous."[9] In this
they were quite sincere.

Satan's plan, you will recall, was to make everybody virtuous, not vicious, and in that he was the model and arche-
type of those monarchs of old who insisted on abolishing all
sin by edict. Time and again the panegyrists hail this or that
emperor for having abolished all sin and nonconformity from
the world. God was against sin; very well, the emperor would
see to it that nobody sinned—he would close the door on sin
and make it possible for the human race to walk one way
and one way only—the way of light, the path of compulsory
virtue. Emperors, sincere and devout men who gave themselves such names as Pius and Felix, sent out their *agentes in
rebus* to teach virtue to the Christians (everybody knew about
their immoral doctrines and secret orgies!), and met with a
surprising rebuff. "What a splendid sight to God," writes
Minucius Felix, "when a Christian stands up to pain, when
he holds his own against threats, tortures, and torments!
When he smilingly faces the multitude screaming for his death
and the grim preparations of the butcher, as he asserts his
liberty against kings and princes, yielding it only to God, to
whom it belongs!"[10] It is not for kings or princes to judge
whether a man's course is a godly one or not; it is for God
alone.

Yet, a hundred years after this was written, the Christian
Roman emperors began their long, futile series of edicts monotonously ordering the whole human race to be good, orthodox Christians on pain of the severest penalities, exactly as
their heathen predecessors had called repeatedly on the human
race to acknowledge their virtuous rule and follow its example—or else. The Emperor Theodosius in a famous edict
declared that all who disagreed with his church's definition
of God could only be treated as extravagant madmen. The
Emperor Justinian announced his intention of forcing even
the devil himself to join the true church and thus achieve
that perfect unity "which Pythagoras and Plato taught." To
this way of thinking, the church itself was completely converted in the fourth century. No more nonsense about *two*

ways—henceforth there was to be only *one* way pleasing to God, and the church would see to it that nobody ever got off the track.[11] St. Augustine had taught that true liberty was not to be able to sin, forgetting that the angels envy man's right to sin if he wants to.

The Reformation and the wars of religion did not abolish the doctrine of compulsory virtue but extended its application, acknowledging the right of princes to take their choice among a number of religions and binding their subjects to the same—*cujus regio eius religio*—or at least giving it such preferential treatment as to make it all but compulsory. The system flourished throughout Europe until World War I.

On July 4, 1776, the ancient law of liberty was again established upon the earth. Everywhere in America, says John Adams, the people received the Declaration of Independence "as though it was a decree promulgated from heaven." And well they might, for it was a strange and wonderful thing. "Freedom hath been hunted round the globe," wrote Tom Paine. "Asia and Africa have long expelled her. Europe regards her like a stranger, and England hath given her warning to depart. O! receive the fugitive and prepare in time an asylum for mankind."[12] It was a radical departure from the established order of things. Ancient precepts were renounced, and men disowned an allegiance to which they had taken oaths, however reluctantly. For that trespass a price was paid, and the right to the "new order of things," the *novus ordo seclorum* that appears on the national seal, was purchased by the shedding of blood.

Both the Declaration of Independence and the Constitution of the United States contain statements of general principles along with specific and particular provisions for their implementation. The principles are the really important thing. Both documents specifically render back to God those rights of judgment and execution which men had usurped. That is why both have a strongly negative tone. "Hands off!" is the theme—there are certain rights which *all* men enjoy which the Creator himself has declared inalienable and with which no man or group of men has any right to interfere. Men may check and admonish each other in their little affairs, but where the great decisions of life are concerned, God alone is the judge. That is the key to the whole thing: "In God we trust." The Founding Fathers *did* trust God. They trusted him enough to give back to him and him alone the right to judge the hearts and minds of men. In the eyes of absolutism, our Constitution is hopelessly soft on sinners. Here, heresy, held for centuries to be the quintessence of subversion and the worst of all crimes, does not fall under human jurisdiction at all; people with wrong ideas are expressly allowed to talk about them and even hold meetings; Congress may never declare one religion more desirable than another (Article VI and Amendment I), or one person more noble than another (Article I, Section 10). God alone knows who is really virtuous and who is not. The king may be right some of the time or even all the time, but that, as Macaulay observes in his "Essay on Civil Disabilities," is beside the point, which, according to the Declaration of Independence and the Constitution, is that men must be free individually and collectively to make their own choices, no matter how bad. That, as we have seen, is the ancient law of liberty.

The kings and priests who rush officiously to the defense of God, with hue and cry against the sinners, do not trust God either to fight his own battles or to make his own judgments. When Pope Stephen III wrote Pepin to come to his rescue because "save for thy mighty arm we have only God to help us!" he certainly rated the power of God very low— "only God," forsooth! And do those who offer to do God's judging for him really trust his adequacy as a judge? God has never delegated his power and office of judging to anyone, Tertullian reminded the Roman clergy on one occasion.[13] When Christ returns in glory, it will be to preside at the judgment, but while he was in the flesh he said, "I judge no man" (John 8:15). God is not easy on sinners; he says he cannot look upon sin with the least degree of allowance, but reminds men that "I the Lord will forgive whom I will forgive, but of you it is required to forgive *all* men" (D&C 64:10). "Judgment is mine, saith the Lord, I will repay" (cf. D&C 82:23, Mormon 3:15). "Judge not, lest ye be judged" (Matthew 7:1). "Man shall not counsel his fellow man, neither put trust in the arm of flesh" (D&C 1:19). We could go on, but the point is clear enough: God does not delegate to any man or institution functions which he has reserved to himself to exercise at an appointed time and place. As Irenaeus says, God wants men to do good, but he forces no man. Until the judgment day, he lets his sun shine upon the just and unjust; he who can do all things does not coerce to virtue—is it the business of men to do it in his name? The Lord was crucified as a blasphemer by people rushing to the defense of God, and those who killed the Apostles were convinced that they were doing God a favor. God asks no such favors of men. The power is his alone, and the judgment. But it remained for the Constitution of the United States to recognize that fact and act upon it. The most important thing about a man is what he thinks; the next most important, his contact—giving and taking—with the thoughts of others; last of all come the busy preoccupations of the organism, its bodily and social functions. It is in the first two of these areas that the despots of the past and present have sought to do their most effective work. And these are precisely the areas in which the Constitution says, "Congress shall make no law . . . ," thus proclaiming in all its purity the ancient law of liberty.

In 1833 the Lord revealed to a modern prophet that he had suffered the Constitution to be established, and that it "should be maintained for the rights and protection of all flesh, according to just and holy principles; that every man may act in doctrine and principle pertaining to futurity, according to the moral agency which I have given unto him, that every man may be accountable for his own sins in the day of judgment. Therefore, it is not right that any man should be in bondage one to another. And for this purpose have I established the Constitution of this land, by the hands of wise men whom I raised up unto this very purpose, and redeemed the land by the shedding of blood" (D&C 101:77-80).

It is more than Fourth of July rhetoric when the Latter-day Saints declare that the Constitution is an inspired document. It actually is the restoration to the earth of that ancient law of liberty which has been preached by the prophets in every age, allowing every man to act in doctrine and principle according to the moral agency which God has given him, to be accountable for his own sins on the day of judgment. Such acts may never be prescribed or judged by any human agency, the Constitution maintains, and we firmly believe that to be the will of God: it was known to the early Christians as the ancient law of liberty.

22

Prophets and Crisis

Secure in their safe and quiet studies, generations of reverend gentlemen have viewed the lives and pondered the words of the prophets in what they fondly supposed was a mood of broad and tolerant humanity, reinforced by that wider intellectual background and scientific detachment which the prophets themselves were never in a position to enjoy. This comfortable and complacent mood is by no means the exclusive product of nineteenth-century smugness. Peace, security, dignity, repose, calm detachment, undisturbed contemplation—such words are constantly on the lips of the Fathers from the third century on. Every Christian would, if he possibly could, spend every moment of his time in the study of philosophy, writes Origen, who regards the distractions of domestic and economic life as an unmixed evil. [1] The argument that is constantly put forth for celibacy from the end of the fourth century on is that family life is an evil since it takes a man's mind away from the single, exclusive, uninterrupted contemplation of God. *Ataraxia*, the state of being undisturbed, became the supreme goal in the life of every philospher in late antiquity, and the search for the *Vita Beata* as the quiet life, the unattached life, the life free of all financial and social obligations, devoted to long afternoons in peaceful garden walks, and endless, ambling conversations with like-minded friends on the search for God and the meaning of life—the ideal of the *nil admirari* and the *fuga mundi*, the flight from the noisy, nasty, everyday world—this pagan ideal became the model of a Christian life, as we see so clearly in the case of St. Augustine.

We cannot blame men for wanting peace and security; but such, as the prophets are always pointing out, cannot be gained by shutting one's eyes to the facts of life. Men insist on treating this world as a permanent, going concern; they would like to think that as it is, so it always was, and so it always will be. That would be nice if we could have it that way here and now, and we do look forward to such security in the world to come; but to make such an assumption the foundation of our thought and action here is to build upon the sand. Consider only the rapid, almost bedizening tempo of our lives, individually and collectively. History moves today, and as far as we can determine, has always moved at a terrible pace: the 1950's are a world removed from the 1940's, but it is so with any two decades you may select in our history. With almost indecent haste we are hustled and bustled into and out of the world through our childhood, youth, maturity, and age into immediate graves. Plainly, we were not meant to stay here for long; we live in the midst of a constant combustion—literally—a ceaseless and remorseless process of oxidation that surely, inevitably, and *not* slowly reduces all earthly things to ashes. Here we have no abiding kingdom.

Unlike prophets, churchmen are the product of institutions. In the safety and permanence of institutions they put their trust. They resolutely oppose the prophets, whom they accuse of disturbing their repose and rocking the boat; and they cultivate in opposition a peculiar "spiritual" type of religion, detached, and unworldly, but not in the sense that the primitive Christians were spiritual, detached, and unworldly. You will recall that the earliest critics of the ancient Christians describe them as noisy, unwashed, seditious, uncooperative, overactive, unabashed in their behavior, and crass, coarse, physical, and literal in their doctrines of heaven and their expectations of blessedness.

Conventional Christian piety is the other kind. The poets and philosophers of the pagans were all for denouncing the pomps and vanities of the world. They talked endlessly about the *fuga mundi* and the blessedness of pure contemplation, and just as the later church took its philosophy from them, so also it took its morality. The result is that the conventional Christian teachings are a fragile and unconvincing sort of thing, a hothouse product, a bouquet of exotic words that wither at a touch. The rich and artificial vocabulary of Christian theology has often been charged by Christian thinkers with being a thing of unreality and an instrument of confusion. The modern liberal Christian has broken loose from the jargon of Scholasticism, indeed, but only to introduce another and equally unconvincing jargon in its place—the copy-desk clichés that call ceaselessly for a "vital, vivid, dynamic, vibrant" religion, as if the endless mechanical repetition of these words would accomplish the thing.

But there is an interesting phenomenon that appears from time to time throughout the whole course of church history. It is the abrupt abandonment of the calm, urbane, academic, and scholastic mood of the clergy whenever the calm and even flow of life itself is rudely interrupted by the facts of history. When sudden reverses of fortune abolish the thought of security in this life, Basil, Chrysostom, Jerome, Hilary, and the Fathers of the Middle Ages all suddenly forget that they are philosophers and turn to conning Revelation and Daniel for the most literal signs of the times. The same churchmen who gloried in the irresistible forward march of their invincible church suddenly remembered, when that church suffered collapse and dissolution before their eyes, that the real church of Christ was not to be a triumphant world church at all; they remember what they had forgotten: that Christ's church is only to be victorious at the end of the world. "The Apocalyptic element of Chiliasm," Harnack wrote, "it is true, lay dormant for long periods, but at critical moments constantly emerged."[2] Not just a few overwrought crackpots in time of world crisis have had a rude awakening to the reality of prophetic utterance: time and again the whole Christian world has gone back to the scripture.

To take an eminent example from the East, it would be hard to imagine more brashly boastful declarations than those with which John Chrysostom announced the complete and smashing victory of his church over all the world. The terms in which he hails the universal triumph of the church are not only naive, they are positively shocking. But it is interesting to see how political and natural calamities sober the man. After a great earthquake at Antioch he asks, "What is this world? A foul nest stuck together of scraps and mud. The greatest houses are no better than swallows' nests: come winter and they promptly collapse. . . . Well, I say this is winter now. God is going to purge the world with great destructions." Then John remembers that "Christ said that when the gospel had been preached to all nations, then the *end* would come; and since the gospel *has* been preached to almost all the inhabited world, there is nothing for it but that the *end* is at the door. Let us fear and tremble, beloved, for the end is very near."[3] And so on. This is an almost comical reversal from John's former confidence in worldly progress.

Left to themselves, the fathers of the fourth century joyfully look forward to long careers of success for themselves and prosperity for the church, and only remember old, outmoded prophecies when calamity comes upon them. Jerome is as good an example for the West as Chrysostom is for the East. He too had gloried in the final establishment of the kingdom of heaven on earth with the ultimate victory of the church over all her rivals. And then overnight everything changes. "Who would have believed it?" he cries in astounded incredulity. "Rome fighting on her home base not for glory but for survival! Not even fighting, in fact, but rather trying to buy off her life with gold and goods. . . . As for the church, our house upon this earth as well as our home in heaven will be lost to us if we are lazy and slow to good works; and the whole structure which was designed to elevate to the peak of heaven shall collapse to earth, bringing ruin to its inhabitants. When our hands weaken, the storms overcome us, and this is as true of the Church as it is of private individuals: that through the neglect of the leaders the whole structure collapses."[4] Gone is all the old buoyant confidence; Jerome will not allow even the favorite consolation—that though individuals might go astray, the church never could be lost. Christ will not destroy his church, Jerome says, but he will uproot it and remove it from the earth to another place. "Christ disestablishes his church because of daily increasing unrighteousness."[5]

Such enforced recognition of truth was always a reluctant one, it is true, and the first opportunity was always taken to return to business as usual. A very early Christian writing describes how at the crucifixion, all the earth was thrown into terrible turmoil, "but the next day after it was all over, the sun came out and shined again, and men went about their everyday business as if nothing at all had happened."[6] That is the normal course of things. But which is the reality—the everyday business, or the eternity that waits to receive us all? Religion should teach that it is the latter, yet conventional Christian doctrine is a denial of that. It is the apotheosis of institutions and routines, of old established ways, a solid and imposing dike to keep out the sea— to shut off the sight and even the memory of the sea which the Christian soul should be exploring. Throughout its long history, the church has been the steady enemy of the old Christian eschatology which, as Harnack says, emerges only at critical moments. When, as has happened in every century, groups and individuals within the church have sought the old literalism in normal times, they have been held to display exceedingly bad taste, and vigorously suppressed.

"The Church is constantly hastening after the saints, . . . "
says Powicke, "so it may . . . control them."[7] Harnack holds
this to be the leitmotif of the whole history of the Christian
church: the constant antipathy between the established
churches and those who insist on taking the scriptures too
literally. In the end, however, no amount of official control
of the scripture had availed to make men forget the true
nature of prophecy. The abstractions of the schools have
never satisfied men. A remarkable illustration of this, quite
unfamiliar to most people, is the strange phenomenon of
"letters from heaven."

At least as early as the sixth century A.D. reports started
circulating in the Christian world of letters that had fallen
from heaven. A great sensation was caused by a letter that
was supposed to have fallen about 583 in Iviza, the smallest
of the Balearic Islands. When the Bishop of Cartegena examined the letter, he declared it to be a silly thing, inelegant in
language and unorthodox in doctrine; he rebuked Vincent,
the Bishop of Iviza (who was later banished) for accepting
the letter as genuine, expressing his amazement that anyone
could accept "new scripture even after the prophecies of the
prophets, the Gospels of Christ, and the letters of his
apostles."[8] Nevertheless the letter started something. Immediately reports of other letters fallen from heaven, usually
upon the altars of churches, and usually in some remote and
inaccessible part of the world, began to turn up everywhere.
Always, the letters were the same: they began with a solemn
attestation that the letter was not written by any man but
was a direct missive from the hand of Christ or from the
heavenly Father. Then followed a surprisingly commonplace
discourse on the importance of not working on Sunday, a
denunciation of vice and wickedness in the church, and a
promise of impending disaster unless the people mended their
ways. It was a pedestrian sermon, but it was not that which
electrified the world—it was the introduction: "I swear," to
quote one of the later letters, " . . . that this letter is *not*

from the hand of a man . . . but from the Heavenly Father, who alone is invisible. Cursed be the man who resists me, and says, that this letter is not from Heaven!"[9] This was the tremendous news that the heavens were again open, against which the church fought in vain. In every century these letters continued to circulate and meet with the wildest enthusiasm and general belief. As late as 1846 such a letter caused an immense sensation in Bohemia, and not only the uneducated multitudes but also the gravest churchmen took them seriously.[10] Few stories from the Middle Ages are more moving than that of the reception of such a letter in Rome. It was, we are told, in the temple of Paul at Rome when all the people were assembled that Theodoton, the assistant of the Roman patriarch, saw the epistle first, hanging in the air over the heads of the people and written on a tablet of *ice*. The multitude of 47,000 people were overwhelmed with weeping, the day was turned to night; in the presence of this missive the people all put on white garments and purified their hearts. Finally the letter descended upon the mantle of the patriarch himself, who was so overcome that he could not speak.[11]

In many instances it is reported that when such a letter is produced, those who behold it are blinded with tears. From all the extensive studies of the letters from heaven, two facts stand out: (1) that they all contain the same commonplace, unoriginal, little message which displays not the slightest spark of inspiration and shows them, in the opinion of all scholars, to be palpable forgeries; and (2) that what gave them their overwhelming popularity through fourteen centuries was not their content, but simply the fact that they were supposed to be a direct communication from God to men. This shows that the abstractions of the schoolmen did not at all satisfy the yearnings of the Christian soul. In spite of all creeds and councils to the contrary, men have persisted through the centuries in taking the scripture at its word, and holding the belief in concrete and literal things which the doctors have discarded since the days of the Alexandrian school.

To come down to the present, it is our privilege to live in another period of world crisis. Again the old ashes are stirred up, and literalism flares up anew. Here is the British scholar and clergyman F. A. M. Spencer, once a leading exponent of what he himself describes as the "liberal, ameliorist, social-gospel," announcing the discovery that by accepting the *literal return* of Christ we remove the strain "of having to contort his message, ignoring a considerable portion of it and making unwarranted deductions from other parts, to suit our preconceptions. It gives a sense of relief, of illumination, of enlargement. We begin to see now. The world has not reformed itself or allowed itself to be reformed by God in love. But then Christ did not say that it would."[12] Spencer notes that the world is desperate; Christ must in some way make himself known to men if anything is to be saved at all, and in the face of grim new reality, this man now recognizes that all the old sentimental phrases about the "Gentle Galilean" count for nothing. "Yet in what way," he asks, "could God most adequately reveal himself to humanity? Surely through a human person. . . . Are we to hope that increasing evangelistic ardour and ecclesiastical efficiency will produce in the near future what preachers and prophets and pastors have not succeeded in accomplishing during all the centuries since Christ appeared on earth?"[13]

Very recently, Austin Birch, a distinguished Anglican, pointed out that every religion has a central doctrine; if that doctrine seems fantastic, one is not obliged to adhere to it, but he reminds the liberal Christians of a thing they have forgotten—that if they do not choose to subscribe to the quaint old central doctrines of the Christian church, they are perfectly welcome to go elsewhere, but they have no right to rewrite those doctrines to suit themselves.[14] It is just such well-meaning rewriting of history and doctrine that has produced modern-day Christianity. Since the last war, we have

seen what Pauck calls "the re-discovery of the church," and
the sudden general admission that Christ really founded a
church. [15] T. W. Manson even reports in 1950 that "there are
signs that the doctrine of Apostolic Succession is in process
of restatement in terms of the idea of a continuing body
whose nucleus is the original Apostles, a body to which new
members can be, as it were, co-opted." [16] In other words, two
thousand years too late, Christians are discovering that if the
church were to continue, the ancient quorum of Twelve Apostles should also have continued, and now at this late date
they are attempting to lock the barn door. In his dispute
with J. B. S. Haldane, the noted Anglo-Catholic, Arnold
Lunn, wrote in 1930: "St. Jerome . . . cites as an illustration
of such nonsense the fact that some Christians are foolish
enough to believe that . . . God really sits [on a throne in
heaven] 'as if he were a commander or judge,' and that the
angels stand around to obey his commands. . . . Literalism,"
Lunn boastfully declares, "is a Protestant, not a Catholic
failing." [17] Yet in 1950 the world saw the publication of the
Bull *Munificentissimus Deus*, the forty-fourth article of which
declares as "revealed dogma" that Virgin Mary ascended to
glory "in body and spirit." [18] Here is a literalness of revelation and a concreteness of heavenly things which would seem
to indicate that in spite of Mr. Lunn, literalism may yet turn
out to be a Catholic failing.

Now, *literalism* better than any other one word sums up
the charges against the restored Church since the first message of its first prophet in these latter days, over a century
ago. And just as the periodic return to literalism in times of
crisis in the past have vindicated the prophets of old and
kept the import of their message from ever being lost, so the
present-day return to literalism in the face of world crisis is a
clear vindication, after a hundred years of fierce denunciation, of the Latter-day Saint point of view. Time has vindicated the prophets.

23

The Prophets and the Scripture

A fundamental teaching common to all Christian churches is that there is on earth no other source of revelation from God to man than what is contained in scripture and tradition. Such an arrangement leaves no room, of course, for present-day revelation direct from heaven, and bars the activity of living prophets whose presence, as we have seen, has always scandalized conventional students of scripture and tradition.

In proclaiming the restored gospel, the Latter-day Saints do not minimize the importance of the Bible. We say the scripture and revelation are *both* necessary; they are not mutually exclusive as some would have us think; they are complementary—they not only can co-exist, but they must. Strange as it may seem, the idea that one might profit from both scripture and revelation at the same time has been in the past a formidable stumbling block to scholars. Not long ago a great controversy raged among the learned over whether any man could possibly possess the gifts of the Spirit and at the same time do anything as worldly as hold an office in the church or concern himself with written records. Nearly all the scholars supported Sohm's thesis that spirit and order were absolute opposites, hopelessly irreconcilable. Law and authority were for Sohm the complete antithesis of the Spirit; the two could not exist together. "Jesus of Nazareth is altogether unliterary," wrote Deissmann in a typical declaration, since "the new thing for which he looked came not in book, formulae, and subtle doctrine, but in spirit and in fire."[1]

Apparently, one cannot have a religion of spirit and fire and still read the scriptures. And yet nothing is more evident from the example of Jesus himself than that the possession of scripture does not preclude revelation and the gifts of the Spirit on the one hand, nor, on the other, does the possession of those spiritual gifts in any way jeopardize the authority of the scriptures. For maintaining this rather obvious point the Latter-day Saints have been attacked from all sides.

The Lord said, "Search the scriptures; for . . . they are they which testify of me"; and when in reply to that the people said in effect, "We have the scripture, so we don't need you at all," he answered, "If you believed the scriptures, you would believe me."[2] Here we have the two witnesses, the scripture and the Lord in person, side by side, testifying of each other. The fact that the Jews had the holy writings did not, as they supposed, make the presence of a living prophet among them superfluous; and the presence of a prophet did not, as the scholars supposed, make the written word superfluous. As a remarkable illustration of this, what did Christ do when he first appeared to the assembled Apostles as the resurrected Lord? There he was, the Son of God in his own person, a glorified and resurrected being who could have told them all things by his own authority; but instead of that, we are told, "beginning at Moses and all the prophets, he expounded unto them in all the scriptures the things concerning himself" (Luke 24:27). Is it surprising, then, that when the Lord and other glorious beings appeared to men in these latter days they again cited the ancient prophets at length? One could not ask for a more powerful recommendation for the sacredness of the holy writings than the Lord's use of them after his resurrection; nor on the other hand, could one have a more convincing demonstration that the scriptures cannot stand alone, for it was only after Christ had expounded their meaning to them in person that the disciples' "eyes were opened, and they knew him. . . . And they said . . . Did not our heart burn within us, while he talked with us by the way, and while he opened to us the scriptures?" (Luke 24:31-32.) Even to the Apostles the scriptures did not convey their full message until they were "opened" to them by their heavenly teacher.

The early Christians did not regard the canon of the scripture as closed. In a recent and important study, Van Unnik has shown that for the earliest Christians, the apostolic office, the gift of revelation, and the bringing forth of scripture were always regarded as going hand in hand; and, with von Harnack, he points out that at least as late as A.D. 200 it was held to be perfectly legitimate "for someone to add something to the word of the Gospel."[3] The Bible itself leaves the door wide open for future revelation in many places, but even if it did not, men fool themselves when they think for a moment that they can read the scripture without ever adding something to the text, or omitting something from it. For in the wise words of St. Hilary, *Scripturae enim non in legendo sunt, sed in intelligendo*: "Scripture consists not in what one reads, but in what one understands."[4] We have just seen that the Apostles themselves "knew not the scripture"—though no doubt they had often read it—until the Lord opened it to them. To read is by very definition to unriddle, to expound to oneself, to interpret. In the reading of the scripture we must always have an interpreter, but who qualifies for the task of interpreting God's word to men? Irenaeus insisted that no special interpreter was needed, the book being self-explanatory so that "the whole of the scripture . . . can be understood clearly and without ambiguity equally and by all."[5] But then he accuses vast numbers of Christians of reading it all wrong, "becoming bad interpreters of the good and correct word."[6] What is one to do when, in the words of a later church father, "there are as many interpretations of the scriptures as there are readers"? In that case, Irenaeus recommends appealing to the opinions of the oldest churches, those who had traditions actually

going back to the Apostles. But when these churches disagree among themselves, what then? Then, says Irenaeus, we
must examine the order of tradition committed to the
churches.[7] All the while, you will note, Irenaeus is looking
for an interpreter for the scriptures, which he began by saying needed no interpreter! If the Bible contained its own
interpretation, the best and wisest of its readers would surely
agree on its teachings, yet those who study it hardest disagree most widely about it. Tertullian pointed out that discussions based on scriptures are a waste of time since the
most hopelessly mistaken person can in all good faith prove
his case from the scriptures "by divers expositions and
commentaries," easily corrupting the sense without having
to corrupt the letter of the text, and picking and rejecting
whatever suits his purpose. If *we* say that the heretics are
playing fast and loose with the Bible, Tertullian reminds us,
we must remember that they in all seriousness believe that
we are corrupting the scripture by false exposition while
they preserve the pure truth of it. For that reason, according
to Tertullian, it is practically impossible to win an argument
by appeal to the scripture alone, and even when we do win,
the whole issue remains uncertain.[8]

Can one interpret the scripture without actually adding
something that was not there before? If the Bible is all-
sufficient, why the huge flow of books and periodicals that
obligingly offer to tell us what the Bible is trying to say?
Can't the Bible speak for itself? The council of Seleucia in
359 solemnly declared that the prophets and gospels are perfect and complete, the absolute guide to the church in all
things, no others being necessary. This point being settled,
the meeting was promptly thrown into an uproar, for the
homoousian party was quick to point out that the keyword
of the opponents' doctrine, the *homoiousia*, was not to be
found in the Bible, while the *homoiousian* faction returned
the charge against them. Each side protested that it was merely
interpreting the Bible, while the opposition was *adding* to

it.[9] It was the suspicion that the Council of Nicaea in interpreting the scriptures had been guilty of adding to them that drove the clergy and general public alike into agonies of doubt and indecision that were never allayed. Even the first and greatest of ecumenical synods was not able to interpret the Bible without adding to it.

Who has a right to interpret the scriptures? Clement of Alexandria asks that question. He says that there are things in his own writings which in the future will be interpreted in all sorts of different ways as men "seek to reveal hidden meanings in them to demonstrate the presence of things unsaid." But who has the right to take such liberties? Only the author himself, says Clement, or a direct and trusted disciple. On one thing he insists—the interpretation must come from *outside*; it cannot be conjured out of the writing itself which is being interpreted. To interpret the Bible by one's own reading of the Bible is to lift oneself by one's own bootstraps.[10] Men have recognized this fact and sought earnestly to establish or discover some authorized *individual* or board or some infallible rules and principles by which the interpretation of the Bible could be made a sure and certain thing, and they have failed. The synods of pious and learned men assembled to give definite interpretations have been scenes of raging controversy through the centuries, each great council sowing the seeds of misunderstanding that lead to the next. The great Tertullian declared with fire and indignation that the authority of the church in such matters does not reside in a number of bishops no matter how great, but only in a man who can speak by the spirit of God.[11]

One of the normal offices of episcopal councils has been to correct the errors and indiscretions of certain individual bishops, those of the great leading communities of Christendom—Alexandria, Antioch, Rome, Constantinople, etc.—who have declared that in their peculiar office as bishops resides the ultimate authority to interpret the scriptures. The holders of that high interpretive office have been convicted of heresy from time to time, [12] and an examination of the *Patrologia*, the writings of the fathers, will show that it has never been the custom of Christians to consult any one particular individual when in doubt on matter of doctrine and authority, no matter what his office. Instead, the Christian church has been guided through the centuries in its reading of the scriptures by doctors of the church whose supreme qualification was their own native wit, regardless of the office they held. These clever men have made repeated attempts to lay down sure and reliable rules by which anyone properly trained could arrive at the true meaning of the scriptures. Of course, we cannot discuss these here, but taking only the greatest of the fathers as an example, we cite Marrou's recent work on St. Augustine's methods of interpreting the scripture wherein he points out what has long been known to scholars: that the rules which Augustine calls "nothing less than the keys to the holy writ" are simply the familiar technique which had been employed for centuries in the pagan schools in the interpretation of Homer and Virgil. [13] When this system found itself—as it did not rarely—in indissoluble opposition to the plain meaning of the scripture, "It was," wrote Turmel, "the interpretation of the text [the Bible] that was sacrificed." [14] "Let us remember," says Gilson, "that a doctor of the Church is not infallible." [15] How then can the ultimate appeal be to such? Time and again we meet with such phrases as "since the authority of the scripture does not specifically declare such and such to be so, it is doubtful whether we should presume to express an opinion on it." No one seems eager or even willing to assume the awful responsibility.

There are churches today which declare for the absolute sufficiency of the Bible as perfect, complete, and infallible. Yet it is precisely the ministers of these churches who concern themselves most diligently with the study of Greek. Why? Because they recognize that our translated versions are not the original, but are imperfect, tainted by the interpretations of men. So our sectarian friends choose a *Greek grammar* as the faithful guide to lead them on paths that do not stray. Alas! a more hesitant and speculating guide could not be imagined, and when we get the so-called original texts of the Bible before us with their stately apparatus of possible corrections, emendations, suggestions, recommendations, and whatnot, we first come to realize that the holy text is a maze of a thousand passages. [16]

In the end, authority cannot reside in man, but, as Tertullian insists, only in a man who speaks by the Spirit of God. Without a living prophet, the scripture is indeed what the medieval church called it: a mystery. The question is not whether or not one shall add to the word of the scripture—thousands of volumes of learned commentary have already done that—but whether such addition shall come by the wisdom of men or the revelation of God. Until recent years, the Latter-day Saints have stood alone in maintaining the latter alternative and in upholding the integrity of *both* the spoken and the written word of God.

24

The Book of Mormon as a Witness

"Search the scriptures," said the Lord, "for in them ye think ye have eternal life: and they are they which testify of me" (John 5:39). The words and deeds of prophets and of angels testify to the divinity of Jesus Christ; so likewise does the written record of those words and deeds. There are many reasons on which we cannot comment here for believing that God gave the miracle of writing to men as a means of keeping records through the ages. Writing is as marvelous and subtle a thing in its operation and in its effects as television. Here we have a means of transmitting not only the deeds but also the very thoughts of men through unlimited expanses of space and time—and this amazingly economical and efficient device has been in the possession of the human race from its very beginning. Writing was not devised by men as a tool to help them in their everyday affairs: successful businessmen have been illiterates, and there is ample evidence that writing was adapted to commercial uses only *after* such uses were found for it. If you bring together all the written records of man's past, you will discover that the overwhelming mass of material is religious in nature, and that the primary purpose to which writing has been put through the ages has not been for business records and correspondence, in which writing is employed awkwardly and without enthusiasm, but for keeping a remembrance of God's dealings with men. The specific purpose of writing, as the Egyptians put it, is to record the *mdw ntr*, the divine words.

We have skirted the fringe of speculation here for a moment only to recall to a generation that has forgotten to read the scriptures that the written word is one of the means chosen and established by God for communicating with his children. It is not the only means or the most direct means— to insist on that is a common fallacy of the sectarian world. A man who can convey his mind to others only through a written letter must be personally inaccessible to them either because of distance, death, or some other obstacle, and to say that God can speak to men no more clearly or directly than in written pages hundreds of years old is to impose upon him the most pathetic human limitations. Of course God can speak to men now as directly as he ever did, and the scripture is but one of his ways of speaking to them. It is a most effective way, however, and one that has peculiar advantages of its own. It overcomes time—the scriptures are the common meeting ground of all the prophets no matter how many centuries apart they may have lived; here they all speak a common tongue and bear witness to each other. The prophets constantly and characteristically quote each other; the New Testament everywhere quotes the Old; after the resurrection the Lord taught using the very words of Moses and the prophets and employing the scriptures for that purpose. He said that those who did not believe those prophets would never believe him.

As no one has a right to limit God's capacity to speak to men with his own voice whenever and wherever he will, neither has anyone the authority to say that God may not, when he will, present his children with his word in writing by dictating scripture to his prophets, by bringing forth forgotten writings of the ancients, by guiding the work of an inspired translator, or in any way he chooses. We have said before that the test of the soundness of men's hearts is their willingness to accept the message of a living prophet; the same applies to their willingness to accept God's word in any form. So the Lord has told us through an ancient prophet how it is when men who reject the prophets because they already have dead ones are confronted with God's written word: "Thou fool, that shall say: A Bible, we have got a Bible, and we need no more Bible. Have ye obtained a Bible save it were by the Jews? Know ye not that there are more nations than one? Know ye not that I, the Lord your God, have created all men, and that I remember those who are upon the isles of the sea; and that I rule in the heavens above and in the earth beneath; and I bring forth my word unto the children of men, yea, even upon all the nations of the earth? . . . Wherefore, I speak the same words unto one nation like unto another. And when the two nations shall run together the testimony of the two nations shall run together also. And I do this that I may prove unto many that I am the same yesterday, today, and forever; and that I speak forth my words according to mine own pleasure. And because that I have spoken one word ye need not suppose that I cannot speak another" (2 Nephi 29:6-9).

These words are those of the prophet Nephi, found in the Book of Mormon, a book which in many such passages opens a window on other worlds. Here we learn that God has been in contact at sundry times and places with nations of whose existence the world has never dreamed, and even with inhabitants of other worlds, for the house of man, we are told, is but one among many mansions. This doctrine of other worlds, though not infrequently indicated in early Christian writings, was one totally strange and foreign to the world into which the restored gospel was introduced. Just as all churches agreed in denouncing as unspeakable blasphemy the proposition that there ever could be any other holy scripture than that contained in the canon of the Old and New Testaments, so all agreed that the idea that there might possibly be any other world than this one, with its heaven above and its hell beneath, was utterly preposterous. The absolute uniqueness and centralness of this our world was basic to the whole philosophy and cosmology of Aristotle and the schools, for example, of Origen, Augustine, and the Middle Ages, culminating in the airtight cosmos of Dante. People forget that fact today, now that churches are finding it expedient to teach otherwise, but at the time the gospel was restored to the world, such a teaching as the doctrine of other worlds was radically opposed to anything taught anywhere. It is another case in which time has vindicated the prophets.

But in its own right, apart from its being proved in our own day, this is a marvelous doctrine. It is what might be called the law of perfect economy: There is no waste in the universe. "There is no space," says the Lord, "in the which there is no kingdom; and there is no kingdom in which there is no space. . . . And unto every kingdom is given a law; and unto every law there are certain bounds also and conditions. All beings who abide not in those conditions are not justified" (D&C 88:37-39). Even the earth, we are taught, is not the exclusive home of man; it is shared by other creatures who fulfill the measure of their existence and have joy in the sphere in which they were created. Man has first claim on the earth and what is in it, but though he makes poor use of that claim the earth is not wasted; it is used by other creatures of whose nature and whose very existence we have hardly an inkling. It is a wonderful doctrine that widens our horizons to infinity, and it was first revealed to the world in modern times in and by the Book of Mormon.

In the Book of Mormon the words of many prophets are brought together for the particular instruction of our own age. Those words are presented to the world in a strange and wonderful form. Go through the whole literature of devotion and you will find no book like this. If the great Christian writings of such widely differing geniuses as the scholastic thinkers of the Middle Ages, Swedenborg, and the author of *Science and Health* were to be printed on loose-leaf, the pages of all of these could be freely shuffled among each other without any serious disruption of style and content. They are all doing the same thing—simply commenting on the Bible—and they all use with mechanical ease and practiced skill one and the same key: the old Neoplatonic formula of "spiritual" interpretation. This is an easy game to play; it is a much harder thing, in fact, to spend many years with the scriptures *without* acquiring the conviction that one is privy to the deeper secrets of their interpretation. But none of these inspired writers, though claiming inside knowledge into the mind of God, will face up to the test of a prophet and speak as one having authority. In the end, the Bible is always their authority, and like the scribes and Pharisees of old they can always pass off onto it the responsibility for whatever they say.

This is not the case with the Book of Mormon. What do we find in it? A wealth of doctrine embedded in large amounts of what is put forth as genuine historical material, not devotional or speculative or interpretive or creative writing but genuine historical fact, stuff that touches upon reality—geographical, ethnological, linguistic, cultural, etc.—at a thousand places. On all of these points the book could sooner or later be tested, as Joseph Smith knew. We cannot possibly deny his good faith in placing it before the whole world without any reservation. Aside from all other considerations it is a staggering work; its mass and complexity alone would defy the talent of any living man or body of men to duplicate today. Its histories are full and circumstantial; yet sober, simple, straightforward—there is nothing contrived, nothing exaggerated, nothing clever in the whole book. For a century and a quarter it has undergone the closest scrutiny at the hands of its friends and enemies, and today it stands up better than ever. Let me illustrate how very recent findings have vindicated the Book of Mormon on two broad and general themes.

From the Book of Mormon we learn that through the centuries the Jews have had as it were a double history. Along with the conventional story of the nation as recorded in the official accounts kept closely under the control of the schoolmen, there has coexisted in enforced obscurity another Israel, a society of righteous seekers zealously devoting their lives to the preservation of the law of their fathers in all its purity and considering the bulk of their nation to have fallen into sin and transgression. These righteous ones lived a life of their own; and while they sought constantly to bring the others into their ways, they were just as constantly resisted with mockery and persecution. Often they took to the desert and lived in family groups or communities there, teaching the law and the prophets to each other and looking forward prayerfully to the coming of the Messiah. There were many dreamers among them and real prophets as well, for they believed—unlike the scribes and doctors of official Jewry— in continued prophecy. Also they practiced rites rejected by the majority of the nation and talked constantly of such things as the resurrection of the flesh and the eternities to come—things which though they figure prominently enough in the apocryphal writings and also the Talmud, are hardly found at all in the official canon of Jewish scripture. They were a sober, watchful, industrious people, sorely distressed by the wickedness of their nation as a whole; and that nation would have nothing to do with them and did all it could to obscure the fact that they even existed. This briefly is the picture the Book of Mormon paints of Lehi and his ancestors, who had from time to time been driven out of Jerusalem for looking forward too eagerly for the Messiah. It is also the picture that now meets us in the abundant and ever-increasing documents which have come forth from the caves in Palestine almost in a steady stream since the first find was made in 1947. For some years the best scholars, Jewish and Christian, fought strenuously against accepting any of the so-called Dead Sea Scrolls as genuine—they must be medieval forgeries, it was argued, since the picture they presented was one totally at variance with the picture which had been delineated by the meticulous labors of generations of devoted

scholars.[1] "It is not *a single* revolution in the study of biblical exegesis which the Dead Sea documents have brought
about," wrote Dupont-Sommer, whose own conclusions, once
judged hasty and radical, have now been remarkably vindicated, "it is, one already feels, a whole cascade of revolutions."
Since those words were published two years ago, the manuscripts have continued to pour forth as cave after cave has
been discovered and opened.[2] And as new scrolls are unrolled,
the picture itself is unrolling—the picture of that other Israel
that lived in obscurity and hope, first sketched out for us in
the Book of Mormon and now for the first time emerging
into the light of history.

The Book of Mormon draws us the picture of another
and totally different type of society which has become a historical reality only within the last thirty years or so. It was
once thought that the world which Homer described was
purely the product of his own inventive genius. Toward the
end of the eighteenth century, however, the shrewd and obser-
vant English scholar and traveler Robert Wood had the idea
of writing "a detailed work in which similarities of the cul-
tures exhibited in the Old Testament, in Homer, and in the
Near East of his own day should be collected, and prove that
a 'Heroic Age' is a real and recurrent type in human society."[3] Wood died before he could produce the work, and it
was not until the 1930's that Milman Parry showed that what
is called heroic poetry is necessarily "created by a people
who are living in a certain way, and so have a certain outlook on life, and our understanding of the heroic will come
only as we learn what that way of living is and grasp that
outlook."[4] Then Chadwick showed that epic poetry cannot
possibly be produced except in and by a genuine epic milieu,
as he called it—a highly developed, complex, very peculiar
but firmly established and very ancient cultural structure.[5]
How ancient may be guessed from Kramer's recent and con-
fident attempt to describe the culture of the earliest Sumer-
ians in detail simply on the basis of the knowledge that they

produced a typical epic literature. Knowing that, one may be
sure that theirs was the same culture that is described in epic
poetry throughout the world,[6] for epic cannot be faked: innumerable attempts to produce convincing epics by the creative
imagination are almost pitifully transparent. Now one of the
books of the Book of Mormon, the book of Ether, comes
right out of that epic milieu, which it faithfully reproduces,
though of course the world of Joseph Smith had never heard
of such a thing as an epic milieu. Here is a good test for the
Book of Mormon. It is but one of many—all awaiting fuller
treatment, and none as yet settled with any degree of finality. But the mere fact that there are such tests is a most
astonishing thing. That one can actually talk about the Book
of Mormon seriously and with growing respect after all that
has been discovered in the last 125 years is, considering the
nature of its publication, as far as I am concerned, in itself
ample proof of its genuineness.

But the Book of Mormon was not meant as a sign and a
wonder to an unbelieving world; though an angel from heaven
were to declare it, we are told, the world would not believe.
It was meant to give instruction to those who should believe
in these last days. It is a book for hard times and for great
times. I have always thought in reading the Book of Mormon, "Woe to the generation that understands this book!"
To our fathers, once the great persecutions ceased, the story
of the Nephites and the Lamanites was something rather
strange, unreal, and faraway—even to the point of being
romantic. The last generation did not make much of the
Book of Mormon. But now with every passing year this
great and portentous story becomes more and more familiar
and more frighteningly like our own. It is an exciting thing
to discover that the man Lehi was a real historical character,
a fact that can now be established from secular sources with
a high degree of probability, but it is far more important and
significant to find oneself in this twentieth century standing
as it were in his very shoes. The events and situations of the

Book of Mormon that not many years ago seemed wildly improbable to some and greatly overdrawn have suddenly become the story of our own times, when we see and shall see the words of those prophets who speak to us from the dust fearfully and wonderfully vindicated.

25

Prophecy and Tradition

The twin pillars of all conventional Christian religion are scripture and tradition. It is the second of these, the Christian tradition, that we shall consider next. Our churches are rooted in tradition; they are conservative institutions; their business is to preserve intact a sacred deposit with a minimum of change. At the time that Joseph Smith brought forth the restored gospel, *no* church would admit that it was the product of change and innovation. It was Newman's "Essay on the Development of Christian Doctrine," appearing in 1845, that, to quote the Anglican Alfred Fawkes, "disposed once for all of the *Semper Eadem* conception of Christianity then common to Catholics and Protestants. 'You are not primitive,' was the charge brought against Rome by Anglican and Puritan alike. Newman was too well informed and too astute to deny it. He met it by an effective *tu quoque*: 'Neither are you.' "[1] The admission that none of the Christian churches was primitive, as all up till then pretended to be, was the real beginning of Modernism, says Fawkes, but "it was like striking a match in a powder magazine."

The realization that all churches have changed requires a reorientation in Christian thinking, for as Eduard Schwartz wrote, "It lies in the nature of a church that claims divine origin, that it can know nothing of a process of historical development."[2] If there is to be any change at all, it must be inaugurated by God himself—by revelation. Only a church claiming continual revelation has a right to change and still

remain God's church. This is clearly illustrated in the controversies of the fourth-century church when men were aware
of many innovations necessary to the operation of the new
imperial church but were very dubious as to whether the
church, in which revelation had ceased, had a right to tolerate such innovations. Thus Athanasius, condemning certain
practices connected with the veneration of relics, writes, "Who
doth behold the corpses of the martyrs and the prophets,
cast out and exposed, and trembleth not? No Christian work
is this; Paul hath not enjoined it upon us, neither did patri-
archs thus, nor prophets aforetime; but the Meletians it was
devised these things for gain."[3] It is a shocking thing for
Athanasius because the Apostles and prophets have not authorized it, and he knows of no one living who can authorize an
innovation. In view of the inevitability of change, this posed
a knotty problem which the churches have never been able
to solve, since the only solution lies in the presence of a living emissary of heaven—a prophet of God.

In every age, prophets have been resisted in the name of
established tradition as religious innovators. We have seen
that the Jews objected to Christ as an upstart. From Arnobius
we learn that the commonest charge against the Christians
by the heathen was that they were guilty of introducing strange
new things into religion.[4] Caecilius, the apologist for the
Roman state religion in the *Octavius* of Minucius Felix, calls
upon his Christian friends to consider the antiquity, the dignity, the beauty, the massive grandeur, and the infinite respect-
ability of the pagan religion of the empire. Its antiquity, he
says, makes it customary to attribute sanctity to its ceremo-
nies and buildings proportionate to their age. The Christians, on the other hand, he points out, are a band of noisy
innovators who would do away with all this wonderful old
stuff.[5]

To this charge of innovation the early Christians had two
answers. The first was that antiquity as such is not important. Justin reminds the heathens that they charged Socrates

with the very crime that was then being brought against the
Christians, that of introducing strange new things into religion. In Socrates' search for truth the argument of antiquity
was entirely irrelevant. Justin begins his apology by reminding the emperor that honest men "love only what is true and
decline to follow traditional opinions."[6] He says that a ruler
who puts established opinion above truth has no more real
authority than a robber in the desert, who takes what he can
get.[7] To the pagans who claimed that the records of their
miracles were older than the records of Christian miracles,
Arnobius replied with a forthright, *Antiquitas plenissima mater
errorum*: "Antiquity is the chief mother of errors!" It is true,
he says, that your religion is older than ours, "but the authority of a religion is not to be measured by time but by
divinity"—*numine*, supernatural power. "You say our name
is new, and the religion we follow was born not many days
ago. . . . You say our religion did not exist 400 years ago;
well, neither did yours exist 2000 years ago. . . . What is
there that does *not* have a beginning in time?"[8]

But the philosophical argument that truth is a timeless
thing and therefore not dependent for its authority on the
accumulation of years is the other face of the second argument, the religious argument, so fully expounded by Eusebius
in the first book of his *Ecclesiastical History*, i.e., that true
religion takes its rise and its authority from heaven; heaven
is timeless; and our doctrines and institutions come from
there. It is an earth-bound religion that is impressed by antiquity.

But when revelation ceases, a religion does become
earthbound. Chavannes has shown how as the church became
less and less dependent on direct revelation, it fell back more
and more on appeals to tradition and antiquity. In the time
of Tertullian, who regrets the loss of the spiritual gifts from
the church, Chavannes finds the first timid intimations that
Christianity had after all not really brought into the world

anything particularly strange or novel.[9] By the fourth century, age had become everything; the church that had once admitted readily enough the charges of innovation against her developed a horror of innovation. The churchmen went all out to become the champions of tradition, both sacred and profane, displaying, says Chavannes, "constant application to save the greatest possible part of the heritage of the past, not allowing any but indispensable changes, carefully reproducing in their literary works the style, the vocabulary, and the methods of composition of the classic writers."[10] During the feverish councils of the fourth century, all parties and individuals were busily engaged in accusing each other of innovation, for a new doctrine was necessarily a false doctrine.

But for revealed religion, innovation is not a crime, on the one hand; nor on the other, is tradition a millstone. As the prophet respects the scripture which in turn supports his mission, so he also respects tradition, and tradition supports his claims. Christ respected the traditional offices of the Jews and ordered his followers to do the same: "The scribes and the Pharisees sit in Moses' seat: All therefore whatsoever they bid you observe, that observe and do; but do not ye after their works" (Matthew 23:2-3). Paul respected the office of the high priest even while the man insulted him. (Acts 23:5.) On the other hand, when the gospel was preached at Jerusalem, "a great company of the priests were obedient to the faith" (Acts 6:7). Some scholars have recently suggested that this great company may have been such a band of holy men as we find described in the newly discovered Dead Sea Scrolls and related documents, if not a group actually named in one of them. These men were prepared by their *tradition* to receive the gospel when they heard it. Without that tradition and training the preaching to them might have fallen on deaf ears.

Eusebius and Clement of Alexandria both suggest that Greek philosophy was meant by God as a sort of preparation to ready men's minds for the reception of the gospel. Eusebius goes further and shares with Justin and Origen the belief that that philosophy, insofar as it is true and its principles sound, is actually a carryover from earlier lost dispensations of the gospel. The gospel has been on earth from time to time, according to the old apocalyptic or eschatological pattern followed by Eusebius, but each time men have fallen from grace and lost its fullness, they have not lost everything. There is always left some memory, some lingering trace of divinely revealed doctrines and institutions, and it is to the presence of these lingering traces, according to Eusebius, that we owe what we have in the world of humane laws, and refined manners.[11] The great tradition of civilization is really the abiding remnant of the true gospel and as such is to be greatly esteemed.

The significance of tradition in God's plan may be illustrated from the case of the synagogue. The synagogue is not the temple; its ministers are not Levites; its rites and ordinances are not those prescribed in the ancient law. The synagogue only came into existence with the diaspora—the dissolution of the proper Hebrew religious practices centering about the temple. It does not represent the ancient order of things established by direct revelation from heaven; yet for all that, it performs a very valuable function, for it keeps alive and warm the memory of great dispensations of the past when God has spoken to men, and it looks forward to that future time when all past glories will be restored, a new Jerusalem will be founded, and the Messiah will come to reign among men. These things must be kept before men's minds so that when it pleases God at any time to send his prophets to earth, they will be able to bear witness to ears that understand them.

The same holds true of the Christian churches. In the famous words of Tertullian, the Christian churches grew up

"in the shadow of the synagogue."[12] Father Duchesne has
described in his work on *The Origins of the Christian Cult*
how the traveling, inspired general authorities of the apostolic age suddenly disappeared from the scene, leaving the
church without a central head or any general authorities.
There were left in their place only officers of local churches,
the highest of which were bishops. It is to these local churches
that the ritual, liturgies, and organization of the later Christian church are to be traced.[13] And these are the churches
that grew up "in the shadow of the synagogue," modeling
their hymns, prayers, sermons, and offices after the Jewish
pattern. This was a good thing. The Christian churches did
the same thing for the gospel of Christ that the synagogues
did for the law and the prophets: they kept the memory alive
through the centuries, though, like the synagogues, they were
completely severed from the original source of authority. So
complete was the gap between the primitive church and that
which emerges in the second century that many scholars
have maintained that the original church, that of Christ and
the Apostles, never existed at all but was an invention of
later writers! When the predicted time of the end came, following the preaching of the Apostles, and the fulness of the
gospel was taken away, it was the Christian churches that
preserved through the centuries the tradition without which
the preaching of the gospel, when the time came for its restoration, would have been meaningless. For that we honor
and respect the churches and the traditions of Christendom.
Actually, we speak the same language that they do with this
difference: *We* believe in their great tradition *literally* as their
ancestors and ours once did, while for them it has become
merely a tradition, an appeal to antiquity for its own sake, a
sentimental or cultural sort of thing. Take for example the
two great poles of the Christian tradition, Christmas and
Easter. Latter-day Saints enter wholeheartedly into the traditional aspect of these things; but when we want to go further
and take the Christmas and Easter stories literally, we part

company with the Christian world. Nothing has more embarrassed and confused the doctors of the church through the
centuries than the presence of God on earth in a physical
body. Origen confesses himself completely at a loss to comprehend such a thing, and to all his successors it has been at
best a mystery. Only the Latter-day Saints honor the great
traditions of Christendom by taking them literally—not as
beautiful allegories, useful social fictions, or sentimental routines—and not with any philosophical limitations and qualifications, or rhetorical legerdemain.

The world pays lip service to the venerable traditions of
our civilization, but who seriously concerns himself with
such? The professor who is paid to do so; the hobbyist, who
in this field is very rare—that is all! The rest of us bestow an
occasional well-meaning nod to the past or feel a passing
twinge of nostalgia for the long ago—that is about all. But
this is not the case with the Latter-day Saints. Thousands of
them are engaged day and night in attempting, at their own
expense, to reconstruct the records of the past—family histories consisting not only of the names and vital statistics of
all their ancestors, but also as far as possible preserving every
detail of their past in letter and spirit. All Mormons are
urged constantly to engage in this work. Each one searches
out as far as the records will allow, the life stories of his own
progenitors—those whose blood actually runs in his veins—
in the firm belief that their salvation is indissolubly linked
with his own. We have been taught that this generation cannot be saved unless the hearts of the children turn to the
fathers and that an exclusive concern with one's own time
and place, where "every man walketh in his own way," is a
sign of degeneracy. Our latter-day prophets, far from brush-
ing aside the noble heritage of the past, have given it a content and a meaning such as it has never had before.

As far as tradition is concerned then, time has vindicated
the Prophet Joseph Smith. At a time when nobody believed
it, he announced the principle that is generally recognized

today, that allowance must be made for change and innovation even in the Church of Christ. More than that, he has shown the world how that principle can be implemented without in any way minimizing the value and influence of tradition.

26

The Prophets and
the Plan of Life

With the restoration of prophecy to the earth, a knowledge of the larger plan of things was also restored. Conventional Christianity, though it talks a great deal today about
man's place in the universe, does not answer the great questions of life with authority or assurance. In the face of such
questions its spokesmen merely repeat traditional formulae
which they have learned by heart, and to support and eluci-
date them, turn to philosophy. This is the famous program
of *fides quaerens intellectum*, the search for intellectual support of the faith, which gave rise to Scholasticism. But this is
no religion of faith. To believe of God's word only what
checks with our own limited experience; to trust God only as
far as we can "control" him by our feeble reasoning; to
accept his revelations only where they square with our calculations—that is not faith, but suspicion and doubt. Scholastic philosophy, nay, all conventional theology, is constantly
laying down the law as to what God can and cannot do;
what is proper and fitting to Deity and what is not. Instead
of being controlled by God, those thinkers who would answer
the great questions of life insist on sitting at the controls. By
their tricks and slogans, they assure us, they are working out
concepts which will be adequately plausible for our acceptance: Then we can rejoice that we have found God!

Meanwhile, however, we have a perfect right to put to
them the little test question that Hamlet put to Guildenstern:
"Can you play upon this flute? [Can you read this text or

solve this equation?] 'Tis as easy as lying," to use Hamlet's phrase; simple little assignments like these instantly detect the limits of man's tiny knowledge and reveal the majestic and unlimited sweep of his presumption. Christian doctrine will go as far as it can go holding tightly to the hand of philosophy, but it refuses to budge an inch farther. In every century the great theologians insist that what philosophy cannot answer is beyond the comprehension of the angels themselves, and though the theologians sometimes profess an obligation to believe things they cannot understand, they are always very unhappy with such a settlement. Is it any wonder that the answers of modern religion to the ultimate question of life are barren platitudes?

In the original Christian church it was all very different. In those days, knowledge came by revelation. The earliest Christian documents, especially those brought forth in recent years, contain frequent references to a remarkable cosmology which the later church lost. As might be expected, people whose contacts with the other world were real and intimate would not settle for philosophical commonplaces when it came to the great plan of eternal life. Behind everything, according to the early Christians, there was a plan agreed on before the foundation of the earth, and our earthly experience was to be explained in terms of prior agreements made before the creation of the earth. A clear indication of this is given in a fragment by Papias. The case of Papias, incidentally, illustrates well how easily and how quickly the church lost the great treasures of revealed knowledge. "I shall not be ashamed," he writes, "to set down for you whatsoever I have correctly learned from the Elders, and well remembered as to their interpretations, having confirmed first their reliability. . . . If any ever came who had been a follower of the Elders, I would inquire into what the Elders had said: what Andrew or Philip or Thomas or James or John or Matthew or any of the Lord's other disciples had had to say about this or that. . . . For I did not think that I would be helped as

much by what was in the books as by those things which
came by the living voices that remained."[1] Of the ten-odd
surviving fragments thus collected, the most important has
to do with the millennium and was, of course, firmly rejected
by the churchmen of a later age; but what interests us here is
the teaching of "the Elders" that "to some of them, that is,
those angels who had been faithful to God (lit. Gods) in
former times, he gave supervision over the government of
the earth, trusting or commissioning them to rule well. . . .
And nothing has occurred [since] to put an end to their
order."[2]

We cite this very brief passage because it definitely traces
the doctrine of the great plan back to the original apostolic
church. The philosopher convert Justin Martyr gives a much
fuller account in his *Apology for the Christians*. "And we
have been taught that in the beginning He of his own goodness and in the interest of man, created everything out of
unformed or unorganized—*amorphos* matter. And if men by
their good works prove themselves to be worthy of His plan,
they are considered qualified, we take it, to return to His
presence and to rule with Him, having become deathless and
immune to suffering (or change—*apathes*). For in the same
way in which He created in the beginning those who were
not, in just such a manner, we maintain those were deemed
worthy of living with Him in immortality who of their own
will chose what was pleasing to Him. For it was not in our
power to accomplish our own birth in the first place; but the
fact that we chose what was pleasing to Him, making use of
those rational faculties with which He endowed us, now convinces us and conducts us to faith."[3]

This is a nearly literal rendering of a passage which,
needless to say, has caused the churchmen a good many
headaches with its undeniable references to other existences
and other creations. The most annoying thing about it is that
Justin insists on reminding us all along that he is not speaking as a philosopher or as an independent thinker. This piece

is his *Apology for the Christians,* and with every other sentence he repeats, "this we believe," "this we have been taught," and so forth. This is the official opinion of the early church.

"We do not teach," says Justin elsewhere, speaking again for the church, "that God made the world for nothing, but in the interest of the human race. . . . And man does not do and suffer what he does by chance or accident, but in accordance with the *proairesis* every man is more or less faithful." *Proairesis,* according to the lexicon, means "*choosing* one thing *before* another," a plan of action laid out in advance, not an arbitrary rule or a predestined thing, but an agreement.[4]

In the *Clementine Recognitions,* Clement, recalling what Peter has taught him, says, "After these things when you were explaining the creation of the world, you said something about God's plan or decree, which he presented as his own will in the presence of all the first angels, and which laid down an eternal law for everyone; and you said that it provided two kingdoms, that is, the present and the future, and fixed the time for each, setting up a future day of judgment, which he himself determined, in which all things and spirits would be judged and sent to their proper place." Clement, paraphrasing Peter, then goes on to describe the creation of the earth, and concludes: "Then after he had commanded these living things to come forth from the earth and the waters, he made paradise, which he called a place of delights. And finally after all these things he made man, in whose behalf all had been prepared by him, and whose real nature (*interna species*) is more ancient [than they], and for his sake all were made and turned over to his supervision and for use as his habitation."[5] Our *Patrologia* editor notes in a footnote to this passage that Justin is here referring to the belief of the early Fathers that the spirit of man is older than his body. This doctrine was very old in the church. According to the *Apostolic Constitutions,* one of the greatest errors common to the heretics is that "they do not believe

that the spirit is immortal by nature,"[6] a position in which
the churchmen of a later day were to concur wholeheartedly
with the heretics.

Clement of Alexandria is dipping back into early Christian doctrine when he writes: "The Logos is not to be despised
as something new, for even in Jeremiah the Lord says, 'Say
not "I am too young," for before I formed thee in the womb
I knew thee, and before thou camest forth from thy mother I
sanctified thee.' It is possible that in speaking these things the
prophet is referring to us, as being known to God as faithful
before the foundation of the world. Only now we have become
babes for the purpose of fulfilling the plan of God. According to this we are new-born as far as the calling and salvation are concerned."[7]

Another doctrine rejected by later churches was that of
eternal progression. When Irenaeus was challenged to explain
how man being created can partake of the uncreated glory of
God, he had to fall back on this old teaching, even though it
contradicted many of his own ideas. This led Irenaeus to the
paradoxical conclusion that though man was not uncreated,
yet in time he could *become* uncreated through an endless
progression that would make him of the same eternal nature
as God himself! If philosophy will not permit him to allow
man's divine nature, religion forces him to, and so he writes:
"Taking increase from his great goodness, and persisting to a
fullness, the glory of the uncreated comes to them as a gift
from God. As they persevere through long ages, they acquire
more and more the virtue of being uncreated, and thus the
begotten and molded man becomes like the image and likeness of the unbegotten God [The scriptures, incidentally, say
man was made in that likeness from the beginning]. . . . It is
necessary for a man first to be born, and having come into
being to increase, and having increased to be strengthened,
and having been strengthened to multiply, and having mul-
tiplied to become great, and having become mighty to receive
glory, and having received glory to behold his Lord. For God

is he who is to be seen. The sight of God is perfect immortality, and immortality makes one to be very near to God."[8]

Tertullian makes much of the doctrine frequently met with in the primitive church (e.g., in the "Letter to Diognetus"), that the Christian "is a pilgrim in a strange land, among enemies: his is another race, another dwelling, another hope, another grace, another dignity."[9] But how can we be out of our element here if this is the only element we have ever known? Here we are lost and ill at ease. Lost from what? The theory of the later fathers is that man has an irresistible urge to get to heaven because he was created for the express purpose of filling the gap left in heaven by the fall of the angels. But the same fathers who maintain this doctrine also hold that the vast majority of spirits thus created will never see heaven—a strange inconsistency indeed.[10] The early Christians thought of the yearnings of the soul for heaven specifically as an urge to return to a familiar home. Origen's reflections on the preexistence are enlightening in this connection.

Speaking of the differences in rank and glory among the angels, Origen writes: "I think therefore, according as it seems to me, that the preceding disputation has sufficiently shown that the ruler holds his principate and the other orders receive their authority not indiscriminately or by chance, but that each receives the rank and honor for which he has qualified by merit, though it is not for us to know or even ask just what the deeds were by which they worked themselves into their various ranks." Origen finds support for this theory in the scriptural teaching that "God is no respecter of persons, but rather," he adds, "dispenses all things in proportion to the merit and progress of the individual. Therefore we cannot allow that the angels hold their offices on any other basis than merit, nor that the Powers exercise any power to which they have not progressed, nor that they administer what are called thrones, that is, the power to judge and to rule, on any other grounds than merit, nor that there is any dominion which is unearned."[11]

Passing from angels to men, Origen sees the same universal system in operation. Why the vast diversity and inequality among the creatures of earth? he asks. "If it is arbitrary, the creator must be unjust. Let us not think that differences of birth and fortune are accidental, but rather distributed to each one according to his desserts." Why was Jacob preferred to Esau? He deserved to be, and so it must be with all other men and all other creatures. Jacob was preferred even in the womb, so "*we believe* that he was even then chosen by God because of merits acquired before this life."[12] The "we believe" here is significant, for while Origen often gets himself into trouble as an incurable speculator, he is scrupulously and uniquely honest in stating at all times when an idea is his own, when he is guessing, when he is assuming a thing for the sake of argument, or when he is expressing a settled opinion. At the beginning of the first passage cited from him, for example, he said, "I think therefore, according as it seems to me, that the preceding disputation has sufficiently shown. . . . " Would that modern scholars were half so honest! When, therefore, Origen specifically says, "we believe," we can be sure that he is speaking (as is Justin Martyr by the same sign) not merely for himself, but for the early church.

Then Origen points out that the merited differences of fortune among men on earth are just like what we find among the angels—in each case the honors must have been deserved. But when and how? This leads him to an interesting speculation. There is no doubt at all that when the human race bids its final farewell to earthly life, there is going to be a judgment, in which to everyone will be assigned a future state of bliss or misery in accordance with his behavior during his earthly probation. So when we behold men *already* enjoying a great variety of privileges and pains, that is, of rewards and punishments (as they needs must do, if God is not arbitrary) on this earth, that strongly suggests that some sort of judgment has already taken place before we came here, and that our places here are assigned us as the result of what was awarded us there for work done in a preexistent state.[13] Perhaps Origen has let his speculative temperament carry him too far here, but that the most important of all theologians next to Augustine could in all seriousness have proposed such things in the first half of the third century is very significant. It shows why the early church never had to wrestle with the agonizing problems of predestination by which alone the churchmen after Augustine tried to explain the facts of life, though it made God seem cruel and arbitrary.

We might go on from the preexistence to discuss the early Christian doctrine of the plurality of worlds (a thing abhorrent to the systems of the later churchmen), or the degrees of glory or eternal progeny. The prominence given these things in the early fragments is the more striking in view of the complete silence of the later church regarding them. We have here a body of doctrine unknown to all but a few. We are only just beginning to learn what the early Christians really talked about, and how they answered the great questions of life. It is all totally foreign to conventional Christianity, but perfectly familiar, I am sure, to most Latter-day Saints, though few if any of them have ever considered the ancients in this regard. This is another certificate of the genuineness of the restored gospel, and as time goes by, a steady stream of new discoveries is vindicating the prophets.

27

A Prophetic Event

The Twenty-fourth of July is the day on which the Pioneers entered this valley. How do we tie *them* up with the ancient church? Very easily. The early Christians thought of themselves individually and collectively as strangers and pilgrims, outcasts from the world, seekers for a promised land. Collectively the churches describe themselves as "sojourning" in this or that place. One of the earliest Christian documents after the New Testament is the so-called First Clement, which begins, "The Church of God sojourning at Rome to the Church of God sojourning in Corinth," where the word for "sojourning" is the familiar and classical expression to denote a stay or visit in a place where one does not regularly belong: "here we have no continuing city" (Hebrews 13:14). The earliest Christian literature is full of this motif, which soon disappears as the church settles down and changes its nature. The passage cited, for example, is paraphrased in the opening sentences of the famous *Pastor of Hermas*, where the angel says, "Your city is far from this city; . . . why do you seek to own lands and build buildings here?"

The faithful have always compared themselves to Abraham who, "when he was called to go out into a place which he should after receive for an inheritance, obeyed; and he went out, not knowing whither he went. By faith he sojourned in the land of promise, as in a strange country, dwelling in tabernacles [tents] with Isaac and Jacob, the heirs with him of the same promise: For he looked for a city which hath foundations, whose builder and maker is God" (Hebrews 11:8-10).

Some of the earliest Christian sects, like the Mandaeans, thought of themselves as wanderers whose search for paradise began the day Adam was put out of Eden, he being the arch pilgrim and stranger on the earth, seeking ever to get back to the presence of the Lord. In this they seem to be following the teaching and example of ancient Jewish sects, such as the Rekhabites and those sectaries whose affairs and teachings in the centuries before the time of Christ have been so wonderfully brought to light of recent years with the discovery of the Dead Sea Scrolls. It is plain from these scrolls that certain particularly pious and devout Jews fled from the wicked society of a nation which they felt had ceased to observe the law in its fulness or in righteousness, going forth to live in the desert in imitation of Abraham, Isaac, and Jacob, who "sojourned in the land of promise as in a strange country, dwelling in tabernacles."[1] Nothing is more natural than that the modern Saints in their wanderings and sufferings should compare themselves to the ancients as the early Christians themselves did. This has been a popular bit of self-dramatization among Christians of every age, but in the case of the modern Saints it has a peculiar validity.

This whole question of religious parallels is a very challenging and significant one. It meets us everywhere in the history of the restored Church. To take the present theme, for example: is not the national epic of the pagan Romans concerned with the wanderings of a very religous man, *Pius Aeneas*, in search of his land of promise? Is not his Greek counterpart (and literary prototype) the good and noble Odysseus, who wanders a stranger and an outcast through the world until by divine aid he regains his rightful kingdom? In the nineteenth century, scholars began pointing to ubiquitous parallels in religion and folklore and acting as if they were very damaging to any claims of revealed religion. Eduard Meyer, for example, one of the profoundest and best informed

of all the searchers after such resemblances, pointed out that
there are definite parallels between Joseph Smith's account of
his first vision and that in the New Testament of the vision
beheld by the three Apostles on the mountain of the Transfiguration. Some scholars viewed that as a very suspicious
circumstance, but is it any more suspicious than the close
resemblance between the Transfiguration, as it is called, and
the story of Moses on Sinai? In both instances we read of the
ascent of a mountain, a dazzling light, a cloud, the transfig-
ured countenance, the terror of the beholders, a holy conversation in which two of the conversants were the same, Moses
and the Lord. Obviously the New Testament account is simply a revamping of the story of Moses on the mountain. But
why should it be? Men change very little and God not at all:
why should their dealings with each other not follow a con-
sistent pattern instead of complying with the passing fads of
the scholars? The schools of Wellhausen and Gressmann,
though diametrically opposed, were each convinced that it
had blasted the supernatural element out of religion forever
by demonstrating that there were everywhere in the ancient
world close ritual parallels to the crucifixion. The now well-
known Year Drama, a ritual found throughout the whole
world, presents everywhere, though with a great variety of
local variations, substantially the same ritual pattern: the
humiliation and sacrifice of the king, his rising from the
tomb after three days to be proclaimed as the god victorious
over death and worthy to rule forever.

But what do such parallels prove? Long before the scholars became aware of them, Jews and early Christians knew
all about them and saw in them not a refutation but a convincing support of the claims of true religion. In the
Clementine writings as in the Jewish Apocrypha, we read
how the priesthood of God and its rites and ordinances
have been deliberately imitated in every age of the world,
following the example first set by Ham, who tried to steal
the ordinances and insignia and used them without authority

in setting up the rule of priest-kings in the world. Jewish and Christian observers thought they could trace the diffusion of this imitation priesthood from a single center, and that is precisely the point to which modern comparative studies seem to be bringing us.[2] But whether or not we choose to be convinced by the growing prestige and authority of the diffusionist school, it is quite plain that the ties which seem to exist among all the religions of antiquity may be interpreted as vindicating as well as condemning the religion of the Bible. Time and again it is pointed out in the New Testament that this or that episode in the life of the Savior is the fulfillment of some ancient prophecy and that what was done in one dispensation had been foreshadowed in another. The whole eschatological pattern of history which is so extremely prominent in Jewish and Christian apocryphal writing calls for the periodic repetition of certain characteristic events—a "visitation," as it was called, from heaven; the making of a covenant; the corruption and the wickedness of men, leading to the breaking of the covenant; the bondage of sin, then the coming of a prophet with a call to repentance; the making of a new covenant; and so around the cycle.[3]

Now the Twenty-fourth of July gives us Israel in the desert again and the entering of the promised land. The parallels between the history of the restored Church and the doings of the ancients are so numerous and striking that even enemies of the Church have pointed them out again and again—what writer has not compared Brigham Young to Moses, for example? But I think in the case of the Latter-day Saints these resemblances have an extraordinary force, and that, for two main reasons: (1) they are not intentional and, (2) they actually are the fulfillment of modern-day prophecy. The history of Christianity has been marked by many and determined attempts by individuals and groups to imitate the example of ancient Israel. I have been to camp meetings of some denominations deliberately designed to resemble the doings of the camp of Israel in the wilderness. The medieval churchmen insisted that all the episodes in the history of Israel even to the slightest detail were allegorical foreshadowings of the institutions and practices of their own church. That they found the imitation not wholly convincing is implied by their great envy of the Jews, an envy which is very apparent in such writers as Ambrose and Optatus. Origen says a remarkable thing on this point: "Had God so willed that the Jews had not broken the law and slain the prophets and Jesus we would by now have seen the type and model of that heavenly city which Plato sought to describe."[4] But it never occurs to him that the Christians might be authorized to set up that city—that first becomes a fashionable doctrine in the fourth century. For the early Christian, the Jews are still the people of the promise.[5]

But conscious imitation of the sufferings and wanderings of Israel and the Saints has never been in the Mormon program. They have never been imitators: they have not needed to be. Nothing is more striking in the history of the Latter-day Saints than the way in which they were constantly pushed and driven around entirely against their own will. It was not their idea to be driven from place to place, and wherever they settled they sought with all their might to establish a permanent order. But all along, God had other plans, and the whole history of the church is his doing. It is easy enough to say in retrospect that whatever happened was God's will, but you can always tell the chosen people because in their case, "the Lord doeth nothing save he revealeth his will to his servants the prophets" (Amos 3:7), and all along, these people enjoyed prophetic guidance which, like the Children of Israel, they often failed to heed. In the case of Kirtland, Benjamin F. Johnson writes: "The Revelation in which God had given but five years of safety in Kirtland for the Saints . . . had been forgotten, and all appeared to feel that Kirtland was to become and remain a great center of business and religious interest for the future. But the Lord had other and greater purposes in view, one of which seemed to be to show us the weakness of human wisdom and folly of our idolatry, by bringing us to see our idols crumble in our hands."[6] Happy is the man whom God correcteth! The people had no intention of fulfilling the five-year prophecy, but it was fulfilled to the letter.

As in Kirtland, so in Missouri and Nauvoo: the people built for permanence, tired of their wanderings and tribulations, while the Lord had other plans, plans which he had clearly announced by the voice of the Prophet. Away back in March, 1831, God had given to men a marvelous revelation setting forth the divine economy of the latter days. That revelation concludes with the announcement of three great historical events which must transpire before the Lord comes again: "But before the great day of the Lord shall come, Jacob shall flourish in the wilderness, and the Lamanites shall blossom as the rose. Zion shall flourish upon the hills and rejoice upon the mountains, and shall be assembled together unto the place which I have appointed" (D&C 49:24-25). This is the language of prophecy, but there is nothing mystical or obscure about it. The members of the Christian church and those pretending to be so have at all times called themselves Israel, but not *Jacob*. That name is reserved for the Jews, and the consultation of a good Bible commentary will show that it is bound intimately to Palestine, whereas Israel refers to the people of the later covenant wherever they are: *Israel kata pneuma*, the earliest Christians called themselves, "spiritual Israel." Jacob was Israel's name before he wrestled with the Lord and received his new covenant. Jacob flourishing in the wilderness is the Jews prospering in their desert places, of that there has never been any doubt in the minds of Latter-day Saints. Nor can there be the slightest doubt what is meant by the Lamanites blossoming as the rose. We all know what the Lamanites are, and the familiar expression from Isaiah 35:1, that the desert shall rejoice and blossom, emphasizes not only a joyful but a totally paradoxical and unexpected event: the dead desert coming to life. Lastly, Zion has been from the very first the familiar code word, so to speak, designating the restored Church. And here we are told that "Zion shall flourish upon the hills and rejoice upon the mountains, and shall be assembled together unto the place which I have appointed." Before the Church was a year old, the Lord announced that he had appointed a place of gathering upon the hills and the mountains. This could not possibly have been any place in the Middle West, and the Prophet knew it. There is ample indication that he knew all along that the Saints would not have rest in Jackson County, however determined they were to have it.

But what we wish to point out is the marvelous sweep and consequence of the prophecy. It would have been hard in 1831 to pick out among all the people of the world three less likely candidates for earthly glory than the Jews, the Indians, and the Mormons. The first named, after centuries of steady persecution, had still to face their greatest trials. Compared to the great slaughterings that were to come, the centuries of torment and danger they had been through were but a rough sort of heckling. In 1831 the Indians, though long in the decline, still held the greater part of the continent, which they were presently to lose rapidly and catastrophically; a hundred years of steady defeat lay ahead of them, ending in near annihilation. The restored Church, less than a year old, had not yet, for all its hardships, learned what persecution could really be. Almost a century of bitter, unrelenting, and often violent opposition lay ahead of it. What a sorry trio! Yet before the Lord should come again these three were to flourish, to blossom, and to rejoice. Somehow the fortunes of all three were to move together and that not by any collusion between them or any plan of coordination among men, but purely by the marvelous power of God. With him alone lay the plan and the power to bring it about.

There is a saying of George Albert Smith, grandfather of the late President Smith, to the effect that the Saints came west of their own free will because they were forced to. That has always been the story. The saints have never been free to plan their own future, because the Lord has done it for them, usually to their extreme discomfort and always to their great advantage. Untold thousands have fallen by the wayside because of this constant testing. After Kirtland there was hardly a summer patriot left in the Church, but the testing went right on, and those who survived the following decade firm and unshaken were truly the very elect. Yet other great trials lay ahead—the crossing of the plains and the settling of the valleys. At every stage they left behind them a considerable population of weaker souls who, sometimes ostentatiously and sometimes quietly, left the Church in hopes of enjoying the riches of new land in safety and security. The little companies that came down the East bench in the ensuing decades had all been tried seven times seven in the fire. The hardships of the journey were the least of the hardships most of them had to face, and what they stood to gain in this world was nothing compared with the opportunities they left behind. The entrance of the Saints into Salt Lake Valley 107 years ago was one of the great moments in world history. It was that moment at which the assembly upon the hills and the mountains began at a place which the Lord had appointed from the beginning. It was the beginning of the final act of what we know as world history. It was a vindication of the prophets ancient and modern. It is a day of days to be remembered.

28

Prophecy and Office

The principal concern of students of Christianity in modern times has been to discover how and to what degree it is possible to reconcile the spiritual aspects of Christianity with the temporal. Debate, speculation, and research have all concentrated on one problem: to what degree, if any, can or must a spiritual message be implemented by physical organization, formal offices, and tangible ordinances? The two extreme points of view have been magnetic poles, and few were the churchmen who were not drawn either to the one or the other. The one pole was the opinion that the operation of the Spirit precluded the existence of any formal organization, any church at all, in apostolic and early Christian times. The other pole was that the operation of the church completely superseded the unpredictable and unreliable offices of direct revelation. To the one school, the Spirit was everything; to the other the church was everything. Let us consider the first pole first.

The war cry of the liberals was that the idea of direction and government through the Spirit absolutely precluded any idea of a physical church set up on this earth. A favorite argument was that the nearness of the expected end obviated the need for a church. "The eschatology of Jesus," to quote one authority, "was the decisive argument against the founding of a Church by him."[1] The fashion of this world passeth away, here we have no abiding kingdom—and here, accordingly, is no place for any such thing as an established church. "If the end was at hand and the Lord was approaching," these men asked, "what need for a church?"[2] To this they added the "spiritual" argument. A leading Protestant divine of our day recently wrote: "The Protestant affirms that God has not placed between Him and man a hierarchy of saints, bishops and priests through whom alone the individual can enter into His presence. On the contrary, we declare that as God spoke to Moses in the burning bush, to Samuel in the temple, to Paul on the road to Damascus by His Holy Spirit, so God still guides men through the still small voice of conscience."[3] Both these proofs for the nonexistence of an original church rest in the end on historical assumptions; and on historical evidence they both break down.

To take the latter point first, the historic illustrations just quoted are quite sufficient in themselves completely to refute their author's stand. God speaking to Moses from the burning bush, to Samuel in the temple, and to Paul on the road to Damascus were personal experiences to which three prophets bore witness. If *this* was God speaking "through the still small voice of conscience," then those three men were grossly abusing that conscience by describing its operation in such extravagant and misleading terms that those who heard their stories were moved to marvel at the strangeness and wonder of them; for though we daily experience the still small voice of conscience, which of us has ever had an experience remotely resembling these? Almost as soon as the *Didaché* was discovered, Harnack was able to show from it that however "spiritual" the primitive church might have been, it was also highly organized. And he went on to ask the question that should have been natural enough even before the great discovery, namely, what in the world is there to prevent a man who holds an office from being directed by the Spirit? And what is there to prevent a spiritual man from being appointed to an office? Nay, it would seem, Harnack concluded, not only that the power and gifts of the Spirit can be possessed by one holding an office in the church, but also very probably as far as the ancient church was concerned, they must be.[4] If the office without the spirit is a dead thing, is not the spirit without the office an ineffectual one?

As to the argument that the primitive Christians would take no thought of any kind of organization, since they expected the immediate end of all things, psychology and the scripture would support the opposite conclusion, i.e., that the fact that they were making a last-ditch stand would tend to draw the saints closer together:[5] "Not forsaking the assembling of ourselves together," says Paul, "as the manner of some is; but exhorting one another: and so much the more, as ye see the day approaching" (Hebrews 10:25).

Forced to admit some sort of organization in the early church, the scholars tended to favor the theory that such organization was a spontaneous local sort of thing—clubs of like-minded individuals spontaneously gathering in various communities, only to be welded into a central church organization through a long process of evolution. Now it is true that modern Christian churches can be plainly shown to be the product of just such a process of growth and adjustment; but it is equally clear that the early Christian church was not an evolved institution. "There," says Harnack, "the development goes from the whole to the part," and not the other way around. "Ecclesia," wrote Sohm, "means *Gesamtkirche* —the general church—of which the local churches were only copies"; the local church was a scale model (*Abbild*) of the main church.[6] This is plainly seen in the fact that originally all the local churches had the same offices and ordinances, which would not have been the case had they grown up independently; it was only after the Apostles passed away and the general authorities disappeared that each church went its own way, so that by the fifth century Sozomen can report that in his own day, no two churches do things the same way.[7] Schermann observed that the mere existence of set rites and ordinances in the early church was itself evidence for a set organization, without which they would be unthinkable.

Of these ordinances Hans Lietzmann pointed in particular to those of initiation into the church as proving beyond a doubt the existence of a close-knit, overall organization. The earliest records speak of definite rules for joining the church, Leitzmann notes, and these rules are fully developed in the Acts and the Epistles, a situation which is quite unthinkable without a rather strict organization.[8] Then Karl Holl, pointing to the well-known fact that the Christian church was from its very inception a missionary organization, drew the obvious conclusion that "no missionary church begins with autonomous branches." Missionary work always spreads from some center or other and is concerned with bringing others into a well-defined group.[9] As late as 1950, T. W. Manson notes that it is in the earliest records of all, the gospels, that "we begin with the fact that Jesus did gather a community round himself *during the course of his ministry*; and we may well ask what it was, if it was not the Church. . . . It will not do to regard this group merely as the more or less regular disciples of a somewhat unorthodox traveling Rabbi. . . . The more the Synoptic evidence is studied, the more clearly the fact emerges that what Jesus created was something more than a new theological school. It was a religious community, of which he was leader."[10] It has taken the Protestant scholars fifty years to come around to this, and today the strong consensus is that the church was not a product of late and gradual evolution. In all camps, the dependence of the individual on the church rather than the church on the individual is being emphasized. This may be taken as a thread characteristic of the times and seems to favor the second or other pole of theory we mentioned at the outset—that which places the operation of the church above all other things.

In the last analysis the two conflicting schools really agree perfectly on a most fundamental premise, namely that you don't need *both* the spiritual gifts and a church organization. The nineteenth-century schools, in the name of the Spirit, abolished the church. Their opponents in the name of the

church had long before ruled out the gifts of the Spirit. The
fathers of the fourth century definitely regard the church as
taking over entirely all the functions once reserved to the
prophets and to revelation. John Chrysostom said that members of the church were always and everywhere asking him,
What has happened to the spiritual gifts? Why do we no
longer have the gift of tongues? Where are the prophets?
Why are men not chosen for office as they were anciently by
direct revelation from above? His answer was always that
the church no longer had these gifts because it no longer
needed them. They were, he said, like a supporting scaffold
which is taken down as soon as the building is finished, or
like a prop with which a gardener supports a young tree: as
soon as the tree becomes strong and vigorous, the prop is
taken away because it is no longer needed. [11] Of course neither John nor his hearers were completely satisfied with this
answer, for the plain implication of it was that the church of
the Apostles was spiritually weaker than the church of their
own day—which they knew very well was not the case. Nevertheless, that was the official answer: The church had taken
over the offices anciently filled by the Spirit.

St. Augustine has a great deal to say on this subject; we
need mention here only his argument that the church has
superseded all revelation. Repeatedly he declares that he
believes only what the church tells him to believe and only
because the church tells him to believe it. This may seem a
paradoxical position for the man who himself was prescrib-
ing the fundamental theology which the church was to follow for centuries to come, but what other stand can he take,
since he insists that revelation has ceased and cannot put
himself up as the ultimate depository of divine authority?
When we read the gospels, Augustine maintains, Christ, the
head, speaks to us through the voice of the church. This is
indeed the opposite pole from the claim that he speaks only
in the still small voice of the individual conscience, but it is
just as far removed from any idea of real revelation. Even

though he *could* speak in his own person, we are told, still, Christ has committed his voice henceforward to the church alone: her voice is his voice. [12] In vain you argue! He tells the Pelagians, "for though no reason can explore or speech explain it, whatever is believed by the whole church is true."[13] Since Augustine well knew in his long controversies with various sects that the whole church never saw eye to eye on any doctrine, he falls back again and again on his favorite argument for the authority of his church—it is the true church because it is the *biggest*; among many competing sects it has the most members and is to be found in the most places—*therefore* it must be the church. [14] That is his favorite and virtually his *only* argument for the authority of his church in his long controversy of the Donatists. It is a strangely geographical, earthbound argument leaving no room for revelation.

But long before Augustine's day the loss of spiritual gifts in the church had caused grave concern in many breasts. Bishop John Kaye of Bristol has written an interesting thesis on this subject. "The miraculous powers conferred upon the apostles were the credentials by which they were to prove that they were the bearers of a new revelation from God to man. . . . We might therefore infer from the purpose for which they were conferred that they would in process of time be withdrawn." This is Chrysostom's theory, a theory for which neither man can give scriptural authority. Indeed, the scripture says, "these signs shall *follow* them that believe" (Mark 16:17). Bishop Kaye continues after discussing the gradual loss of gifts in the church, "that the power of working miracles was not extended beyond the Disciples, upon whom the Apostles conferred it by the imposition of hands." As the number of those disciples gradually diminished, the instances of the exercise of miraculous powers became continually less frequent, and ceased entirely at the death of the last individual on whom the hands of the apostles had been laid, at a date which Bishop Kaye places before the middle of

the second century. [15] The good bishop then proceeds to dis-
prove his own theory of the purpose of miracles by noting
that the early Christians were not at all reconciled to the loss
of the "spiritual gifts," but missed them sorely. After all, did
the missionary work of the church come to an end "before
the middle of the second century?" Most Christians would
say it was just beginning, and that the specific purpose of
miracles was to foster that work. If the church were really
being set up on the earth, miracles should not have ceased
then of all times! "What, then, would be the effect produced
upon the minds of the great body of Christians by their
gradual cessation?" our author asks, and answers: "Many
would not observe, none would be willing to observe it; for
all must naturally feel a reluctance to believe that powers,
which had contributed so essentially to the rapid diffusion of
Christianity, were withdrawn. . . . The silence of Ecclesiastical history, respecting the cessation of miraculous gifts in
the Church, is to be ascribed," Bishop Kaye says, ". . . to
the combined operation of prejudice and policy—of prejudice which made them reluctant to believe, of policy which
made them anxious to conceal the truth. . . . I perceive in
the language of the Fathers, who lived in the middle and end
of the second century . . . if not a conviction, at least a
suspicion, that the power of working miracles was withdrawn,
combined with an anxiety to keep up a belief of its continuance in the Church. They affirm in general terms, that
miracles were performed, but rarely venture to produce an
instance of a particular miracle. Those who followed them
are less scrupulous, and proceeded to invent miracles." [16]

A most remarkable witness to the cessation of heavenly
gifts in the church, and especially of prophecy, was the celebrated Tertullian, the first and in many ways the greatest of
the Latin Fathers. He seems to have been a convert—joining
the church at about the age of forty in Carthage—and was
one of the greatest lawyers of his day. Tertullian was not a
man to be fooled; he wanted to know things for himself, and

he made himself the foremost authority on the nature and institutions of the original Christian church. Like Clement and Justin Martyr before him, he was predisposed by long and laborious study in the schools of the pagans to recognize and appreciate those special characteristics of the Christian teaching which set it off sharply from all other doctrines. He knew, as they knew, that philosophers, administrators, journalists, scholars, orators, and teachers, if not quite a dime a dozen, can be trained up in any desired numbers. But not so with prophets! The gift of prophecy was for Tertullian the strongest recommendation of the divinity of the Christian church, and it was only when painful experience had convinced him beyond a doubt that the main church no longer possessed that gift that he did an amazing thing: Tertullian, commonly called the Puritan of the early church, the man who placed zeal for salvation above all other considerations and who showed by word and deed that no sacrifice was too great provided only he gain that salvation—Tertullian *left the church!* In doing so he did not change his mind about the gospel. What he did was to join the Montanists, a strictly orthodox sect which differed from the main church in one important thing: They preached that the gift of prophecy *must* be found in the church if it is the true church. That was what Tertullian was after. At the time of his going over he wrote a remarkable work in which he accused the main church of having supplanted the authority of revelation by the authority of office and numbers. Because they have the teaching (*doctrinam*) of the Apostles, he reminds the clergy, it does not follow that they have their authority (*postestatem*). All men are governed by *discipline*, but *power* comes only from God by the Spirit. The Apostles worked not by the formal operation of discipline but by direct power from God. "Show me therefore, you who would be apostolic, some prophetic examples, and I will acknowledge the divinity of your calling." It is true, they have *ministerium*, an official calling, but that is not *imperium*, the actual possession of power. The spiritual power of the church is that exercised only by Apostles and prophets, for "the Church is the spirit working through an inspired man; the Church is *not* a number of bishops. The final decision remains with the Lord, never with the servant; it belongs to God alone, not to any priest."[17] Tertullian says much more in this vein. Whether one agrees with him or not, he shows us that the issue was clearly drawn at a very early date. Already there were two factions in the church, those who precluded office by spirit, and those who supplanted spirit by office. The only solution to the problem, as Tertullian clearly sees, is the presence of the power of prophecy in the church.

29

What Makes a True Church?

The Church of Jesus Christ is a church of prophets. To realize that, we need only ask ourselves, What would the Church be without a prophet? The answer is frightening. Let us imagine that the scholars of our time had enough reliable information regarding the primitive church at their disposal to enable them to reconstruct a perfect full-scale model of that church. As a matter of fact, frequent attempts have been made, especially in the nineteenth century, to do just that, with results as unconvincing as that imitation Gothic with which modern churches have tried to capture an ancient mood. Such reconstructions, like those Shinto temples and Torgut shrines that are sometimes transplanted for exhibition to worlds' fairs in great western cities, are remarkably cold and lifeless things, as they needs must be, torn out of their original warm human context. What would an imitation church of Christ need to make it real? We maintain that neither the human touch nor anything that men can devise could effect that miracle; only the presence of a true prophet could do it. Let us illustrate this.

At a very early date, men started setting up imitation churches of Christ, saying, "Lo, here is Christ! and lo, there!" They felt that all that was necessary to have the real church was to have a society that went under the *name* of Jesus Christ. "It is not enough," cry the "apostolic fathers" over and over again, "to be called by the name of Christ in order to be his followers." "Many shall come in my name," the Lord had said, "and deceive many." Ignatius complains that everywhere people are mixing the name of Jesus Christ with their false religion as they would mix good wine with poison; everywhere they are stamping the true name of Christ as a mark of pure value on false and debased coins.[1] The implicit faith people have in labels is a remarkable thing, and never has the power of a label been so exploited as that of the Lord's holy name. When told of the restoration of the gospel, people remark with surprise and wonder that the church of Christ can never have left the earth, since societies professing his name have not ceased to flourish from the days of the Apostles. They conveniently ignore the many predictions of the Lord and the Apostles on this head which make it clear that the persistence of the name of Christ by no means guarantees the claims of the churches that use it.

A name, however, may be considered, like any office, ordinance, or liturgy, to be a mere outward sign. Everybody will admit that in religion it is not the outward sign that counts but the inner life. Right here we run into an insurmountable obstacle to those who would endow a church with sanctity, for, as the school of Sohm insisted, the inner life must remain covert: it cannot be brought out into the open for inspection, exhibition, criticism, or control else it ceases to be an inner life; it defies all rules and regulations accordingly, and it is beyond the reach of office or authority because, like the mystical experience, it is incommunicable. The inner life, to which religionists so often appeal when confronted by questions of authority and credentials, is an appeal to the intangible and the imponderable. Socrates heard an inner voice which to him was very real; it was the infallible guide of his own behavior, but he never presumed on its authority to give orders to other people. To have a church you must have something more than inner voices; the ancient Apostles were not called by such but by a living prophet, and they in turn as prophets actually gave orders to others.

No one will deny that the true Church must have the *Spirit*, for the Spirit giveth life. But how would we go about getting the Spirit for our model church? The only definitions I have ever seen of spirit have been purely negative, and all boil down simply to an absence of matter. Plato and his followers showed how by removing all the accidentals and material qualities of a thing one can arrive at the pure idea of it which is its real essence. And that, we are told, is spirit. I believe the immense influence of Plato and Aristotle on the theology of the later church is to be attributed primarily to the inestimable service they performed in enabling the churchmen to talk meaningfully about spirit, that all-important thing of which they had lost all comprehension in the old Christian sense. Let us recall how grateful Augustine was to Plato, who alone opened his eyes to the reality of immaterial being and thus made it possible for him to believe on God and join the church. [2] In modern times it has become popular to identify spirit with mood, atmosphere, feeling, etc., and to describe its workings in terms of aesthetic or emotional experiences. But to do that is to make the spirit a very common thing indeed, yet nothing is more evident than that the spirit of which the real Christians spoke was a very rare and special thing known only to the saints. A man-made spirit might add a lot to a man-made church, but it could not convert it into the Church of Jesus Christ.

In order to operate in an orderly fashion, our visible church must have some recognized *authority*, but since all organizations have that, we must go still further: ours must be a *divine* authority. Surprisingly enough, this can be rather easily supplied in two ways, historically and rationally. To establish divine ecclesiastical authority on historical grounds is actually the main business of church history. In the fourth century, as we have seen in an earlier chapter, thinking men seriously doubted whether the church still had authority to act in the name of God. To settle doubts on this head the great Eusebius established the study of church history as it has flourished ever since his day, with the deliberate intention of proving that the church that survived in the world could trace its lines of authority in unbroken succession right back to the Apostles. Right at the outset, Eusebius tells us that he finds the materials quite inadequate. It was therefore necessary, as Eduard Schwartz, Caspari, Voelker, and others have pointed out, to reconstruct the record backwards, rewriting church history in retrospect, selecting, altering, and inventing whatever evidence was necessary to prove the case of the church. "One cannot escape the suspicion," wrote Harnack summing up the whole period of early church history, "that present-day historians are still much too trusting in their attitude towards this whole literature. . . . We stand almost everywhere more or less helpless in the face of a systematically fabricated tradition."[3] If men want to prove the authority of their churches by historical evidence, systematic fabrication can meet any demands; however, the resulting proof can hardly endow any organization with genuine authority.

The rational foundation for claims to divine right are as easily established as the historical. The classical formula is given by Anselm: *fides quaerens intellectum*; you first decide what you are going to believe and then you set out to find intellectual demonstrations that will support it. And such proof comes easily and mechanically to hand if one has been "steeled in the school of old Aquinas," who gives us the useful rule: "Since the faith rests on infallible truth, it would be impossible to bring forth a valid demonstration against it; for it is obvious that any arguments brought forth against the faith are not really proofs but soluble arguments."[4] Thus I might state as a true principle that any coin when tossed will always come down heads. I toss the coin, and it comes down tails, but according to St. Thomas' convenient rule, that toss does not count—it must be ruled out since it refutes a true principle; and so by disqualifying all unfavorable tosses I can exhaustively demonstrate my doctrine that any coin when tossed will always come down heads. With an arsenal of such useful weapons at their disposal, it is not surprising that the schoolmen can come up with any proofs they want in matters of authority or anything else. There is no more powerful *argumentrix*, Tertullian reminds us, than self-interest.

Ever since the third century, the schoolmen have insisted that the Spirit of God can be found in its fulness in the church wherever holy men engage in *intellectual* contemplations. Since God is mind, it is argued, the operation of the mind gives the surest and most direct access to God. It is the highest form of revelation, surpassing the crude physical demonstrations of the primitive church even as mind surpasses matter. With this we cannot agree. The exercise of the intellect is a field open to the basest as well as the best of men, and the worse the villain the more clever and ingenious his arguments may be. With his free agency man enjoys the right to use his wits for evil as well as for righteous ends. In the *Clementine Recognitions* Peter assures his followers that the wicked Simon Magus can out-reason him any day. Simon had to be sharp to stay in business; if figures can't lie, liars *can* figure, and the voice of reason is by no means exclusively the voice of God: "Now the serpent was more subtil than any beast of the field" (Genesis 3:1).

Where does this leave us with our model church? We have set it up with all its offices and fixtures, given it the proper label, provided it with a synthetic spirit, established its claim to authority by strong historical and rational demonstrations, and put on it the stamp of the divine through the supernal operations of the intellect. What more is lacking? Everything. As yet our church has not been endowed with a single thing that human wit and will cannot provide. It has the form of godliness, to be sure, but the power is not there. And we can go on digging up the past, devising clever arguments, and holding splendid synods for a thousand years, and the power will still not be there. God alone can provide it, and he always does so in the same way. Let us repeat our question: What would an imitation church of Christ need to make it real? The regular scriptural term to describe the leaders of all unauthorized congregations is *false prophets*.

The fatal defect of such congregations is that they are led by false prophets, and we are told that these would abound in the earth, all claiming to be followers of Christ.

What is a false prophet? He is one who usurps the prerogatives and the authority which by right belong only to a prophet of God. The false prophet need not claim to be a prophet; indeed, most false prophets do not believe in prophecy or even in God, nor do they want anyone else to. Those who would lead the Russians into the promised land are plainly false prophets, but how much faith do they put in prophecy? The scriptural term "pseudo-prophet" designates one who is not a prophet, but who occupies the place that rightly belongs to a prophet, regardless of whether he has been put there by himself or by his followers. Fool's gold, the glittering yellow pyrites that one finds sometimes on the beach, is so called not because *it* pretends to be gold, but because fools take it for gold. A pseudo-prophet is one to whom foolish people accord the obedience and attention due only a true prophet, whether he or they actually take him for a prophet or not.

Even good, devout, sincere men and women can be false prophets. We can illustrate this point by recalling the attitude of Socrates toward his friends Gorgias, Protagoras, and other great Sophists. He respected and admired them for their powerful minds, their moral fervor, and their sincere desire to improve the character and the minds of youth. Yet for all that, these men were, in Socrates' opinion, dangerous deceivers, all of them, for they were teachers of false doctrine. Socrates did not consider himself qualified to guide the lives of his fellows; all his life he sought for one so qualified—what he was looking for was a prophet, as Professor Jaeger has indicated in the case of his disciples[5]—and when he insisted that he had never found such a man, and that those who thought themselves most qualified were even less worthy than he, his boldness cost him his life. His pupil

Plato poked fun at the way the Sophists accepted the wor-
shipful adulation of the multitude and of their disciples, for
nothing disturbed him more than the incurable tendency of
the schools to make false prophets out of good men. By his
standard we still live in a world of false prophets. Anyone
whose work competes with God's work, who makes claims
on the time and energies of men which rightly belong to
God, who puts the word of God in second place to the theories of men, or forces the teachings of true prophets to yield
precedence to his own discourses—anyone, in a word, who
puts his own knowledge above or on a level with revelation
from heaven is a false prophet.

Since we have mentioned the *Apology* of Socrates (a
work, incidentally, dear to the early Christians), we may
appeal to that immortal dialogue by way of answering one
of the commonest charges brought against the Latter-day
Saints, the charge of narrowness. Through the centuries students reading the *Apology* have sighed and shaken their heads
in sorrowful regret that one of the greatest men who ever
lived had to get himself executed by being so narrow and
uncompromising. He had nothing but love and good feeling
for the solid citizens of Athens, and they knew him as the
most harmless and righteous of men—yet he virtually forced
them to put him to death. "I firmly believe that God wants
me to spend my life seeking wisdom," he said in his farewell
address, "scrupulously examining myself and others."[6] This
is what annoyed the Athenians, who begged him to give up
the practice and live; to them his final word was: "My dear
Athenians, I rejoice to be with you and I love you, but I will
obey God rather than you."[7] And on the same day he drank
the hemlock. He was very narrow. "This Socrates," they said
of him, "thinks he is the only one who 'knows the score.' "

This is akin to the common charge made against the
Mormons, at a time when many of them were paying with
their lives for their stubbornness. It is the charge that Caecilius
and Celsus and all broad-minded heathens brought against

the early Christians: "Why this smug insistence," they would ask, "that you are the only ones who have the truth? Why this narrow-minded claim that your religion is better than any other?"

The first answer to this question today is an historical one. Every church that has an independent organization once claimed exclusive possession of the saving truth. If it did not, it should never have been organized, for the organization of every church creates division in Christendom, and nothing will justify that, short of a peculiar and special claim to enlightenment on matters vital to salvation. In the days of their pristine vitality and conviction, all the churches that now accuse others of thinking they have something better than anybody else thought the same way themselves. If Christianity is anything more than an ethical code or an agglomeration of sentimental attitudes and platitudes, it must be specific in its teachings and clear and uncompromising on matters which by its own profession are of transcendent importance. It is a sorry day when churches apologize for ever having been definite and outspoken on the subject of salvation. Today the fashion is to be neither hot nor cold—and that is the worst state of all. The alternative to being firm and specific is a slippery relativism that leads to nothing but paralysis. Because equally intelligent and gifted people disagree on what makes good music, it does not follow that all music is equally good or that all music is vanity. Because scientists in the same field often contradict each other, it does not follow that all science is a joke or even that the work of the wrangling scientists themselves is thereby discredited. Because what seems wise and moral behavior in one society may be frowned upon in another, it does not follow that all morality is an illusion or that all actions are equally moral. Why then should we assume that since people of equal intelligence and devotion take different views on religion one religion is as good as another, and it really makes no difference what a man believes?

All prophetic religions, like all true disciples, are marked by a kind of narrowness, for strait is the gate and narrow the way that leads to eternal life. But the charge is a false one that the followers of the prophets would exclude all the rest of mankind from their little circle of the elect. Of all the Christian religions in the world today, the only prophetic one, that of the Latter-day Saints, is that one which alone provides salvation for all the human race, living and dead. It alone has been taught by prophets that it is absolutely wrong to think of God as limiting his blessings and manifestations to but one small portion of his human family: all creatures, we are taught, were meant by God to have joy in the sphere in which they were created, and in every age and in all parts of the world men have been given all the joy and all the glory that they have been willing to receive. One of the most wonderful chapters in the history of the restored Church has been that which tells of the innumerable miracles and manifestations, visions and revelations by which the way has been opened up for the missionaries everywhere. The recipients of some of the most marvelous of these dispensations were what the Victorian world chose to call savages, living in the wilderness or on the islands of the sea, yet God had filled their whole lives with blessings. It was so in the ancient church. Cornelius, the Ethiopian, the righteous jailer and his family, the "great company of priests . . . obedient to the faith" (Acts 6:7), all these and many more were so near to the gospel that they recognized it instantly on sight—God had never deserted them but poured out his Spirit on them even in their pre-Christian days. Yet when they heard the gospel, they joyfully accepted it. Because God had remembered them, they did not conclude that they needed no more. It was precisely because they were searchers for more light that God had blessed them as richly as he did: "To those that have shall be given," said the Lord, not, "to those that have there is no further need."

There is nothing narrow, arbitrary, or ungenerous in revealed religion. In the end all the human race will hear the fulness of the everlasting gospel. But meantime, all things must be taught in order, and milk must come before meat. The Lord must work through his established Church, which must unfailingly be under the guidance of his servants, the prophets.

30

Prophets and Glad Tidings

Even when they preach repentance and thunder words of warning, the prophets bring nothing but good news. In every age joy is the keynote of their message: "Sing and rejoice, O daughter of Zion: for, lo, I come, and I will dwell in the midst of thee, saith the Lord" (Zechariah 2:10). Like the angels, the prophets bring glad tidings of great joy, the assurance that our Redeemer lives and that he has come to earth and taken upon himself the task of atoning for our inadequacy. In the boundless jubilation that comes like a vast sigh of relief with that assurance, all other cares and worries shrivel to insignificance. As we all know, the word *gospel* comes from the classic *evangelium*, "the joyful news," "the glad tidings." In his darkest hour the Lord told the Apostles, "These things I have spoken unto you, that in me ye might have peace. In the world ye shall have tribulation: but be of good cheer; I have overcome the world" (John 16:33). Then he left them to tread the winepress alone, to do the work that no one else could do. We are commanded to be joyful because he has borne our sorrows. He was a man of sorrows and acquainted with grief so that we need not be. Our own sins and limitations are the things that make us sad. He had no sins and limitations; he was not sad for his sake, but wholly for ours. Only one could suffer for others who did not deserve to suffer for himself. If we remain gloomy after what he did for us, it is because we do not accept what he did for us. If we suffer, we deserve to suffer because there is no need for it if we only believe in him.

But shouldn't we pay the price of our own sins? Isn't it only right and proper that we do so, and does it not weaken our character to be given something we do not deserve? In answer to this we might imagine the human race to be in the position of a mountain climber on a precarious ledge. The man has been climbing mountains all his life; he has never yet (or else he wouldn't be alive) found himself in a position from which his will and his wit have not been able to extricate him. But now at last he *is* in such a position. Whose fault is it? Strictly speaking the climber is wholly responsible for getting himself in a "jam," for he took the risk. Yet it is only by taking such risks—some of which seemed greater even than this one—that he has become the able climber that he is; his very virtues have led him into a death trap. It was inevitable that his courage and enterprise should someday lead him to overreach himself and turn to his destruction. This is the heroic situation so familiar from the Classics and the Sagas—the very essence of our human tragedy: because the hero does not sit at home and vegetate, because he has godlike aspirations, he is doomed to death. His very virtues encompass his destruction, for he has one fatal weakness— he is human.

In the first lecture we showed that the Greeks, much wiser and more thoughtful than we are, saw with terrifying clarity and conviction after they had examined the question from all sides with their peculiarly searching intensity, that man is simply not up to the task of assuring himself a good life on earth, let alone in eternity. And so after all our planning and toil we find ourselves clinging exhausted to the face of the cliff, forced to admit at last in one terrible flash of insight and despair that our strength is hopelessly inadequate to getting us home again, even if we had not wasted our powers in anger and debauchery.

Then at this moment a helping hand is reached down to us. Now the question is, should we refuse the hand for fear of weakening our character? Will we still, in spite of what we know, insist that we can go it alone—that our own intelligence will be enough to save us? Should we protest that the appearance of the hand at such a time and place is illogical and highly improbable, or debate whether the owner of the hand has strength enough to give us aid? Take the advice of the Greeks, who knew far more about the problems and ambitions of men than we ever will: man can never save himself. Grasp the helping hand while you have a chance, and ask questions afterward. In the novel *The White Tower*, the Nazi mountain climber falls to his death because he is too proud and independent to grab the helping hand of another climber—he is the superman who doesn't need anybody's help; he has been taught since childhood that his own iron will can overcome all things. The moral is plain: "Wherefore, all mankind were in a lost and in a fallen state, and ever would be save they should rely on this Redeemer. Behold, he offereth himself a sacrifice for sin, to answer the ends of the law, unto all those who have a broken heart and a contrite spirit; and unto none else can the ends of the law be answered" (1 Nephi 10:6; 2 Nephi 2:7).

One thing we must recognize, and that is that the fact of man's fallen state is real, whether or not one can think offhand of a good logical explanation for it. The schoolmen can argue the universe itself out of existence—after all, the multiplicity and disorder of the stars is a good argument against their existence, and it is simply absurd to suppose that anything at all can really exist and have life except the one God. We, however, accept existence as one of the facts of life; we begin with the universe as a given quantity—it is not our business to ask whether there could or should be such a thing: *there it is*. Anselm, giving a strictly feudal interpretation of the atonement, says we cannot pay for our sins since, being an affront to majesty, they exceed in enormity anything we can atone for. An awareness of the preexistence, on the other hand, puts the thing in another light. We become parties to the whole plan of salvation from the first. Our

elder brother Jesus Christ has proposed that he should help
us to rise above ourselves, and this does not weaken our
characters since our part of the bargain requires that we take
no credit for the achievement, standing upon new heights
not as haughty conquerors but with broken hearts and contrite spirits. We claim no unearned glory for ourselves, but
we are the richer for the part we have been allowed to play
in our own salvation.

But aside from the life-and-death issue, are not toil and
suffering in general good for us? Did not God condemn Adam
to drudgery and Eve to much sorrow? Is not man born to
trouble as the sparks fly upward? True enough, sorrow is the
lot of man. No one escapes it, and so the question is not
whether man shall suffer or not in this world, but only how
much he shall suffer. And how much should that be?—as
little as possible, is the assurance of the prophets. The ancient
saints were often reminded that if they must suffer their sufferings would be brief, not protracted a moment longer than
necessary. The sorrows of the Apostles are compared to the
sorrows of Eve—inescapable but brief: "Ye shall be sorrowful,"
Christ told them at his leavetaking, "but your sorrow shall
be turned into joy. A woman when she is in travail hath sorrow, because her hour is come: but as soon as she is delivered of the child, she remembereth no more the anguish, for
joy that a man is born unto the world" (John 16:20-21). No
man knows a thousand years of pain. As soon as one realizes his position fully, he is ready to be saved from it. As
soon as our climber grasps the seriousness of his situation in
one clear-sighted instant and repents of his rashness and
folly, then he is ready to receive the proffered hand—his
pride gives way to humility, and he joyfully accepts salvation. No need to have him clinging to the rock indefinitely:
he has learned his lesson! God does not play cat and mouse
with us; our sufferings are not drawn out; they are but for a
little moment, says the scripture, to those who are ready to
accept deliverance.

Since we have used the figure of the cliff, we should, in view of Toynbee's famous allegory, be careful not to fall into a superficial historical interpretation of salvation. Few will deny today, it is true, that the human race is standing on a very narrow ledge with a precarious fingerhold above and a yawning gulf below. But we are not talking about historical salvation at all. Men take themselves and their historical doings altogether too seriously. Those who turn from the daily paper and the news broadcasts to con the scriptures for signs of the times, revise their charts of prophetic world events, and plot the course of God in history are wasting their time. This is a shabby little show down here—read a last month's newspaper if you don't think so. As a matter of fact, the human race is at this moment as near to an earthly paradise as it can ever expect to be—unless you honestly think that more televisions and cars and play-school education are going to endow man with the wisdom and forbearance of the angels. After every conceivable improvement and correction in our world has been made, we are still at a loss to imagine any institutional setup or scientific attainment that can make men permanently happy. Even though we were drunk with permanent prosperity, we would learn with the poet Housman, that

> . . . men at whiles are sober
> And think by fits and starts
> And if they think, they fasten
> Their hands upon their hearts.

If the race were to gain all its earthly desires, it could only exclaim with the bitterness of a Roman emperor, utterly satiated with all he could think to ask for: *Omnia fui et nihil expedit*—"I have been everything, and nothing is worth anything!"

If the things of this world are all an empty show, "a tale told by an idiot, full of sound and fury, signifying nothing," what is important? The atonement of Jesus Christ—that is

the one supreme reality of our life upon this earth! Men have
forgotten about it, I grant you; it sounds strange and unfamiliar in our ears, this joyful news of the redemption—a
technical jargon, the quaint survival of a solemn terminology from another day of simpler and more gullible souls, the
laboring of a forced and unnatural situation, and so forth—
if that is what the atonement has become to this generation,
so much the worse for us. Atonement indeed! Of course it
has no compelling application in modern life—*we* have fixed
that. The vast and variegated stage setting of the modern
world, like that of the ancient, with its impressive props and
ingenious effects, is carefully designed to conceal the truth
that men haven't the courage to face.

What are we afraid of? What do men fear most? Believe
it or not, it is joy. Against joy, society erects its most massive bulwarks. The gospel is a message of terrifying joy.
What is the culmination of all joy? To stand in the presence
of God and behold his face—we don't need to argue that
point. Yet what is the most frightening prospect that mortal
man can imagine? Certainly, to stand in the presence of God
and behold his face! The presence of Jesus was an unbear-
able torment to wicked men and devils alike; rather than
look upon the face of the Lord, the wicked shall beg the
rocks and the mountains to cover them; the Apostles who
cheerfully faced death at the hands of devilish men were
"sore afraid" at the approach of God the Father on the mountain; and when Moses descended from another mountain,
the people fell down in deadly fear at the presence of one
who had been talking face to face with God, though Moses
himself at an earlier time had "hid his face; for he was afraid
to look upon God" (Exodus 3:6). It is not hell that men fear
most, but heaven. Plainly the joy for which man was created
is no light and trivial thing. It has more substance to it than
all the rest of our existence. We live here, as many a philosopher has noted, in a shadow world of half-lights and unre-
alities. Everything in our society conspires to dampen and

control joy. Our sordid little pleasures are carefully chan-neled and commercialized; our pitiful escapes to alcohol and drugs are a plain admission that we will not allow ourselves to have joy in our right senses. Only little children can face up to it—they have no hidden guilt to admonish cautious behavior or make joy appear unseemly. The kingdom of heaven is one of joy, and it is literally true that unless we are as little children we cannot possibly inherit it.

Why do we insist on taking ourselves so seriously? Because we are frightened to death of being found out. Men have turned their backs on the atonement of Jesus Christ to make for themselves a world of humbug. To lend dignity and author-ity to the pretentious fraud, they have invented the solemn business and drudgery of everyday life. To avoid answering questions, we pretend to be very busy—my, how busy! In every conservatory of music there is the student who prac-tices scales and exercises with dedicated zeal for eight or ten hours a day or works away for months and years with terri-fying persistence at a single piece. This is the devoted grind who impresses others by his matchless industry. But don't be fooled: This drudge is not working at all—he is running away from work! His ferocious application to dull routine is but a dodge to avoid the novel and frightening effort of using his head. And never, never, for all his years of toil, does he become a real musician. In the manner of this poor dupe, the whole majestic world goes about its ostentatious enterprises, the important busy-work of everyday life which includes, alas, nearly all its religious activities as well. And all this expenditure of effort inevitably culminates in the supreme effort of all—the effort of war. William James got the cart before the horse in his famous essay on the "Moral Substitutes for War": It is war that is the super-substitute, showing the fantastic extremes to which men are willing to go to escape their true calling.

In such a busy and dedicated world the prophets appear as loafers and tramps, as maladjusted vagrants with no visible means of support. One of the commonest, if not the commonest, charges against Joseph Smith was that he was lazy and easygoing, yet he accomplished far more than any ten men of his generation. He was called by his critics a merry prophet—always cheerful and sweet-tempered, he never took himself too seriously and sometimes, for all his unfailing courtesy, offended visiting dignitaries by his lack of solemnity. In ancient times the saints impressed outsiders the same way, were often charged with unnecessary levity, and even accused of being drunk with new wine. We all know how the learned doctors shook their heads at Jesus' informal manner—but if he did not take seriously the things which were important to them, they on their part despised the things of the kingdom which were all-important to him.

Sorrow is a negative thing, a matter of defects and failures, shortcomings and frustrations, waste, triviality, and inability; to live with it requires only resignation. The Russian novel shows us the almost unlimited capacity of the human race for suffering, and anyone can make his own statistical researches to prove that humanity in a thousand ways declares its almost unanimous preference for drab and depressing routines. If the world is a dark and dreary place, it is because we prefer it that way, for there is nothing in the world that can keep a man from joy if joy is what he wants. Direct access to our Father in heaven through prayer is always open. But right there we draw back; as soon as we gain a distant glimpse of it, we are not so sure whether we want this joy. It is altogether too much for us to bear. We must learn by degrees to live with it. It is not strange that we are afraid of so great and overpowering a thing—that we are overawed by the feeling that all this is too good for us. The fact is that it *is* too good for us—much too good, and the message of the prophets and the Church to us here is that we

must awake and prepare ourselves as good and faithful servants to enter into the *joy* of the Lord. We are not ready yet.
It was the glory of the Lord shining round about them that
made the shepherds sore afraid, so that the angel had to
reassure them that he was bringing only joyful news, good
tidings of great joy, for he had been sent to announce, as all
the prophets have, the coming to earth of the Redeemer.
That has been the joyful message of all the prophets. That
we may come to support not the burden of great suffering,
but the much greater impact of limitless joy is the purpose of
our training here. "In the world ye shall have tribulation,"
says the Lord to his prophets, "but be of good cheer: I have
overcome the world." Let no one imagine that there is no
conflict between the World and the Prophets—throughout
the centuries each has been an affliction to the other. What
the World teaches us, if we would believe its wisest men
(how often the Latin poets have said it!), is to live gracefully
in the wan shadow of ever-present sorrow. To the Prophets
such teaching is posturing pretense and lame surrender, for
they know better; theirs is the far harder task of persuading
men to accept, and to live with, boundless and everlasting
joy.

31

The Doctors' Dilemma

Since World War II there has been a "new look" in religion, fundamental to which has been what one eminent scholar calls "the rediscovery of the importance of eschatology within the New Testament."[1] And what is eschatology? A parable can best explain:

There was once a man who went to see a play at the theater. He arrived an hour and a half late, and had barely taken his seat when an emergency call obliged him to leave. The next day a friend asked him how he liked the play. What could the man answer except that he saw almost nothing of it? What he saw may have been gay or depressing, colorful or exciting, but it was no play at all; it was only a three-minute glimpse of what might or might not be a meaningful drama. Such is our position in the world. We come late to a play which has been in progress for ages, and we never stay long enough to find out what is really happening. We get a glimpse of the stage and the actors and hear a few lines of speech or music, and then we are hustled out of the house. From what we have seen we may rack our brains to reconstruct some sort of plot, but our speculations can never be anything but the wildest guesses. Yet unless we know both how the play began (that is *protology*) and how it ends (that is *eschatology*), the whole show remains utterly meaningless to us, "a tale told by an idiot, . . . signifying nothing." And not to know what the play is about is an intolerable state of things; it is not to be borne. For not only do we find the drama strangely engrossing, but we are actually pushed out onto the stage and expected to participate intelligently in what is going on. We are much too involved in the thing to settle for a play without a meaning, but who can tell us what it is all about?

Literature and Art can help us enjoy or endure the play; they harp everlastingly on the tragic transience of our stay in the theater, help us to appreciate the quickly passing beauty of the scene before us, and incite us to speculate and wonder whether there is any meaning to the thing at all and what it might be. But by their own confession (and the greater the artist the greater the frustration) the masters can only tell us that we are such stuff as dreams are made of and that as far as they can see this world, "the cloud-capped towers, the gorgeous palaces, the solemn temples, the great globe itself, yea, all which it inherit, shall dissolve, and, like [an] unsubstantial pageant faded, leave not a rack behind." What went before? What comes after? Don't ask the artist: he has seen as little of the play as you have. Philosophy would like to tell us what the play is about, but will not allow itself to run out of scientific bounds; it remains too often the pariah dog, snapping at the heels of religion and scavenging in the camp of science. It is to science and religion that we must turn for definite answers. First, of course, to Science.

And the first thing we learn when we turn to Science is that its peculiar strength lies in its formal renunciation of any attempt to deal with the problems of eschatology. The scientist speaks with authority only because he pays strict attention to the problem at hand, limiting himself to the laboratory situation over which he has control and rejecting all else as extraneous and irrelevant. "For scientific procedure," Courant and Robbins remind us, "it is important to discard elements of a metaphysical character. . . . To renounce the goal of . . . knowing the 'ultimate truth,' of unraveling the innermost essence of the world, may be a psychological hardship for naive enthusiasts, but in fact it was one of the most fruitful turns in modern thinking."[2] *Modern* thinking? That

was exactly the program of Thales and the Ionian school; it
was what made Science Science. And the Ionian school had
no sooner got started than the wise Heraclitus pointed out
that the objectivity that the scientists thought they had
achieved by barring the Other World from their calculations
was an illusion; and indeed before long one scientist after
another was issuing solemn pronouncements on the *ultimate*
substance and the *ultimate* cause of everything. The basic
illusion was that the scientific observer, free of all prejudice
and preconception, simply let the evidence work on him and
saw things as they were. But Heraclitus knew better: it is the
observer who really decides what he is going to see.

The ancient Sophists looked at the starry heavens and
immediately perceived that the vast ordered mechanism, moving inexorably and endlessly without cause or hindrance,
was direct and irrefutable evidence against the existence of a
God—things just happen. Aristotle gazing at the same starry
heavens immediately perceived that the vast ordered motion
and structure of things left no possible room for doubt that
there is a directing mind behind it—things don't just happen.
Here are the two classic schools of thought that still divide
the world between them: the one says that things just happen, the other that things don't just happen—and both appeal
to the same evidence to prove their case! Which is the more
deluded? The religious, their opponents constantly remind
us, are guilty of seeing more than the evidence justifies. But
what about the scientists? Do they let the evidence tell its
own story? They say they do, but a recent study by the head
of an important scientific organization spills the beans: "I
have known intimately a number of creative scientists and I
have studied the behavior of a great many more as revealed
by the record of history," he writes; "I have never encoun-
tered one of any importance whatever who would welcome
with joy and satisfaction the publication of a new theory,
explanation, or conceptual scheme that would completely
replace and render superfluous his own creation." Instead of

embracing new truth at any price, "the scientist actually tries—
often in vain—to fit each new discovery or set of discoveries
into the traditional theories" as he "clings to conceptions or
preconceptions as long as it is humanly possible." Hence
"any suggestion that scientists so dearly love truth that they
have not the slightest hesitation in jettisoning their beliefs is
a mean perversion of the facts. It is a form of scientific idolatry, supposing that scientists are entirely free from the passions that direct men's actions, and we should have little
patience with it."[3]

Listen to the great Galileo reporting his observations of
Saturn. Others had suggested that there were rings about the
planet, but there was no place in Galileo's system for such
nonsense; he speaks as the pure observer: "I have resolved
not to put anything around Saturn except what I have already
observed." Couldn't he *see* the rings, then? He could indeed;
his telescope was quite adequate for the task, and yet, looking right at Saturn, he *did* not see them: "I, who have observed
it a thousand times at different periods with an excellent
instrument, can assure you that no change whatever is to be
seen in it. And reason, based upon our experiences of all
other stellar motions, renders us certain that none ever will
be seen."[4] On the strength of *direct observation* this great
scientist categorically denied that the rings of Saturn existed,
though they were as plain as day before him; he denied that
there ever was any change in the planet's appearance—though
it was constantly changing before his eyes; and he declared
that no changes ever would be seen in it to the end of time.
How could he speak with such finality? Because his past
"experiences of all other stellar motions" had completely conditioned him to what he should see and not see. "The efforts
of perception," writes Polanyi, "are induced by a craving to
make out what it is that we are seeing before us"—the evidence does not convey its unerring message directly to our

minds, we have to figure out for ourselves what we are looking at, and in the process our past experiences, conditioning,
and prejudices are a deciding factor.[5]

"Amstutz (1960) has pointed out," for example, that the
definitions which geologists take into the field with them
"restrict our ability to see relationships, and even predeter-
mine the relationships we will see. This, of course, is a common failing; once we think we know a relationship [e.g., an
evolutionary pattern], we continue to see it, even though the
relationship may change."[6] Even our most elementary awareness of things is conditioned to a degree we dream not of,
according to Professor Bridgman: "The perceptions of time
and space . . . we acquire . . . only by arduous practice. Yet
we take our space and time with a deadly seriousness. . . .
Perhaps when we learn to take them less seriously we will
not be so bedeviled by the logical contradictions in which
they sometimes now involve us, as when we ask questions
about the beginning or end of time or the boundaries of
space."[7] These are those very eschatological questions which
tied up the Ionian physicists, and Heraclitus was right: they
cannot be answered by science because there is no such thing
as observation without a conditioned observer. As Polanyi
says, in science "pursuit of knowledge [is] based largely on
hidden clues and arrived at and ultimately accredited on the
grounds of personal judgment."[8] The clues are not self-evident
but hidden, and the ultimate proof is not detached observation and pure reason but personal judgment.

As if the admission of the human element in science were
not alarming enough, we are often being told today what
each generation seems to discover for itself, that science after
all is as firmly founded on faith as religion itself. "Newton's
first law," one scientist reminds us, "illustrates [the] point,
that the physical sciences are based on an act of faith. 'Every
body continues. . . . ' This can never be proved. . . . If we

look carefully at science we see that it is full of these theoretical concepts, these creations of the human mind."[9] If science is based on faith, is it not possible that the present much-lamented sterility in science, that is, the inability to come up not merely with new reports and demonstrations, but to discover what W. H. George calls "the essentially new," is due to a lack of faith and an over-concern with being "scientific"? Many older scientists are suggesting some such thing. A. P. Elkin now reminds us that science progresses only by "forgetting for the time at least the abstract methods, the images and models, the selected and prepared specimens of the scientific student," which are the essence of his trade.[10] Disturbed by the lack of real creativity in science, the British government recently sponsored an ambitious study of scientific creativity in the past. The result was a shocker, showing that the great original scientists have had a disturbing way of combining in their persons remarkable scientific skepticism with an equally remarkable religious gullibility. The creative scientist is a scientific heretic who "must refuse to acquiesce in certain previously accepted conclusions. This argues a kind of imperviousness to the opinions of others, notably of authorities"; the true scientist throws that sacred cow, Scientific Authority, out of the window, and this "sets him free to speculate and investigate."[11] On the other hand he tends to display what our report calls "a curious credulity" in unscientific areas and to favor ideas which have "that touch of offending common sense which is the hallmark of every truly scientific discovery."[12] Newton, the greatest genius of them all, is the classic example. "Most of Newton's biographers," Dr. Ernest Jones informs us, "have suppressed the important fact that throughout his life theology was much more important to him than science, and moreover, theology of a peculiarly arid and bigoted order"; that is, *not* the theology of the Church of England, but a literal acceptance of the Bible, in which Newton "was especially engrossed in unraveling the obscure symbolism of the Books of Daniel

and of Revelation."[13] Eschatology was what really interested
Newton; Dr. Jones is upset by this and treats it as a serious
defect in the great man's character. It does not seem to occur
to anyone that Newton might have been the great scientist he
was just *because* of his constant concern with the gospel,
and not in spite of it, which is all the more likely, since
many other great creative geniuses display the same peculiar
and regrettable tendency to believe in the Other World.

To judge by the more popular scientific journals, there
seems to be a growing suspicion among scientists that perhaps Hume was right—there may be absolute limits to our
scientific knowledge. The mathematician Le Corbeiller points
out that just as there were no more continents to discover
after Columbus, so "there are just so many ways of combining certain things, and no more,"[14] and Gödel has proved to
the world that it is impossible to "prove the consistency" of
any significant set of postulates.[15] Warren Weaver suggests
that "the mysteries of life—perhaps they are intended to
remain mysteries,"[16] and a famous biologist warns us to be
"prepared for the possibility that the human brain will never
be able to understand itself, or consciousness or perhaps the
nature of life itself."[17] Where does science go once it realizes,
with Professor Bridgman, that "the world is not constructed
according to the principles of common sense"?[18] Grand Old
Men in various fields remember the exuberant days of their
youth, when "always just around the corner was the answer
to all the riddles," and ruefully admit that the long years
have not fulfilled the promise.[19] More alarming still, what
was once regarded as the chief strength and virtue of science, namely its ability to reject old ideas and accept new, is
now viewed as an indication of a fatal deficiency. It is all
very well to admit that we were wrong yesterday, but can we
in the same breath insist that we are right today? We cannot.
"The great lesson of the Piltdown business for me," wrote the
anthropologist Hooton, "is that it is unwise to accept current

scientific decisions and 'proofs' as final, irrevocable, and con-
clusive, no matter how authoritative they may sound or
look."[20] The renowned philosopher of science Karl Popper
recently wrote: "Science is not a system of certain, or well-
established statements; nor is it a system which steadily
advances toward a state of finality. . . . The demand for scientific objectivity makes it inevitable that every scientific
statement must remain *tentative forever.*"[21] The italics are
Popper's, and they give us furiously to think. Today's science may be better than yesterday's, but the final answers
are *just as far away as ever.* "This is a rather shocking thing
to say," says Weaver, "—that science does not furnish any
really ultimate or satisfying explanation. . . . Science is
superbly successful at dealing with phenomena, but . . . it
possesses the inherent defect . . . that it cannot furnish ultimate explanation. . . . Scientists—even the greatest ones in
the most advanced field of physics such as Einstein and Bohr
and Planck and Dirac—cannot agree as to whether and how
science explains anything."[22]

So we are back where we started. The scientist studies
the stage and even the actors, the costumes and properties of
the play, the temperature of the building and the composition of the paint and canvas—but the play itself is none of
his business. Like Omar Khayyam, he even gets the idea at
times that there *is* no play; for it is but a step from renouncing the pursuit of eschatology (as the Ionian school did) for
the sake of testing a particular hypothesis, to renouncing
eschatology itself—permanently. Once we find or think we
can do without it, it becomes excess baggage, nay, an imped-
iment to science, an evil hold-over from the past. Henceforth
if there is to be any eschatology at all, science will supply it,
and no nonsense, as Freud announced in ringing tones: "It
would be an illusion to suppose that we could get anywhere
else what Science cannot give us."[23] And so after grandly
announcing that Science is Science because it has done with
eschatology once and for all, we find the scientists right back

in the eschatology business for themselves. "Here we are," cries a leading biologist, "and we had better find some meaning or invent one for ourselves so that we have some definite mission to lend dignity to our life."[24] Without that, science can only offer us what one noted psychologist calls "a bittersweet philosophy of despair."[25] No wonder the scientists have always yielded to the weakness of human nature and constructed their universe—backwards! By all the rules, the *last* question anyone should attempt to answer scientifically is the question How did it all begin? The answer can only lie at the very end of the long trail of research. Yet what science has not *begun* its career by coming up with an answer, to which it has then forced subsequent evidence to comply? It is not surprising that scientists cannot escape the vortex of eschatology: that very curiosity which leads them into science in the first place points them inevitably and irresistibly to those greater questions to which they so often feign indifference. But who is authorized to answer? "My greatest lesson," said a great biologist in his farewell address recently, "was these words spoken by David Starr Jordan: 'Authority? *There is no authority!*' "[26]

So let us turn to religion. If the student hopes to find in the tomes of the theologians another world from the limited twilight zone of science, he will be sorely mistaken. For the doctors of the Christian church simply abhor eschatology. The history of the Christian church, as Albert Schweitzer has shown us, has been the story of one long, progressive process of "de-eschatologizing" the gospel message; since the victory of the University of Alexandria in the days of Clement and Origen, the Doctors of the church have worked steadily and devotedly on the project of emancipating Christianity from all traces of the old eschatological teachings, and they have dealt most severely with those fanatical sects which from time to time have attempted to revive them. The official position of the Fathers, once they had taken the measure of the primitive Christian teachings, was that the only

sound doctrine was that which the trained intelligence of
educated men could give the Church. Just as the scientific
fraternity disclaimed any concern with eschatology and then
gravitated towards it as the needle to the pole, so the religious, claiming exclusive concern *with* the eschatological message of the scriptures, employed all their skill and authority
to *de*-eschatologize that message, paralyzing all the eschatology
in the Bible with powerful injections of tropism, allegory,
and all the other subtle drugs and devices of the schools. The
church and eschatology were mortal enemies![27]

The Christian Doctors put all their faith in the combination of Scripture and Intellect—*tertium non datur*. No scientists were ever more skillful or determined in preventing the
intrusion of extraneous, incalculable or other-worldly elements into the neatness and precision of their thinking; nay,
as Arnold Lunn has boasted, they excluded even experimen-
tal science from their studies in the interest of preserving
perfect rational consistency. The recent reprinting of Martin
Grabmann's big *History of the Scholastic Method* is a timely
reminder that the Roman Church has always been committed to that method, which is simply the application of science to the Scriptures. When ancient, medieval, and modern
theologians speak of revelation in the church they are referring simply to the Scriptures: the Bible *is* God's revelation to
man, and the true doctrine is that which is derived from the
Scriptures by a sound and instructed intelligence following
correct and recognized rules of logic. In his first volume
Grabmann never tires of reminding us that while we do not
need any more revelation than the Scriptures, we do need
trained minds, established authority, and above all a soundly
reasoned "scientific" method in order to understand it cor-
rectly.[28]

But here is a strange state of things indeed, for as we
have noted, science is singularly unsuited for dealing with
matters of eschatology which are ostensibly the first concern
of religion. In swearing allegiance to the Scientific Method

the churchmen had to forswear eschatology, and they did it with a will. They could not, of course, eliminate the Bible, but they could give it the Old School Treatment. It is significant that it is the intellectuals of the church who have always insisted on the apparently fundamentalist doctrine of a complete, perfect, final, and unalterable Bible; R. H. Charles can tell us why this is so: "God had, according to the official teachers of the Church, spoken His last and final word," and the policy of the doctors "so far as lay in its power, made the revival of such prophecy an impossibility."[29] The theory of complete, finished, and absolute scriptures was simply a door banged in the face of future prophets by the doctors. In a recent and important study Van Unnik has shown that until the third century the Christians had no objection whatever to the idea "that someone might still add revelations to the writings of the Gospel."[30] There was originally no moral objection or mystic principle barring the production of more scriptures whenever God should see fit to reveal them; it was only when "the Church believed that the time of Revelation and *therefore* also the time of bringing forth new holy scriptures had come to an end with the Apostolic Age," that the expectation of more holy writings was discouraged and condemned.[31] After that it was to the interest of the scholars to cry out with alarm at any suggestion of going beyond the Bible and the human mind.

There are just two sources of revelation, the Roman Catholic Church declares: "No other source of [public] revelation exists except the canonical books and the apostolic tradition."[32] The Protestants go even further: "We believe . . . that the sole rule and standard according to which all dogmas together with all teachers should be estimated and judged are the prophetic and apostolic Scriptures of the Old and New Testaments alone."[33] So an eminent Protestant divine declares today: "I boldly assert, therefore, that God does not

speak today because of the supreme character of His revelation of Himself made once for all in His Christ. . . . We
must . . . recognize His voice in his *final written Word.*"[34]

But just as scientists insist that the evidence speaks for
itself, only to discover that it speaks with different voices to
different scientists, so those who maintain with Irenaeus,
that the Bible speaks its own message clearly, directly, and
unequivocally to all soon discover themselves in wild disagreement as to what it says. Vincent of Lerinum, author of
the famous Vincentian canon, notes that "although the canon
of the Scripture is complete, 'and of itself is sufficient and
more than sufficient for all things,' yet tradition is needed for
a proper *understanding* of the Scripture."[35] Already we are
questioning the vaunted self-sufficiency of the holy page to
convey its own message; yet the churchmen dare not change
their position, lest they lower the bars to revelation. But how
can they presume to add their comments and explanations to
the Bible, supplying that information without which, they
assure us, the holy Word cannot be understood, and at the
same time insist that they are adding nothing, but simply
letting the book speak for itself? Like the scientists, they are
not letting the evidence alone at all; they are officiously helping it to say the things they think it should say. But how,
short of revelation, will we ever know the real word of God?
That is a question that greatly exercised St. Hilary. "We are
quite aware," he says, "that most people think the mere sound
of the words or the letters are enough," but of course that
won't do: *Scripturae enim non sunt in legendo sunt, sed in
intelligando*—The Scriptures don't consist in what you read
but in what you understand.[36] But how can our weak intel-
lects, our *humana imbecillitas*, ever be sure of understanding
aright? Only by revelation, is Hilary's sensible conclusion.[37]

Now surely the fat is in the fire, but Hilary deftly snatches
it out again by defining revelation as the reading of the
Scriptures "not as men interpret it, but as it is," with no private human opinions allowed to color or distort it, and "no

human interpretation stepping an inch beyond the bounds of what is divinely constituted."[38] Since our fatal weakness lies in our inability to interpret the Word of God, Hilary will simply dispense with all interpretation and read the Word as it is. But the same Hilary has just announced that the Scripture is not as you read it but as you understand it; on what ground, then, would *he* interpret it? He is good enough to tell us: our "revelation" should be founded on right reason, good historical knowledge, and a sense of correct doctrine.[39] To this day the clergy have never been able to solve the problem of how to enjoy inspired guidance while renouncing all claim to revelation.[40] "The Word of God," writes E. C. Blackman, "is in the words of the Bible, but is not to be identified with them . . . but interpreted out of them. . . . The Bible is not itself revelation but is the record of revelation."[41]

Interpreted, but how? Well might the Catholics challenge the Protestant position with the argument: "The Bible is a difficult book, it is full of dark places and apparent inconsistencies. How do you Protestants think you can manage without the authoritative guidance of the Church when you come to interpret it and to build doctrine upon it?"[42] To which the proper answer is: "How do you Catholics think you have solved the difficult problem of interpretation simply by agreeing (after centuries of hot debate) on *who* is to do the interpreting, without the vaguest idea of how he is to do it, apart from the normal fallible processes of human intelligence?" For Catholic theologians often repeat St. Augustine's lament that "men of the most outstanding piety and wisdom very often disagree in their interpretation of the Scriptures."[43]

We have noted above that Augustine knew of no higher court of appeal; but even in much later times "the medieval mind, indeed, was much perplexed by the possibility of error in the interpretation of the will of God."[44] At present Catholic journals are full of articles on "The Inerrancy of the Scripture," "The Consequent Sense of the Scripture," "The

Sensus Plenior of Scripture," etc., with one scholar asking, Do the Scriptures "perhaps contain a deeper meaning expressed by God and left to the ingenuity of the human mind to detect?"[45] And another proving that Genesis 3:5 refers to Mary with the observation: "The text, if paraphrased, reads simply enough, once cleared of the unnecessary accretions which have been read into it."[46] Here we see both the ultimate appeal to the human intellect and the way it is answered—by a critic who removes from the text what annoys him personally and then proves his case by paraphrasing what is left. Aquinas insisted that the Bible is "the only sure and binding authority. But one uses the authority of canonical scripture properly and in arguing from necessity,"[47] that is, by employing the old techniques of the schools. St. Thomas warns us especially against getting any fancy ideas about revelation: "For our faith rests upon the revelation given to the apostles and prophets who wrote the canonical books, but *not* upon revelation, if such there were, given to other teachers."[48] It is learned, not inspired, exegesis, which is recognized: "In the philosophical interpretation of its eschatological hope," an eminent Catholic theologian has very recently written, "Christian theology from the very beginning clings to Aristotle."[49] Aristotle was not a prophet, but a scientist; what would a pagan professor know about the "eschatological hope"?

A French Protestant scholar reminds us that in the Middle Ages there were so many legitimate ways of interpreting the Scriptures that they really meant nothing at all—since they could mean anything you pleased—and boasts that it was the Reformation "which was to give its objectivity and its dignity back to the sacred text."[50] But that was no solution to the problem of interpretation, as the rapid multiplication of conflicting Protestant sects demonstrated, and today the words of a leading Protestant theologian are strangely reminiscent of Hilary: "The Bible has to be interpreted from its own centre. It is not concentric with Aristotle, as Roman

theology posits, nor with modern rationalism, as theological
liberalism has assumed. . . . It . . . authenticates itself . . .
to the man who comes in faith and prays for the inward witness of the Holy Spirit."[51] The old double-talk again: it authenticates *itself*, but it does *not* authenticate itself—a higher
authority is needed, "the inward witness of the Holy Spirit."
Why not break down and call it revelation?

Today there is cautious but unmistakable edging toward
an acceptance of the long-forbidden idea of modern revelation. This has followed upon a growing realization that the
Bible alone is not enough. The Apostles, we are now being
told, had no intention of writing all their knowledge down in
a book; what they did write "was only meant to complement
the spoken word: they had no intention of supplanting it."[52]
Furthermore, what they wrote was meant for the initiated
alone and may never be deciphered by the learning of men.[53]
They wrote, moreover, with no idea of canonicity in mind:
"The idea that any book was written with the conscious purpose of securing a place in the sacred corpus," says Rowley,
"rests on the most unreal conception of the process of
canonization."[54] Nay, the New Testament, we now learn,
was only a sort of substitute for living witnesses and for a
long time remained a very plastic document.[55] So today we
find Catholic and Protestant scholars agreeing that "the inadequacy of the doctrine of the inerrancy of Scripture has demonstrated itself"—that favorite official doctrine of Protestant
and Catholic alike!—"It is too narrow to fit the facts; it cannot be carried through in the exegesis of Scripture without
resorting to special pleading; it does not explain the admitted
imperfection of the Old Testament; it involves a materialistic
notion of the truth. Above all, in being a negative word, it is
quite inadequate to express the glory of the revelation of
God in the Scripture."[56] But even if the Scriptures were inerrant, where is their inerrant interpreter? That is the question,
and D. M. Mackay assures us that we won't find it among
the scholars or scientists when he writes: "Our position, then,

in attempting to make any comprehensive or systematic statement about God, is logically very insecure. It is just no good
quoting a series of inspired scriptures and then supposing
that the guarantee of inspiration will extend infallibly to all
our apparently logical deductions from them."[57] Yet such is
the fundamental thesis of scholasticism, and scholasticism is
the way of the Doctors.

The dilemma of the Doctors is that while they must
renounce eschatology in order to qualify as scientists and
scholars, they cannot as people with curious minds leave it
alone, nor as human beings can they live without it.

32

The Return of the Prophets?

Some years ago in a series of articles in the *Improvement Era* this writer sifted the jewels of anti-Mormon literature to determine what specific charges have been brought against Joseph Smith and the Mormons in the past.[1] From the very first the searcher in this field is aware of a singular lack of variety and imagination in the accusations, all of which can be readily reduced to one standard indictment, monotonously repeated and mechanically transmitted from one writer to the next: the crime of believing in continuous revelation. Claims to the possession of prophetic powers, to exclusive knowledge of the true Gospel and the Priesthood that goes with it and to all the other charismatic gifts, are simply corollaries of the basic proposition that God still speaks to men. Since the attitude of the Christian churches toward the reality of revelation is undergoing a radical transformation at the present time, it is in order to point out here and now that for over a century the Mormons have been assailed from all sides for the sole unforgiveable sin of having prophets to lead them.

Let us cite a few of the most eminent critics of Mormonism, beginning with E. D. Howe (1840), who declared it his mission to rescue his "worthy fellow citizens [who] have been seduced by the witcheries and mysterious necromancies of Smith and his colleagues, from the paths of wisdom and truth, into folly and madness." "It is not your *peculiar opinions*, as you well know," wrote Professor Turner (1842) to Joseph Smith, "but your *impious pretentions*, which honest

and Christian men reject, with loathing and abhorrence."
And Thomas Gregg (1890) declares that the acceptance of
the Book of Mormon "as a Revelation from God to man, is
indeed a moral phenomenon unparalleled in the nineteenth
century," whose effect "is to eschew holiness and goodness,
and to dethrone the Almighty." "No argument, or mode of
reasoning," John Reynolds (1855) asserts, "could induce anyone to believe that in the nineteenth century, in the United
States, and in the blaze of science, literature, and civilization, a sect of religionists could arise on *delusion* and
imposition."[2]

   A learned author in the first volume of the *American
Anthropologist* (1899) informed the scientific world that while
there is not a single immoral teaching in the Book of Mormon, it is nonetheless a deadly menace, since "its adherents
have discovered a most dangerous weapon against the moral
world in the doctrine of '*a continuing revelation*' . . . a portentous danger sign to enlightened civilization."[3] In what has
often been called the first really scientific study of Mormonism, W. E. Linn (1901) advises students to read the Book of
Mormon "rather as a means of proving the fraudulent character of its pretention to divine revelation than as a means of
ascertaining what the members of the Mormon church are
taught."[4] The Fallows (1903) settled the issue once and for all
by asking, "What sane person can believe that this man really
believed that a glorious angel came from God and revealed
to him the hiding place of these golden plates?"—a question
later echoed by Professor La Rue: "How could three rational
men address 'all nations, kindreds, tongues and people,' and
say that God had told them that these plates had been 'translated by the gift and power of God'?"[5] Professor Meinhold
(1954), though obviously impressed and disturbed by the
Book of Mormon, will not even consider the question of its
authenticity, since, he says, "to presume to believe on the
existence of the 'golden plates,' is in spite of the witnesses,
simply unthinkable (*unerhört*)."[6]

In 1833 a large and important public meeting expressed
vivid alarm at the thought of admitting to government men
who are so ignorant and superstitious as to believe that they
"have been the subjects of miraculous and supernatural cures;
hold converse with God and his angels, and possess and
exercise the gifts of divination and of unknown tongues."[7]
And shortly after, the Honorable Judge Rydland "addressed
the Mormons, warning them against the danger of suffering
themselves to be led by pretenders to the high prerogatives
of the Prophets of God."[8] Charles Dickens (1851) neatly dis-
patched Mormonism with the devastating comment "seeing
visions in an age of railways!"[9] In 1898 the League for Social
Service, under the direction of such immortal idealists as
Washington Choate, Jane Addams, Margaret Sanger, and
the Reverend Edward Everett Hale, issued a declaration which
had already been passed by the leading churches of the land
under the title of *Ten Reasons Why Christians Cannot Fellowship the Mormon Church*. The document disclaims any
objections to Mormons on social, political, or moral grounds,
and insists that "the question is purely a religious question."
The first five reasons are the most important: 1) That Mormons claim that they alone have the true Gospel, 2) that
"their so-called revelations of the present are put on the same
level with the Bible," 3) that they regard "Joseph Smith as a
prophet of God," 4) that their priesthood alone has "authority to officiate in the gospel," being "invested with the very
power of God himself," 5) that the Mormon concept of God
is "dishonoring to the Divine Being and debasing to man."[10]

That will do for a sampling of Mormon perversity. But
what is the situation in the churches today? A revenant from
just twenty years ago reading the present-day journals of
religion—Catholic, Protestant, and Jewish—could hardly
believe his eyes. Everywhere he would see evidence of a growing interest in revelation and a deepening suspicion that even
the intelligence of this enlightened age is not up to handling
the ultimate problems of religion. Typical is the confused

though resounding declaration of H. A. Kelly: "I boldly assert, therefore, that God does not speak today," because we have "His final written word," which renders it "impossible that He should ever speak again." There Mr. Kelly should stop, but he does not; he goes on to specify that God will never "speak again more clearly, more positively, or more directly" than he has in the Bible; and after leaving the door thus open for God to speak again after all, provided only he doesn't do it *more* clearly than he already has, Mr. Kelly proceeds to go through it himself: "I do affirm . . . that He does to-day speak indubitably to the hearts of men in each succeeding generation as He never spake of old."[11] So now God speaks but he doesn't speak. The men of old who spake with him face to face didn't, of course, know what it meant to have God speak to them in their hearts—that is a prerogative, as the doctors of the church often remind us, reserved for the cultivated Christian of a better-educated generation,[12] and Professor Enslin can hail Clement of Alexandria "as a man who prized brain and insight, who preferred the voice of reasoned conviction to the braying of Balaam's ass."[13] "No new prophetic or apostolic testimony is to be expected," writes Dr. Bromiley, but like Kelly he too is careful to leave the door open as he adds: "But since their works [i.e., the Bible] are written in the Spirit, they must also be read in the Spirit if they are to accomplish their primary function. . . . In other words, the minds and hearts of the readers must be enlightened by the same Spirit by whom the writings themselves were inspired."[14]

Plainly (after due lip service to the party line) the intellect of an enlightened age is not enough—a new ingredient is being subtly introduced into the recipe. An eminent Lutheran scholar assures us that it is high time to give up the illusion of pure objectivity in our religious studies,[15] but the question is, what is to take its place? "Can we be open-minded and deeply committed? Can we be religious and intelligent? Can God be 'Wholly Other' and *Our* God?"[16] It is too late in

the day to report Professor Schilpp to the League for Social
Service for dishonoring God and debasing man with such
questions; even the skeptical Professor Rowley now smiles at
our naive confidence in the scholarly method: "It has always
seemed to me curious that these 'students of prophecy,' as
they are often called, are firmly persuaded that by the exercise of their ingenuity they can break the seal which is on
these books, and lay bare their secrets."[17] Some, like N.
Ferré, are even blurting out the ultimate admission: "Liberalism was the voice of secular confidence in science, education
and culture. It accommodated its claims to fit human expectations. Certainly it was grounded in man's general experience and best thought. But for this reason it failed to find
wings. Theological accommodation is a parasite dependent
on its host. It dies with its host. Liberalism is dead, or dying,
as secular confidence wanes."[18] Up until now, this "theological accommodation" has been the rule in the churches, which
have constantly adjusted their teachings to the learning of
the times. "The result of the continued repetition of this
undignified retreat, during many generations," wrote
Whitehead, "has at last almost entirely destroyed the intellectual authority of religious thinkers."[19] The so-called "neo-
Orthodoxy" has sought to avoid this disastrous accommodation by cutting religion loose from all that is concrete and
literal, leaving it worse off than ever, as one critic notes,
"flounder[ing] in the abyss of irrationalism and sub-
jectivism,"[20] ignoring (says another) the inescapable fact "that
the original Chrisitianity was a very concrete quantity."[21]

    With the realization that "mere inwardness" and "cul-
tural optimism" are not enough[22] comes the discovery that
the Gospel is more than an Ethical Gospel, and the Scriptures more than a beautiful allegory. Today scholars smile
indulgently at the naive "Social Gospel" of a few years back,
the product, says F. C. Grant, of the "too sanguine, too
puerile views" of the early decades of the century.[23] Not
only have "liberal social ethics" proved hopelessly unstable,

but as a writer in *Harper's* reminds us, "the clergy have failed to furnish the nation with moral leadership."[24] The doctors have known all along that the Christianity they have been preaching differs radically from that of the primitive church, and have congratulated themselves, Catholic and Protestant alike, on their emancipation from the ignorance and superstition of the Early Christians.[25] But today many are asking, How can we call ourselves Christians if we don't believe what the original Christians believed? "Can we repudiate what he [Christ] embraced?"[26] If not we must prepare to face the verdict, as C. S. Lewis puts it: "Either this man was, and is, the Son of God: or else a madman or something worse. . . . But don't let us come with any patronizing nonsense about His being a great human teacher. He hasn't left that open to us."[27]

Open or not, that is the way the doctors have taken, and now they are brought up with a start: "The rediscovery of the importance of eschatology within the New Testament has been one of the most outstanding achievements of historic theology. It is also one of the factors which has led to a new understanding of the New Testament Church; we have learned to see the Church as an 'eschatological community.' "[28] That is a revealing statement by a first-rate scholar; it tells us that the original Christianity definitely was eschatological, and that subsequent Christianity has definitely NOT been—the great secret had to be rediscovered in our own time. The two things that have ever rendered eschatology odious to the intellectuals have been 1) its literalism and 2) its supernaturalism. They can accept the supernatural—if they don't have to take it literally; and they can be literal enough, provided one omits the supernatural. It is the combination of the two that is necessary to genuine eschatology. E. G. Selwyn reminds us that we might as well admit this and reconcile ourselves to the use of words like "supernatural" and "transsubjective"— "though the scientific naturalist . . . may boggle at them, they are indispensable."[29]

J. Rowland traces back to about 1944 this new drift to literalism, and reports that "in the place which may be regarded as the home of modern science—the University of Cambridge—recent statistics show that the most popular religion is a sheerly fundamentalist religion."[30] That we should live to see the day! "When literal meaning is brushed aside as poetic license," writes no less an Old Testament scholar than Cyrus Gordon, "in order to make room for predilection, prejudice, theory, or outside parallels, the results are bad."[31] There is a strong trend towards vindicating the literal histories of both the Old and New Testaments; Professor Albright notes that the peculiar strength and virtue of the Judaeo-Christian religion lay in its historical (as against spiritual) orientation, and demonstrates this by pointing to the Book of Mormon as the prize example of the old historical orientation.[32]

Scholars who a few years ago laughed at the idea of a literal return of Christ now accept it as the only way to avoid "having to contort his message, ignoring a considerable portion of it and making unwarranted deductions from the other parts, to suit our preconceptions."[33] Even the idea of a literal temple is viewed today without the horror and loathing once bestowed on so crass and unspiritual a concept.[34] Indeed, it is not literalism but the old weakness of "spiritualizing" everything that is now coming in for criticism, as when Dr. G. C. Berkouwer writes: "We speak rather glibly about the self-evidence of the Gospel; we talk about the *sword* of the Spirit. But we do not entertain the expectation that something is actually going to happen by the power of the Spirit."[35] This concern with power is an interesting thing, and K. Prümm points out that the real power of God is never dissociated from revelation, while there can be no real authority in the church without both.[36] The heretofore unlimited license of the clergy to play around with words is now being curtailed, and Oscar Cullman questions our right

"in interpreting the first Christian documents" to "make mythical and timeless what they regarded to be real and
temporal."[37] "It is not the New Testament that needs to be
demythologized," writes Anders Nygren, turning the tables,
"but our modern conception of Christianity."[38] "False," says
a leading Orientalist, "is the spiritualization of Old Testament ideas in the interest of their better utilization for religious purposes."[39] Professor McCasland still wants it both
ways as he calls for "the application of reason to historical
evidence" as a means of abolishing belief in miracles and all
such "outmoded concepts of ancient peoples," but in the
same breath laments the "pernicious anemia" that "secular
naturalism" has produced on our campuses.[40] But the forthright Professor Burrows cries: "I do not want my eschatology
de-eschatologized!"[41] If he is serious he will have to take
along with the Bible a lot of unpopular things that come in
the eschatological package.

He will have to accept the ancient gifts of the Spirit—
tongues, healing, prophecy, and the rest—which are always
supposed to have passed away with the Apostles. Protestants
and Catholics are expressing a need for those gifts today
with increasing boldness.[42] A leading Episcopal journal even
hails with delight the report that "*glossolalia* (speaking in
tongues) has appeared in the Episcopal Church, of all bodies,"
and protests that to curtail such gifts "is to impoverish a
faith to which they inalienably belong."[43] The most prized
gift of all, because the most necessary, is revelation, and it is
truly astonishing to see the frequency of articles on the subject in all the leading religion periodicals today. "The return
to ideas of inspiration and revelation," writes McCasland,
"may be put down as one of the marked trends of our biblical scholarship of the last decade."[44] Bromiley even holds
that "the doctrine of inspiration continues to be in many
ways the critical issue underlying all other issues in the
Church today."[45] Nay, according to H. D. McDonald, "the

fundamental question of all theological reconstructions is 'What do we mean by revelation?' "[46]

Naturally the more cautious churchmen have sought to modify the implications of the new trend to revelation by giving revelation its old intellectual definitions, such as the "deeper meaning . . . left to the ingenuity of the human mind."[47] And while Father Herbert and E. Blackman both call for a "truer, richer understanding of the nature of revelation," both agree that such "can only be reached by going through what sometimes seems to be the weary desert of critical inquiry."[48] Revelation still belongs to the seminary and the university, and Augustine and Anselm still give the official definition of it. According to them we can never know God as he is; we can only know analogies to him; this means (and we are following Grabmann) that "it is the rationally endowed mind alone that has the capacity to achieve a concept of the Divine. At the same time the rational mind is the image of God: therefore the more it contemplates its own nature the better it understands God. The human mind is its own mirror in which it beholds that which it cannot see face to face."[49] Anselm defines truth as "that rightness which is perceptible only to the mind." Anselm's famous Ontological Argument Grabmann calls "the expression of a mind convinced of the omnipotence of Philosophy," a mind that "eliminated religion, revelation, and faith from the realm of reason, thought and knowing, because he was convinced of the power of unaided reason, holding fast to the infallible fundamentals of metaphysics, to discover the solution . . . which he held possible and which he sought for on the grounds of pure intellect."[50] And this man is the Father of Scholasticism, the official theology of the Roman Church.

But the religious of today are not satisfied with the old intellectual definitions. "Behind these modern ideas of revelation," says McDonald, "stand a deliberate renunciation of the 'traditional' doctrine and a departure from what the Church has from the first believed concerning special revelation."[51] That is pretty strong, but A. Van den Born gives us no hope of escape: "Of course it is highly discouraging that not a single aspect of biblical prophetism can be explained by means of our western rationalism and psychologism, but so matters are situated and we shall have to submit to it."[52] Our current theology, B. M. Reardon assures us, insists upon "objective" revelation. Revelation, we are told, is something more than the progressive self-realization of Spirit in history; nor is it the mere embodiment of a capacity rooted in human nature itself.[53]

The return to eschatology has meant a revived interest in prophecy, for as many recent studies have announced, prophecy and eschatology are inseparable, since "religion involves essentially the element of prediction."[54] By prophecy we no longer mean merely pious utterances or moral platitudes but specific predictions of things to come: "That the prophets were not merely preachers of righteousness, but foretellers of the future, is plain to every reader," says the leading student of ancient prophetic literature.[55] For the ancient Jews " 'Holiness means nothing else than prophecy' "—"a gift from heaven bestowed upon man by an act of grace."[56] After the loss of the prophetic gift, the Jews were left with a mere echo, the Wisdom of the Doctors, the bath-qol, which "was far from being equivalent to the word of the Lord which came to the prophets of old: it was only a poor substitute left to Israel after prophecy had ceased."[57] "In Jesus' day there were no Jewish prophets. For the Jew the return of the prophetic spirit was inextricably related to the messianic times. . . . The term 'prophet' had become an eschatological term."[58] It was Christianity, R. H. Charles has shown, that restored the lost gift of prophecy, and thereby enraged the Doctors of the Jews— the scribes and Pharisees,[59] but the Christian schoolmen soon got rid of it,[60] and it was, as we have seen, the return of that gift that brought the curses of the Christian world upon the heads of the Mormons.

Yet today Christian ministers are asking with straight faces: "Why not Prophetic Apocalyptic?" "The Silence of God: How is it to be explained?" and reminding us that "if Christianity is, as it were, congenitally prophetic, the prophetic charisma [gift] must always have existed in some authentic form among Christians."[61] God's people must always and necessarily be "the bearers of revelation," E. Käsemann has discovered,[62] and W. C. Klein reminds us that "Christianity must always be pneumatic, but it cannot be exclusively pneumatic."[63] Who said it must be? The Mormons were attacked for being "pneumatic" at all, but at the same time vigorously ridiculed for being intensely practical in a sphere as "spiritual" as religion. Anyway, Protestants are proud now of "the Rediscovery of the prophetic Tradition in the Reformation,"[64] and Jewish and Catholic writers assure us that their churches have never really denied the gift of Prophecy.[65]

Along with the "rediscovery of the importance of eschatology in the New Testament" has gone what Bornkamm called "the present day rediscovery of the Church by the Protestants."[66] After long debate on the merits of "office" versus "inspiration," the scholars came to a consensus that viewed the Christian church as an inspired organization whose leaders were chosen by revelation and led the church by the power of prophecy.[67] Even the Catholics have moved in this direction, and A. Ehrhardt claims that in basing the "succession of her bishops upon the succession of the High Priests of Israel since Aaron," his church "claims for herself also the prophetic Spirit of Ancient Israel."[68] When Haupt affirms that "only the Charisma [the gift of the Spirit] has any real authority in the Church,"[69] we must ask him where he locates that authority. As Tertullian long ago insisted, you cannot claim to have spiritual gifts simply because you hold an office—you must first show that the gifts are there; then you can talk about office![70] Christians, who up until now have deplored the evil doctrine of "dispensationism," now clamor to identify themselves with ancient Israel: "The question *Who is Israel?* stands at the frontier where the question is asked *Who is Jesus?*" writes the historian Muilenberg,[71] and according to T. W. Manson, "the deepest instinct of the early Church, as of our Lord himself, was to insist on the continuity of the Christian movement with the previous history of Israel."[72] And so we are now being told that the church is *Versus Israel*, whose right it is to "Inherit the Promise" and make "The Ascent to Zion."[73] The two basic ideas which Christianity took over from the Jews, according to the celebrated Eduard Schwartz, were the idea of God's Chosen People and the possession of the Spiritual gifts, the two being inseparably joined.[74] Yet if the reader will take the trouble to look back a few pages, he will discover that it was for claiming the validity of these two heritages that the Mormons were formally ostracized by the churches of America.

After centuries preaching the "once-for-all" story of the Redemption, the Christian world now wants to bring old Israel back onto the stage again! What next? Why, the Apostles, to be sure—Christ's Church should have real Apostles, not just Bishops with dubious credentials, but a real "quorum of Twelve made present in the Church."[75] J. G. Davies addresses himself to the problem of Apostolic succession by noting that even if the establishing of a historical "pipe-line" right back to the Apostle could be achieved it would not necessarily establish the authority of any modern church, since "authorization may be withdrawn,"—and who could prove that in the course of the centuries it has not been withdrawn? No group, says Davies, "can be said to possess it in its wholeness," it (Apostolic succession) "is not preserved unimpaired by anyone." Since everybody's credentials are full of holes, and since we cannot know just who has how much authority, the best we can do, Davies suggests, is to pool all the authority we have: "The ministers of the one would have to receive authorization from those of the other and vice versa if any reunion . . . were to be effected."[76] But must there be just *one* church? There must: "To preserve continuity, catholicity and stability in the Church, notably in matters of Christian doctrine, some authority there must be. . . . Unhappily, so much misunderstanding, prejudice and confusion still exists in all denominations, that something more is needed than argument."[77] The reader need hardly be reminded that the most damning charge brought against the Mormons by the League for Social Service was their belief that there could be only one true church.

Today churchmen are writing long articles on "Steps to Revival" and "Church Renewal";[78] today Professor Cadbury declares that "the Church is seeking for authority which will have the sanction of history and which thus will render a service towards providing a norm for modern interdenominational unity."[79] We seek authority. Where? In history. In whose history? In our history. And who authorizes that history? We do. And where do we get that authority? From history. "The ultimate problem, I suppose, is one of authority, the authority of revelation, the authority of Scripture, the authority of the church," writes R. M. Grant, who admits that nobody knows yet where that authority is to be found, and desperately asks: "Is there a way out?"[80] If one dares to claim revelation, it follows, as Bultmann points out, that one must claim to have the only true church, since revelation is necessarily *the* truth.[81] Accordingly, with the "rediscovery of the 'church,' Christians," so Pauck informs us, "have come to realize that . . . they represent a minority. . . . They have been compelled to understand themselves again, like their predecessors of old, as a 'peculiar people.' "[82] O those awful Mormons, pretending to be the only true church! "After centuries of dispute," writes one distracted scholar, "questions persist concerning . . . what religion is the true religion, its true content, and the true interpretation of that content. It is as if the question had no real answers. . . . Yet the religious life depends on there being answers."[83]

It is because "it claims to be a final revelation," someone now suggests, that Christianity "does seem to mark the end of the religious road which Western Man has trod during his recorded history."[84] The intellectual search seems to have reached its limits and led nowhere—it is the "search for the historical Jesus who turns out to be either a deluded apocalyptist or the product of early Christian reinterpretation."[85] Marenck's question, "How can we have a religion for people who are convinced that we can never know anything about the other world?" has been answered: We can't![86] In the palmy days before the War, men could live comfortably with a religion of nonreligion and cry triumphantly with Dr. Wingren: "Eschatology has no more power over us!"[87] Back in the 1920's Bevan could write: "The skies, as far as the utmost star, are clear of any malignant Intelligences, and even the untoward accidents of life are due to causes comfortably impersonal. We have never been thoroughly frightened. . . . The possibility that the Unknown contains Powers deliberately hostile to him is one the ordinary modern man can hardly entertain even in imagination."[88] And in 1925 Whitehead wrote: "[The] appeal to the ready instinct of brute fear is losing its force. It lacks any directness of response, because modern science and modern conditions of life have taught us to meet occasions of apprehension by a critical analysis of their causes and conditions. . . . The old phraseology is at variance with the psychology of modern civilization."[89] This is exactly what Dr. Hippocrates said in his paper on the Sacred Diseases twenty-four centuries ago. Such happy people did not need the gospel; it never occurred to them that it was God who was supporting them on the narrow margin of nothing, sustaining their life from moment to moment. For them there was no mind beyond man's, and man's mind, of course, reached its peak of perfection in the scientist: the pleasing creed of the doctors for centuries was (and this is neither exaggeration nor sarcasm) that their minds were literally the greatest force in all the boundless expanse of the universe. Who would want to give up a creed like that?

But at last some of us *have* been thoroughly frightened. It is only the older men whose days have been spent in the quiet shelter of ivy halls and academic tenure who still assure us that it is useless to seek further than their offices for the answers to the questions of life. But a new generation of scholars can discuss without a blush or a snicker the present need for revelation, and survey with straight faces the possibility of a return of the prophets. Surely, "we have seen strange things today."

Notes

Key to Abbreviations

PG   J.-P. Migne, *Patrologiae Cursus Completus . . . Series Graeca* (Paris: J.-P. Migne, 1857–1866), 161 volumes.

PL   J.-P. Migne, *Patrologiae Cursus Completus . . . Series Latina* (Paris: J.-P. Migne, 1844–1864), 221 volumes.

Note: More recent and serviceable editions of the texts found in *PG* and *PL* are becoming available in *Corpus Christianorum, Series Graeca* (Turnhout, Belgium: Brepols, 1977–); *Series Latina* (1954–).

Foreword

1. See below, ch. 7.

2. Maurice Wiles, *The Making of Christian Doctrine* (Cambridge: Cambridge University Press, 1967), 33.

Chapter 1

1. Stobaeus, *Eclogue* III, 9, 23: Solon. The text is given in Ivan M. Linforth, *Solon the Athenian* (Berkeley: University of California Press, 1919), 166–67.

2. Pindar, *Olympian Odes* XII, 5–9.

3. This is the closing chorus of *Oedipus the King* by Sophocles, lines 1524–30.

4. No less than five plays of Euripides end with these lines. They are the *Alcestis, Medea, Andromache, Helena,* and *Bacchae.*

5. Justin Martyr, *Cohortatio ad Graecos* 8, in *PG* 6:256–57.

6. Justin Martyr, *Dialogue with Trypho* 82, in *PG* 6:669.

7. Origen, *Contra Celsum* II, 8, in *PG* 11:805–8.

8. *Epistle of Barnabas* 4; cf. 14.

9. Kirsopp and Silva Lake, *An Introduction to the New Testament* (New York: Harper, 1937), 62.

Chapter 2

1. Justin Martyr, *Dialogue with Trypho* 7, in *PG* 6:492.
2. *Clementine Recognitions* I, 3, in *PG* 1:1208.
3. Ibid., I, 15–16, in *PG* 11:1214–15.
4. Origen, *Peri Archon* I, 1, 5, in *PG* 11:124.
5. Tertullian, *De Anima* 2, in *PL* 2:689–91.
6. *Clementine Recognitions* I, 32–33, in *PG* 1:1226–27.
7. Ibid., I, 16, in *PG* 1:1215.
8. *Jeffersonian Republican*, Missouri, August 17, 1833. Other accounts of the meeting and resolution, differently, but more vehemently worded in the *Missouri Intelligencer and Boon's [sic] Lick Advertiser* for August 10, 1833, and *History of Missouri* (St. Louis, 1876), 105. Here, incidentally, is a reference to Joseph Smith's first vision ten years before that story is supposed, by Arbaugh and others, to have been invented in Nauvoo.
9. Charles Dickens, "In the Name of the Prophet—Smith!" *Household Words* (July 19, 1851): 385 (emphasis added).

Chapter 3

1. Origen, *Contra Celsum* I, 27, in *PG* 11:713.
2. Ibid., I, 32, in *PG* 11:721.
3. Eduard Meyer, *Ursprung und Geschichte der Mormonen* (Halle: Niemeyer, 1912), 68–75, quote on p. 69, n. 2; published also as *Origin and History of the Mormons*, trans. H. Rahde and E. Seaich (Salt Lake City: University of Utah Press, 1961), 44–49.
4. Ibid., 71, n. 1; 47, n. 1, in English translation.
5. Ibid., 80–81; 54 in English translation.
6. Ibid., 81–82; 55 in English translation.
7. Ibid., 82; 55 in English translation.
8. Ibid.; 55–56 in English translation.
9. Eduard Meyer, *Geschichte des Altertums* (Stuttgart: Cotta, 1944), 4:168, 170; see also (1937 edition), 3:113, n. 1.

Chapter 4

1. Justin Martyr, *Dialogue with Trypho* 7, in *PG* 6:492.
2. John A. Widtsoe, ed., *Discourses of Brigham Young* (Salt Lake City: Deseret, 1954), 38 (emphasis added).
3. Clementine (dubia), *Epistle of Peter to Jacob* 2, in *PG* 2:28.
4. Clement of Alexandria, *Stromata* I, in *PG* 8:704.
5. Eusebius, *Ecclesiastical History* III, 24, in *PG* 20:263–67.
6. Origen, *Contra Celsum* I, 62, in *PG* 11:773–78; III, 39–40, in *PG* 11:969–71; VIII, 47, in *PG* 11:1585–86.

Chapter 5

1. Etienne Gilson, *La philosophie au moyen âge* (Paris: Payot, 1944), 15.

2. Rufinus of Aquileia, *Preface* to *Clementine Recognitions*, in *PG* 1: 1205–7.

3. Robert M. Grant, *Second-Century Christianity* (London: SPCK, 1946), 10.

4. *Clementine Recognitions* I, 1–5, in *PG* 1, 1207–9.

5. Ibid., I, 4, in *PG* 1:1209.

6. Ibid., I, 7a–10, in *PG* 1:1210–12.

7. S. V. McCasland, " 'The Image of God' According to Paul," *Journal of Biblical Literature* 69 (1950): 95.

8. John Morris, "Early Christian Orthodoxy," *Past and Present* 3 (1953): 9–10.

9. Eusebius, *Ecclesiastical History* V, 28, 13–16, in *PG* 20:511.

10. C. N. Cochrane, *Christianity and Classical Culture* (London: Oxford University Press, 1944), 162.

11. Justin Martyr, *Apology* I, 59, in *PG* 6:416; II, 8, in *PG* 6:457; *Cohortatio ad Graecos* 32, in *PG* 6:300.

12. Irenaeus, *Contra Haereses* II, 14, in *PG* 7:750–52.

13. Tertullian, *De Praescriptionibus* 7, in *PL* 2:22.

14. Minucius Felix, *Octavius* 19–20, in *PL* 3:204–312.

15. Clement of Alexandria, *Stromata* I, 5, in *PG* 8:717, 720.

16. Walther Völker, *Der wahre Gnostiker nach Clemens Alexandrinus* (Leipzig: Hinrichs, 1952), 321.

17. The passage is given in Karl Heussi, *Kompendium der Kirchengeschichte*, 6th ed. (Tübingen: Mohr, 1928), 51.

18. Justin Martyr, *Cohortatio ad Graecos* 8, in *PG* 6:256–57.

19. Tatian, *Orationes* 3, in *PG* 6:812.

20. Minucius Felix, *Octavius* 5, in *PL* 3:251, paraphrased.

21. Tertullian, *De Spectaculis* 2, in *PL* 1:705, paraphrased.

22. Tatian, *Orationes* 3, in *PG* 6:812.

23. Hastings Rashdall, *The Universities of Europe in the Middle Ages* (Oxford: Clarendon, 1895).

24. Clement of Alexandria, *Cohortatio ad Gentes* II, in *PG* 8:229.

25. Irenaeus, *Contra Haereses* II, 7, in *PG* 7:754–55.

26. Tertullian, *De Anima* 2, in *PL* 2:689–91.

Chapter 6

1. Socrates, *Ecclesiastical History* I, 5–6, in *PG* 67:41.

2. Ibid., I, 7, in *PG* 67:56–57.

3. Ibid., I, 8, in *PG* 67:64.

4. Ibid., also citing Eusebius' letter, in *PG* 67:68, 72.

5. Ibid., under heading *Symbolum*, in *PG* 67:76.

6. Athanasius, *De Synodis*, in *PG* 26:684.

7. Ibid., in *PG* 26:688.

8. Ibid., in *PG* 26:689.

9. Ibid.

10. Ibid., in *PG* 26:760. This is the summary.

11. Hilary, *Epistle to Constantine* II, 4–5, in *PL* 10:566–67.

12. Ibid., II, 6, in *PL* 10:567–68.

13. Sozomen, *Ecclesiastical History* I, 18, in *PG* 67:917.

14. Hilary, II, 5, in *PL* 10:566–67.

15. Ibid., II, 6, in *PL* 10:568.

16. Ibid., II, 5, in *PL* 10:567.

Chapter 7

1. Rufus Jones, *Pathways to the Reality of God* (New York: Macmillan, 1936), vii.

2. Justin Martyr, *Dialogue with Trypho* I, in *PG* 6:473.

3. Ignatius, *Epistle to the Trallians* VI, in *PG* 5:679.

4. Ignatius, *Epistle to the Smyrnaeans* IV-VI, in *PG* 5:710–12.

5. *Apostolic Constitutions* VI, 10–11, in *PG* 1:954.

6. Irenaeus, *Contra Haereses* I, 2, in *PG* 7:451.

7. Origen, *Contra Celsum* IV-VI, in *PG* 11:1036.

8. Melito, *Fragmentum*, in *PG* 5:1230.

9. Hilary, *De Synodis* 63, in *PL* 10:522–23.

10. Lactantius, *De vero Cultu* 9, in *PL* 6:662.

11. Edward Gibbon, *The History of the Decline and Fall of the Roman Empire* (New York: Harper, 1836), 440–41.

12. Ignatius, *Liturgia*, in *PG* 5:969.

13. Basil, *Epistle* 16, in *PG* 32:280.

14. John Chrysostom, *De Incomprehensibili Dei Natura* II, 3, in *PG* 48:714; III:3–4, in *PG* 48:721, 723–25.

15. Michael Buchberger, *Lexikon für Theologie und Kirche* (Freiburg i/B: Herder, 1960), 4:1081, 9:599.

16. Arnold Lunn and John Haldane, *Science and the Supernatural: A Correspondence Between Arnold Lunn and J. B. S. Haldane* (New York: Sheed & Ward, 1935), 304, 314.

17. Hilary, *On the Trinity (De Trinitate)* IX, 71–73, X, 55, and XI, 67, in *PL* 10:338, 387, 395.

18. John Chrysostom, II, 2, in *PG* 48:710; see also 705–9.

19. Heinrich Denzinger, *Index Systematicus*, 19.

20. Thomas Aquinas, *Summa Theologica* (Turin: Marietti, 1932), Question I, Article ii (quoting Augustine, *De Trinitate*, XIV, 7, in *PL* 42: 1042–44).

21. Justin Martyr, *Dialogue with Trypho* III, in *PG* 6:481–84.

22. Karl Heussi, *Kompendium der Kirchengeschichte*, 6th ed. (Tübingen: Mohr, 1928), 34.

Chapter 8

1. Willem Cornelis van Unnik, Jan Waszink and C. De Beus, *Het oudste Christendom en de antieke Cultuur* (Haarlem: Tjeenk, Willink & Zoon, 1951), 2:84. The subtitle of vol. 2 is "Life and Thought of the Early Christian Church up to Irenaeus."

2. Eugene de Faye, *Gnostiques et Gnosticisme* (Paris: Ernest Leroux, 1913), 431.

3. Eusebius, *Ecclesiastical History* I, 1, in *PG* 20:48.

4. Kirsopp and Silva Lake, *An Introduction to the New Testament* (New York: Harper, 1937), 149.

5. Eusebius, II, 1, 4, in *PG* 20:136.

6. Thus, the so-called Testament in Galilee, the Pistis Sophia, the Gospel of the XII Apostles, the Apocalypse of Peter, the *Testamentum Domini Nostri (Testament of Our Lord)*, etc.

7. Eusebius, *Ecclesiastical History* III, 32, 7, in *PG* 20:283.

8. Ibid., IV, 7, in *PG* 20:315; Irenaeus, *Contra Haereses* I, 29, 1, in *PG* 7:691.

9. Walther Völker, *Der wahre Gnostiker nach Clemens Alexandrinus* (Leipzig: Hinrichs, 1952), 439–40.

10. Gilles Quispel, in *Het oudste Christendom en de antieke Cultuur* (Haarlem: Tjeenk, Willink & Zoon, 1951), 1:152.

11. Eusebius, *Ecclesiastical History* V, 16, in *PG* 20:464–72.

12. Paul Alphandery, "Le gnosticisme dans les sectes médiévales latines," *Revue d'histoire et de philosophie religieuses* 7 (1927): 395–411.

13. August Neander, *Antignostikus, Geist des Tertullianus* (Berlin: Dümmler, 1849), 5–6; R. A. Lipsius, *Der Gnosticismus, sein Wesen, Ursprung und Entwickelungsgang* (Leipzig: Brockhaus, 1860), 66.

14. Adolf Harnack, *Lehrbuch der Dogmengeschichte*, 3rd ed. (Freiburg: Mohr, 1894), 1:241.

15. Ibid., 241–43.

16. Irenaeus, *Contra Haereses* 2, preface, in *PG* 7:707–9.

Chapter 9

1. Augustine, *Confessions* I, 10, in *PL* 32:668.

2. F. Schemmel, "Die Hochschule von Athen im IV. und V. Jahrhunderten," *Neue Jahrbücher für das klassische altertum Geschichte und deutsche Literatur und für Pädagogik* (1908), 494–513; and "Die Hochschule von Alexandria in IV. und V. Jahrhunderten," ibid. (1909): 438–57; Albertus Müller, "Studentenleben im 4. Jahrhundert nach Christus," *Philologus* 69 (1910): 303ff.

3. Adolf Harnack, *Lehrbuch der Dogmengeschichte*, 3rd ed. (Freiburg: Mohr, 1894), 1:590.

4. Clement of Alexandria, *Stromata* I, 9, in *PG* 8:740–41; quote from 741.

5. Harnack, 601.

6. Ibid. The italics are Harnack's.

7. Ibid., 602.

8. Photius, *Bibliotheca* cix, in *PG* 103:383.

9. A good discussion in Friedrich Überweg, *Geschichte der Philosophie der patristischen und scholastischen Zeit* (Berlin, 1877), 64–65.

10. Harnack, 607–11.

11. Ibid., 601.

12. Cited in Überweg, 63.

13. Harnack, 650: "Origenes hat die kirchliche Dogmatik geschaffen."

14. Both authorities are cited in Carolus Delarue, *Preface* in *PG* 11:13.

15. The best life of Origen is in the *Ante-Nicene Christian Library* 23 (Origen, Vol. II), (Edinburgh: Clark, 1872), xiii–xxxviii.

16. Minucius Felix, *Octavius* 3, 16, 18, 19; quote is from 20, 34–36.

17. Origen, *Peri Archon* II, 4, 3, in *PG* 11:204.

18. Harnack, 612.

19. Origen, *Peri Archon* I, 2, in *PG* 11:115–16.

20. All these passages in the prologue of the *Peri Archon* I, 1–10, in *PG* 11:115–21.

21. Origen, I, 3, 3, in *PG* 11:148.

22. Ibid., II, 6, 2, in *PG* 11:210–11.

23. Ibid., II, 3, 4, 7, in *PG* 11:192–93, 197–98.

24. Ibid., II, 8, 4–5, in *PG* 11:224.

25. Ibid.

Chapter 10

1. Arthur McGiffert, *A History of Christian Thought* (New York: Scribner's, 1932–33), 2:124.

2. Martin Grabmann, *Mittelalterliches Geistesleben* (Munich: Max Hüber, 1936), 2:46, who quotes many authorities in praise of St. Augustine. (Translation by the author.)

3. George Coulton, *Studies in Medieval Thought* (London: Nelson, 1940), 24.

4. Ferdinand Lot, *La fin du monde antique et le début du moyen âge* (Paris: A. Michel, 1927/1951), 181 = *The End of the Ancient World and the Beginnings of the Middle Ages* (London: K. Paul, Trench & Trubner, 1931), 158.

5. Adolf Harnack, *Monasticism: Its Ideals and History, and the Confessions of St. Augustine* (London: Williams & Norgate, 1901), 125.

6. Grabmann, 2:45.

7. Ernst Troeltsch, *Augustin: Die christliche Antike und das Mittelalter*, Historische Bibliothek 36 (Munich: Oldenburg, 1915; reprinted New York: Arno, 1979), 50.

8. Augustine, *Confessions* III, 10, in *PL* 32:691.

9. Ibid., VII, 1, in *PL* 32:733, and *passim*.

10. Grabmann, 2:3-4.

11. Quoted in Ibid., 2:1.

12. Ibid., 2:13, citing Richard Reitzenstein.

13. Gustave Combès, *Saint Augustin et la culture classique* (Paris: Plon, 1927), 87.

14. Franz Eggersdorfer, *Der heilige Augustinus als Pädogoge und seine Bedeutung für die Geschichte der Bildung* (Freiburg i/B:Herder, 1907).

15. Combès, 127-28.

16. Louis Duchesne, *Early History of the Christian Church From Its Foundation to the End of the Fifth Century*, 3 vols., translated from the 4th French edition by C. Jenkins (London: J. Murray, 1909-24), 3:1.

17. Eduard Norden, *Die antike Kunstprosa* (Leipzig: Wissenschaftliche Buchgesellschaft, 1898), 2:623; Combès, 75; Frederick Raby, *A History of Christian-Latin Poetry* (Oxford: Clarendon, 1927), 7.

18. Henri Marrou, *Saint Augustin et la fin de la culture antique* (Paris: Boccard, 1938), 275, 517-18.

19. Duchesne, 3:3-4.

20. Arnold Lunn, *The Flight From Reason* (New York: Dial Press, 1931), 25.

21. Grabmann, 2:44.

Chapter 11

1. John 10:2-24.

2. Martin Grabmann, *Mittelalterliches Geistesleben* (Munich: Max Hüber, 1936), 2:51.

3. Coulton, *Studies in Medieval Thought* (London: Nelson, 1940), 34-37.

4. Gustave Combès, *Saint Augustin et la culture classique* (Paris: Plon, 1927), 102.

5. Augustine, *Confessions* VII, 12, in *PL* 32:743.

6. Etienne Gilson, *Introduction à l'étude de Saint Augustin* (Paris: J. Vrin, 1929), 294–95.

7. Augustine, *The City of God* XIX, 18, in *PL* 41:646.

8. Augustine, *Confessions* VII, 9, 20, 21, in *PL* 32:740, 746–48.

9. Augustine, *The City of God* VII, 35, in *PL* 41:223.

10. Ibid., IV, 3; VII, 6, in *PL* 41:114, 199–200.

11. Arthur McGiffert, *A History of Christian Thought*, 2 vols. (New York: Scribner's, 1933), 2:76.

12. Augustine, *Confessions* IX, 10, in *PL* 32:774–75. (Italics added.)

13. Louis Duchesne, *The Early History of the Church* (London: J. Murray, 1931), 2:521.

14. Ibid., 2:522.

15. Augustine, *Confessions* VI, 4, in *PL* 32:721. (Italics added.)

16. Ibid., VI, 5, in *PL* 32:722.

17. Ibid., VI, 11, in *PL* 32:729.

18. Ibid., VII, 1, in *PL* 32:733.

19. Ibid.

20. Ibid., VII, 9, in *PL* 32:741.

21. Ibid., VII, 18, in *PL* 32:746.

22. D. Thomasius, *Die Dogmengeschichte der alten Kirche* (Erlangen: Deichert, 1886), 1:281.

23. Ibid., p. 281, n. 2, and p. 282.

24. Ibid., 283.

25. Ibid., 283–88; the last passage is from *De Trinitate* V, 8; VII, 4, cited in ibid., p. 287, n. 3.

26. Ibid., 287.

27. Origen, *Epistle* 11, in *PL* 33:75–76.

28. Grabmann, 2:44.

29. Wilhelm Christ, *Geschichte der Grieschen Literatur* (Munich: Beck, 1924), 2:955.

30. John Bligh, "The 'Edict of Milan': Curse or Blessing?" *Church Quarterly Review* 153 (1952): 309.

Chapter 12

1. Johannes Edvard Lehmann and A. Bertholet, eds., *Lehrbuch der Religionsgeschichte*, 2 vols., 4th ed. (Tübingen: Mohr, 1925), 1:77–79, 126–30. Lehmann's definition is in James Hastings, ed., *Encyclopaedia of Religion and Ethics*, 13 vols. (New York: Charles Scribner's Sons, 1951), 9:85. Appendix A of William Inge's *Christian Mysticism* (London: Methuen,

1899), 335–48, lists twenty-six "Definitions of 'Mysticism' and 'Mystical Theology.' "

2. Nicol MacNicol, in Hastings, 9:114.
3. Joshua Abelson, in Hastings, 9:109.
4. Rufus Jones, in Hastings, 9:84.
5. John Chapman, in Hastings, 9:91.
6. Origen, *Contra Celsum* VII, 39, in *PG* 11:1477.
7. Sources given in Friedrich Überweg, *Geschichte der Philosophie des Altertums* (Berlin, 1876), 281ff.
8. Adolph Harnack, *Lehrbuch der Dogmengeschichte*, 5th ed. (Tübingen: Mohr, 1931), 452.
9. Ibid., 499.
10. Chapman, in Hastings, 9:93.
11. Dionysius Areopagitae, *De Mystica Theologia* I, in *PG* 3:997–1000; the translation is Chapman's.
12. Rufus Jones, *Pathways to the Reality of God* (New York: Macmillan, 1936), 22–23. It is, he says, "bafflingly incommunicable," p. 37.
13. See generally, William James, *Pragmatism* (New York: Longmans, Green & Co., 1907), 151.
14. Chapman, in Hastings, 9:90.
15. Jones, 43–46, and in Hastings, 9:84.
16. Jones, 40.
17. Chapman, in Hastings, 9:99.
18. Fitz Roy (Lord) Raglan, *The Origins of Religion* (London: Watts & Co., 1949), 21–22.
19. See generally, Inge, *Christian Mysticism*, "Lecture I," 3–36, cited by Rufus Jones.
20. Louis Poussin, and Edward Thomas, in Hastings, 9:86.
21. Jones, in Hastings, 9:84.
22. Chapman, in Hastings, 9:97.
23. Ibid., 9:99.
24. Ibid., 9:94.
25. Jones, 26–38.

Chapter 13

1. An excellent treatment in Franz Eggersdorfer, *Der heilige Augustinius als Pädagoge* (Freiburg, 1907), 1ff.
2. Wilhelm Schmid, and Otto Stählin, *Geschichte der griechischen Literatur* (Munich: Beck, 1924), II, ii, 949ff.
3. Gustave Combès, *Saint Augustin et la culture classique* (Paris: Plon, 1927), 49.

4. For these and other definitions, Hugh Nibley, "The Unsolved Loyalty Problem: Our Western Heritage," *Western Political Quarterly* 6 (1953): 652–53.

5. F. Schemmel, "Die Hochschule von Alexandria in IV. und V. Jahrhunderten," *Neue Jahrbücher für das klassische altertum Geschichte und deutsche Literatur und für Pädagogik* (1908), 494–513.

6. Clement of Alexandria, *Stromata* I, 8, 376, in *PG* 8:736.

7. Eggersdorfer, 2. On Boethus of Tarsus, see Strabo, *Geography*, Horace Jones, ed. (Cambridge: Harvard University Press, Loeb Classical Library, 1970), XIV, 5, 14.

8. Lucian, *Harmonides*. Lucian attacks the rhetoricians in many writings.

9. Walter August Müller, "Studentenleben im 4. Jahrhundert nach Christus," *Philologus* 69 (1910): 249, 308.

10. M. Schanz, *Geschichte der römischen Literatur* (Munich, 1914), Pt. IV, 515, cf. 502ff, 514–20, 527–37, etc. Combès, 54–55; Augustine, *De Ordine* II, 9, in *PL* 32:1007–8.

11. F. J. E. Raby, *Secular Latin Poetry* (Oxford, 1934), 1:7, 49.

12. Johannes Zellinger, "Der Beifall in dem altchristlichen Predigt," *Festgabe A. Knopfler* (Freiburg, 1917), 403.

13. Ibid., 404.

14. Eduard Norden, *Die antike Kunstprosa* (Leipzig: Wissenschaftliche Buchgesellschaft, 1898), 2:623.

15. Raby, 1:48.

16. Schanz, Pt. IV, 500.

17. Gibbon, *Decline and Fall of the Roman Empire*, ch. 27, n. 101.

18. Henri Marrou, *Saint Augustin et la fin de la culture antique* (Paris: Boccard, 1938), 275; cf. 54–59, 85–89, 237ff; 354–55.

19. Cicero, *Orator* 69:231.

20. Augustine, *Confessions* III, 3, in *PL* 32:685; "hoc laudabilior quo fraudulentior"; cf. V, 3; *De Doctrina Christiana* II, 36, in *PL* 34:55.

21. Augustine, *Confessions* VI, 9, in *PL* 32:726–27; Petronius, *Satyricon* I, 3; IV, 1; VI, 1.

22. Augustine, *Confessions* I, 17, in *PL* 32:673.

23. Dio Chrysostom, *Orationes* XXXVI, 18; XXXVIII, 40.

24. Augustine, *Ennaratio in Psalmum LXVIII*, in *PL* 36:865.

25. Gibbon, ch. 20, n. 125.

26. Augustine, *De Doctrina Christiana* IV, 18, 35–37, and 26, 56–58, in *PL* 34:105–6, 117–18.

27. For references, see *PL* 46:544–45.

28. John Chrysostom, *In Epistola I Corinthios Homilia* 35, in *PG* 61: 297–98.

29. Augustine, *Confessions* V, 13, in *PL* 32:717.

Chapter 14

1. Heinrich Bornkamm, *Grundriss zum Studium der Kirchengeschichte* (Gütersloh: Bertelsmann, 1949), 31.

2. Louis Duchesne, *Early History* 2:519.

3. Quoted by Eusebius, *Ecclesiastical History* III, 32, in *PG* 20:281–86.

4. A good illustration of this is *Clementine Recognitions* I, 55, in *PG* 1:1209, where the Jewish leaders try to win over the Christian movement.

5. Bornkamm, 64.

6. Ibid., 90.

Chapter 15

1. Quoted by Alexander Kaun, *Soviet Poems and Poetry* (Berkeley: University of California Press, 1943), 15.

2. A classic treatment of the subject is Lecture II in William James, *The Varieties of Religious Experience* (London: Longmans, Green, 1952), 27ff.

3. Rufus Jones, *Pathways to the Reality of God* (New York: Macmillan, 1936), 48–49. Jones appears to be dealing only with the early works of Barth.

4. Arnold Lunn and John Haldane, *Science and the Supernatural* (New York: Sheed and Ward, 1935), 394.

5. Cornelius Bouman, "Variants in the Introduction to the Eucharistic Prayer," *Vigiliae Christianae* 4 (1950): 114.

6. Paul Kahle, *The Cairo Geniza* (London: Oxford University Press, 1947), 175ff.

7. Theodor Schermann, *Die allgemeine Kirchenordnung frühchristliche Liturgien und kirchliche Überlieferung* (Paderborn: Schöningh, 1915), 2: 143.

8. See generally, August von Gall, *Basileia tou Theou* (Heidelberg: Carl Winter, 1926), 1–47.

9. "Piltdown Hoax Clumsy, Fresh Evidence Shows," *Science Newsletter* 66 (July 17, 1954): 40.

10. F. Bridgman, "Science and Common Sense," *Scientific Monthly* 79 (July 1954): 35–36.

11. Ibid., 36.

12. An enlightening remark by Whitehead on this theme may be found in Lucien Price, "To Live Without Certitude," *Atlantic Monthly* 193 (March 1954): 58.

13. William F. Albright, *The Archaeology of Palestine* (Baltimore: Pelican, 1949), 244ff.

14. Frank Moore Cross, "The Manuscripts of the Dead Sea Caves," *Biblical Archaeologist* 17 (February 1954): 3.

Chapter 16

1. Reginald Garrigou-Lagrange, *De revelatione per ecclesiam catholicam proposita* (Rome: F. Ferrari, 1931), 2:335.

2. *Quaestiones ad Antioch Ducem*, in PG 28:665.

3. Garrigou-Lagrange, 2:331.

4. Ibid., 2:335.

5. John Kaye, *Ecclesiastical History of the Second and Third Centuries Illustrated from the Writings of Tertullian* (London: Griffith-Farran, 1893), 93–95.

6. Robert M. Grant, *Second-Century Christianity* (London: SPCK, 1946), 14–15.

7. Ibid.

8. Cited by Ambrose, *Epistle 64*, in PL 16:1271–72.

9. Franz Dölger's important works, *Antike und Christentum*, 5 vols. (1929); *Ichthys: der heilige Fisch in den antiken Religionen und im Christentum*, 5 vols. (Münster: Aschendorffs, 1910); and *Sol Salutis* (1925).

Chapter 17

1. For a good summary of the question, see Sigmund Mowinckel, *Religion und Kultus* (Göttingen: Vandenhoeck & Ruprecht, 1953), and Fitz Roy Raglan, *The Origins of Religion* (London: Watts & Co., 1949).

2. Ludwig Eisenhofer and Joseph Lechner, *Liturgik des römischen Ritus* (Freiburg: Herder, 1953), 5–6 [see also the English translation by A.J. and E. F. Peeler, *The Liturgy of the Roman Rite* (Freiburg i/B: Herder, 1961), 4–6]. The present translation is the author's, taken from the German edition.

3. Kurt Goldammer, "Christliche Archäologie," in Heinrich Bornkamm, *Grundriss zum Studium der Kirchengeschichte* (Gütersloh: Bertelsmann, 1949), 101ff.

Chapter 18

1. Gregorius Magnus, *Epistle 76*, lxxvi, in PL 77:1215–16.

2. See editor's note on the above, ibid.

3. Clement of Alexandria, *Cohortatio ad Gentes*, in PG 8:153, 157, 160.

4. Jerome, *Epistle 128*, in PL 22:1099.

5. Sozomen, *Ecclesiastical History* II, 4, in PG 67:944; Eusebius, *De Vita Constantini* III, 51–53, in PG 20:1116B, 1112.

6. Silva Aquitana or Egeria, *Peregrinatio ad Loca Sancta* XX, 8.

7. John Chrysostom, in *PG* 49:363–65; 51:143–45; 56:257, 263; 57: 384ff; 64:461–62, 623–25, 629.

8. Ignatius, *Epistle to the Smyrnaeans* 3, in *PG* 5:709.

9. Ibid., *Epistle to the Trallians* 9, in *PG* 5:681.

10. Ibid., 9, in *PG* 5:681. (Other codices: F, O, U, V.)

11. Origen, *Peri Archon* II, 6, 2, in *PG* 11:210.

12. Ibid., II, 3, in *PG* 11:188–91.

13. Ibid.; Jerome is summarizing, not defending, the doctrine.

14. Augustine, *Questiones ex Utroque mixtim* 114, in *PL* 35:23, 45; *Sermon* 109, 2 in *PL* 39:1961; *Dialogus Questionum LXV*, Question 27, in *PL* 40:743; *De Civitate Dei* xiii, 19, in *PL* 41:392–93; *De Trinitate* IV, 17, 23, in *PL* 42:903.

15. Ibid., *Ennaratio in Psalmum 88*, in *PL* 37:1134.

16. Ibid., *Epistle* 147, 19–21 (Class III), in *PL* 33:618–19.

17. Ibid., *Epistle* 164, 3, in *PL* 33:712, cf. 38:944; 39:1614, 1628.

18. Ibid., *Epistle* 147, 19–21, in *PL* 33:618.

19. Clement of Alexandria, *Cohortatio Ad Gentes* XI, in *PG* 8:229. See above, Chapter 10.

20. Karl Holl, "Urchristentum und Religionsgeschichte," *Zeitschrift für systematische Theologie* 2 (1924): 403.

21. Fletcher Watson, *Between the Planets* (Philadelphia: Blakiston, 1945), 172–73; reprinted (Cambridge: Harvard University Press, 1956), 147.

Chapter 19

1. Minucius Felix, *Octavius* 8, in *PL* 3:269.

2. Ignatius, *Letter to the Romans* 8, in *PG* 5:816.

3. Basilius, *Epistles* 5 and 6 (Class I), in *PG* 32:237–44.

4. F. J. E. Raby, *A History of Christian-Latin Poetry* (Oxford: Clarendon, 1927), 420.

5. Ibid., 445.

6. Ibid., 444.

7. For a preliminary treatment of this subject, Hugh Nibley, "Baptism for the Dead in Ancient Times," *Improvement Era* 52 (1949): 24.

8. Clement of Alexandria, *Homilia* 14, in *PG* 11:345.

9. *Clementine Recognitions* I, 52, in *PG* 1:1236.

10. Bruno, *Expositio in Epistolam I ad Corinthios xv 29*, in *PL* 153:209; for the perplexities of the later Fathers, see Nibley, "Baptism for the Dead," 91.

11. Ibid., 24ff.

12. *Hermae Pastor (Shepherd of Hermas)* III, Similitude IX, 16, in *PG* 2:995–96; cf. Nibley, "Baptism for the Dead," 90.

Chapter 20

1. Tertullian, *Scorpiace* 10, in *PL* 2:167.

2. John Henry Evans, *Joseph Smith: An American Prophet* (New York: Macmillan, 1936), 12.

3. The case is discussed by Robert Eisler, *Iesous Basileus ou Basileusas* (Heidelberg: Carl Winter, 1930), 2:530–51.

4. Brigham H. Roberts, ed., *History of the Church of Jesus Christ of Latter-day Saints*, 2nd ed. (Salt Lake City: Deseret, 1950), 6:605–7.

5. Peter Cartwright, *Autobiography of Peter Cartwright, the Backwoods Preacher* (New York: Carlton & Porter, 1857), 346.

6. L. B. Cake, *Peepstone Joe and the Peck Manuscript* (New York: L.B. Cake, 1899), 82.

7. John C. Bennett, *History of the Saints: An Exposé* (Boston: Leland & Whiting, 1842), 83.

8. Pomeroy Tucker, *Origin, Rise and Progress of Mormonism* (New York: Appleton, 1867), 15.

9. T. W. P. Taylder, "The American Mahomet," *American Whig Review* (June 1851), 556.

10. Taylder, *The Mormon's Own Book* (London: Partridge, 1857), li–liii.

Chapter 21

1. Irenaeus, *Contra Haereses* IV, 37, 1, in *PG* 7:1099–1100.

2. Ibid., 37, 3–6, in *PG* 7:1101–3.

3. *Clementine Recognitions* II, 23–25, in *PG* 1:1260–61.

4. Ibid., III, 26, in *PG* 1:1294–95.

5. Ibid., III, 59, in *PG* 1:1307; IV, 24, 34, in *PG* 1:1324, 1330.

6. Ibid., III, 49, in *PG* 1:1303.

7. Willem Cornelis van Unnik, Jan Waszink and C. De Beus, *Het oudste Christendom en de antieke Cultuur* (Haarlem: Tjeenk, Willink & Zoon, 1951), ch. 2, pp. 92–93.

8. Hugh Nibley, "The Hierocentric State," *Western Political Quarterly* 4 (1951): 231–35.

9. For a general treatment, Hugh Nibley, "The Unsolved Loyalty Problem: Our Western Heritage," *Western Political Quarterly* 6 (1953): 637–41.

10. Minucius Felix, *Octavius* 37, in *PL* 3:367–68.

11. For references, Nibley, "The Unsolved Loyalty Problem," 641–46.

12. Both quotations from Homer Hockett, *Political and Social Growth of the United States: 1492–1852*, reprinted as *Political and Social Growth of the American People: 1492–1852* (New York: Macmillan, 1940), 200–201.

13. Tertullian, *De Pudicitia* I, 20–22, in *PL* 2:1031–35, 1074–84: "quis permittit homini donare quae Deo reservanda sunt?"

Chapter 22

1. Origen, *Contra Celsum* I, 9–10, in *PG* 11:672–75.

2. Adolf Harnack, *Monasticism, Its Ideals and History, and the Confessions of St. Augustine* (London: Williams & Norgate, 1901), 69.

3. John Chrysostom, *On the Epistle to the Colossians* 2, 4, in *PG* 62:314; *On the Epistle to the Hebrews* 21, 3, in *PG* 63:152; see also *Homily After the Earthquake*, in *PG* 50:713–14; *On Saint Bassus the Martyr* (dubia), in *PG* 50:723–24; *On the Epistle to the Hebrews* 32, 3, in *PG* 63:222.

4. Jerome, *Epistles* 60 and 123, in *PL* 22:600–602, 1058; *Commentary on Ecclesiastes* 10, in *PL* 23:1154.

5. Jerome, *Commentary on Isaiah* 7, in *PL* 24:275.

6. *Clementine Recognitions* I, 42, in *PG* 1:1231.

7. Frederick Powicke, "The Christian Life," in *The Legacy of the Middle Ages*, Charles Crump ed. (Oxford: Clarendon, 1951), 39.

8. Robert Priebsch, *Letter from Heaven on the Observance of the Lord's Day* (Oxford: Blackwell, 1936), 1–2. Translated by the author.

9. Maximilian Bittner, *Der vom Himmel gefallene Brief Christi in seinen morgenländischen Versionen und Rezensionen*, in *Denksehriften der kaiserlichen Akademie der Wissenschaften: Philosophisch-Historische Klasse* 51 (Vienna: Hölder, 1906): 71.

10. H. Delehaye, "Un exemplaire de la lettre tombée du ciel," *Recherches de science religieuse* 18 (1928): 168. Cf. Frank Branky, "Himmelsbriefe," *Archiv für Religionswissenschaft* 5 (1902): 149–53. All writers here cited give general surveys of the whole subject.

11. Bittner, 107ff.

12. Frederick Spencer, "The Second Advent According to the Gospel," *Church Quarterly Review* 126 (1938): 18.

13. Spencer, "The Imminence of the Parousia," *Church Quarterly Review* 148 (1949): 241–42.

14. Austin Birch, "The Creeds: How Shall We Take Them?" *The Hibbert Journal* 51 (1953): 176–80.

15. Wilhelm Pauck, "The Idea of the Church in Christian History," *Church History* 21 (1952): 192.

16. T. W. Manson, "The New Testament Basis of the Doctrine of the Church," *Journal of Ecclesiastical History* 1 (1950): 11.

17. Arnold Lunn and John Haldane, *Science and the Supernatural* (New York: Sheed & Ward, 1935), 52–53.

18. Josef Ternus, "Theologische Erwägungen zur Bulle 'Munificentis-simus Deus,' " *Scholastik* 26 (1951): 11–35.

Chapter 23

1. G. Deissman, *Light from the Ancient East*, 2nd ed. (New York: Doran, 1927), 245–46.

2. See, e.g., John 5:39, Matthew 22:29ff, Acts 18:28.

3. Willem Cornelis van Unnik, "De la Regle *mete prostheinai mete aphelein* dans l'histoire du canon," *Vigiliae Christianae* 3 (1949): 32ff.

4. Hilary, *Ad Constantium Augustum* II, 9, in *PL* 10:570.

5. Irenaeus, *Contra Haereses* II, 27, in *PG* 7:803.

6. Ibid., I, 1, in *PG* 7:437.

7. Ibid., III, 1–3, in *PG* 7:844–48.

8. Tertullian, *De Praescriptionibus* 14–19, in *PL* 2:31–36.

9. Socrates, *Ecclesiastical History* II, 39–40, in *PG* 67:336–37.

10. Clement of Alexandria, *Stromatum* I, in *PG* 8:704–5.

11. Tertullian, *De Pudicitia* 21, in *PL* 2:1080.

12. Frederick Powicke, "The Christian Life," in *The Legacy of the Middle Ages*, Charles Crump ed. (Oxford: Clarendon, 1951), 43, speaking specifically of Rome.

13. Henri Marrou, *Saint Augustine et la fin de la culture antique* (Paris: Boccard, 1958), 494–98.

14. J. Turmel, "Histoire de l'interpretation de I Tim. II, 4," *Revue de l'histoire et de litterature religieuses* 5 (1900): 392–93.

15. Etienne Gilson, *La philosophie au moyen âge* (Paris, 1944), 14.

16. There are more than 8,000 ancient manuscripts of the New Testament, no two of which read exactly alike!

Chapter 24

1. Hugh Nibley, "New Approaches to Book of Mormon Study," *Improvement Era* (March 1954): 148ff.

2. André Dupont-Sommer, *The Dead Sea Scrolls: A Preliminary Survey* (New York: Macmillan, 1952), 96. For a description of later finds, Frank Moore Cross, "The Manuscripts of the Dead Sea Caves," *Biblical Archaeologist* 17 (February 1954): 2–21.

3. H. L. Lorimer, "Homer and the Art of Writing: A Sketch of Opinion between 1713 and 1939," *American Journal of Archaeology* 52 (1948): 14–15.

4. Albert B. Lord, "Homer, Parry and Huso," *American Journal of Archaeology* 52 (1948): 39.

5. See generally, Hector and Nora Chadwick, *The Growth of Literature* (Cambridge: Cambridge University Press, 1932).

6. Samuel N. Kramer, "New Light on the Early History of the Ancient Near East," *American Journal of Archaeology* 52 (1948): 156–64.

Chapter 25

1. Alfred Fawkes, "The Development of Christian Institutions and Beliefs," *Harvard Theological Review* 10 (1917): 111.

2. Eduard Schwartz, *Kaiser Constantin und die christliche Kirche*, 5th ed. (Stuttgart: Teubner, 1969), 18.

3. Athanasius, *Epistle* 39, cited by W. E. Crum, "Some Further Meletian Documents," *Journal of Egyptian Archaeology* 13 (1927): 23.

4. Arnobius, *Disputation Against the Gentiles* II, 66, in *PL* 5:913, and below, note 8.

5. Minucius Felix, *Octavius* 6–8, in *PL* 3:258–69.

6. Justin Martyr, *Apology* I, 5–6, 10, in *PG* 6:336–41.

7. Ibid., 2, 12, in *PG* 6:329, 341.

8. Arnobius, ibid., I, 57, and II, 69, and 71, in *PL* 5:796, 922, 925–26.

9. P. Chavannes, *Revue d'histoire de littérature religieuses* 4 (1899): 398.

10. Ibid., 334.

11. Eusebius, *Ecclesiastical History* I, 2, 23, in *PG* 20:56.

12. Tertullian, *Apologeticus Adversus Gentes pro Christianis* 21, in *PL* 1:449–65.

13. Louis Duchesne, *Origines du culte chrétien* (Paris, 1898), ch. 1.

Chapter 26

1. Cited by Eusebius, *Ecclesiastical History* III, 39, in *PG* 20:297.

2. Papias, *Fragmentum* vi, in *PG* 5:1260 (Andreas Caesareae, *Commentary on the Apocalypse* 34, 12).

3. Justin Martyr, *Apology* I, 10, in *PG* 6:340–41. Cf. I, 59, in *PG* 6: 416–17; II, 4–5, in *PG* 6:452–53.

4. Justin Martyr, *Apology* II, 7, in *PG* 6:456.

5. *Clementine Recognitions* I, 24, in *PG* 1:1220 and I, 28, in *PG* 1: 1222.

6. *Apostolic Constitutions* VI, 10, in *PG* 1:933.

7. Clement of Alexandria, *Paedogogus* I, 7, in *PG* 8:321.

8. Irenaeus, *Contra Haereses* IV, 38, in *PG* 7:1107–08.

9. Tertullian, *Apologeticus Adversus Gentes pro Christianis* 1, in *PL* 1:307–8.

10. Thus Anselm in Book 1 of *Cur Deus Homo?*

11. Origen, *Peri Archon* I, 8, 4, in *PG* 9:179.

12. Ibid., II, 9, 6–7, in *PG* 9:230–31.

13. Ibid., 7–8, in *PG* 9:231–32.

Chapter 27

1. André Dupont-Sommer, *The Dead Sea Scrolls: A Preliminary Survey* (New York: Macmillan, 1952), 61ff.

2. For a summary of the whole question, Fitz Roy Raglan, *The Origin of Religion* (London: Watts, 1949).

3. The best-known general treatment of the much-treated subject is Hermann Gunkel, *Zum Religionsgeschichtlichen Verständnis des neuen Testaments*, 3rd ed. (Göttingen: Vandenhoeck and Ruprecht, 1910).

4. Origen, *Contra Celsum* V, 43, in *PG* 9:1249.

5. Thus, I Clement 31 and 41; Romans 11:2.

6. Benjamin F. Johnson, *My Life's Review* (Independence: Zion's, 1947), 27.

Chapter 28

1. The whole problem has been treated by Olaf Linton, *Das Problem der Urkirche in der neueren Forschung* (Uppsala: Almquist and Wiksell, 1932), 121.

2. Ibid., cf. Kirsopp Lake, "The Shepherd of Hermas and Christian Life in Rome in the Second Century," *Harvard Theological Review* 4 (1911): 37.

3. Gardiner Day, *Our Protestant Heritage* [pamphlet] (Cambridge: Cambridge University Press, 1953).

4. Linton, 123.

5. This is the "Noah's Ark" and "Rock of Refuge" theory of the Church, treated especially by Scheel and discussed by Linton, 179, 180.

6. Ibid., 51, 136, 196.

7. Socrates, *Ecclesiastical History* V, 22, in *PG* 67:628.

8. Hans Lietzmann, *Geschichte der alten Kirche* (Berlin: de Gruyter, 1975), 1:55.

9. Linton, 63–64.

10. T. W. Manson, "The New Testament Basis of the Doctrine of the Church," *Journal of Ecclesiastical History* 1 (1950).

11. John Chrysostom, *De Sancta Pentecoste*, in *PG* 50:453, 455–56, 459, 488; *In Inscriptionem Actorum* 2, in *PG* 51:81–82, 85; *Expositio in Psalmum* 135, in *PG* 55:402; *On Matthew* 46 (47), 3, in *PG* 58:479; *On Epistle I to the Corinthians* 32, 4–5, and 33, 3, in *PG* 61:269–71, 279–80; *On Epistle I to Timothy* 6, in *PG* 62:529–30; *Extracts from Diverse Homilies* 9, in *PG* 63:623, 627.

12. Augustine, *Sermon* 129 III, 4, in *PL* 38:722.

13. Ibid., *Contra Julianum Pelagianum* VI, 5, 11, in *PL* 44:829.

14. Numerous references to this argument in Augustine are given in the main index, *PL* 46:264. The argument is lavishly exploited by Optatus and Lucifer against the Donatists and Novatians.

15. John Kaye, *The Ecclesiastical History of the Second and Third Centuries Illustrated from the Writings of Tertullian* (London: Rivington, 1825), v.

16. Ibid., 92–95.

17. Tertullian, *De Pudicitia* 21–22, in *PL* 2:1077–82.

Chapter 29

1. Ignatius, *Epistle to the Magnesians* 4–5, in *PG* 5:665–68; and *Epistle to the Trallians* 6, in *PG* 5:679.

2. Augustine, *Confessions* III, 4; IV, 15–16; V, 10, 14; VII, 9, 19, etc., in *PL* 32:685; 32:703–6, 714–18, 740–42, 746.

3. Adolf Harnack, *Dogmengeschichte*, 5th ed. (Tübingen: Mohr, 1931), 2:64.

4. Thomas Aquinas, *Summa Theologica* (Turin: Marietti, 1932), Question I, Article viii.

5. Werner Jaeger, *Aristotle* (Oxford: Clarendon, 1948), 132–136, 390–93.

6. Plato, *Apology* 28e.

7. Ibid., 29d–30b.

Chapter 31

1. N. A. Dahl, "Christ, Creation and the Church," in W. D. Davies & D. Daube, *Background of the New Testament and Its Eschatology* (Cambridge: Cambridge University Press, 1956), 422.

2. Richard Courant and Herbert Robbins, *What is Mathematics?* (Oxford University Press, 1941), xvii–xviii.

3. I. Cohen, "Orthodoxy and Scientific Progress," *Proceedings of the American Philosophical Society* 96 (1952): 505–6.

4. S. Drake, ed., *Discoveries and Opinions of Galileo* (New York: Doubleday, 1957), 101–2.

5. M. Polanyi, "The Unaccountable Element in Science," *Philosophy* 37 (1962): 14.

6. L. Platt, "Cause and Effect, A Fable for Geology Teachers," *Journal of Geological Education* 10 (March 1962): 28.

7. F. W. Bridgman, "Science and Common Sense," *Scientific Monthly* 79 (July 1954): 36.

8. Polanyi, 14.

9. F. Vick, "The Making of Scientists," *The Listener* 61 (January 29, 1959): 196.

10. Adolphus Elkin, "A Darwin Centenary and Highlights of Field-Work in Australia," *Mankind* 5 (1959): 333, quoting J. T. Merz, *Religion and Science, A Philosophical Essay* (Edinburgh: Blackwood, 1915), 103.

11. Ernest Jones, "Nature of Genius," *Scientific Monthly* 84 (1957): 80.

12. Ibid., 77.

13. Ibid., 81.

14. P. Le Corbeiller, "Crystals and the Future of Physics," *Scientific American* 188 (January 1953): 51.

15. Warren Weaver, "The Imperfections of Science," *American Scientist* 49 (March 1961): 109.

16. Ibid., 100.

17. W. O. Fenn, "Front Seats for Biologists," *Bioscience* (December 1960): 16.

18. Bridgman, 33.

19. A. W. Herre, "Letters," *Bioscience* (December 1960), 5–6.

20. E. A. Hooton, "Comments on the Piltdown Affair," *American Anthropologist* 56 (1954): 289.

21. Weaver, 112.

22. Ibid., 106–7.

23. Sigmund Freud, *The Future of an Illusion* (New York: Doubleday, 1957), 102.

24. Fenn, 16; cf. R. M. Frumkin, "Scientific Millennialism as the Coming World Ideology," *Journal of Human Relations* 10 (1962): 145, 157.

25. I. Galdston, "Existentialism as a Perennial Philosophy of Life and Being," *Journal of Existential Psychiatry* 1 (1960): 379.

26. Herre, 6.

27. Heinrich Bornkamm, *Grundriss zum Studium der Kirchengeschichte* (Gütersloh: Bertelsmann, 1949), 83: the conflict began long before Augustine.

28. M. Grabmann, *Die Geschichte der scholastischen Methode* (Graz: Akademische Druckanstalt, 1957), I, chs. 1 and 2.

29. R. H. Charles, ed., *Apocrypha and Pseudepigrapha of the Old Testament* (Oxford University Press, 1913) 2:viii.

30. Willem Cornelis van Unnik, "De la Regle *mete prostheinai mete aphelein* dans l'histoire du canon," *Vigiliae Christianae* 3 (1949):1–2.

31. Van Unnik, 3–4, citing T. Zahn, *Geschichte des neutestamentlichen Kanons* (Erlangen: Deichert, 1888–1890) 1:112–16. Italics ours.

32. Heinrich Denzinger, *Enchiridion Symbolorum* (Freiburg: Herder, 1957), No. 783, cf. No. 785: cf. *Tridentinum* iv. See especially O. Chadwick, *From Bossuet to Newman* (Cambridge: Cambridge University Press, 1957), ch. 2.

33. M. H. Franzmann, "The Apostolate: Its Enduring Significance in the Apostolic Word," *Concordia Theological Monthly* 28 (1957): 174. The statement of a Lutheran conference, quoting from the Lutheran Confessions.

34. H. A. Kelly, "The Silence of God: How Is It to be Explained?" *Journal of the Transactions of the Victoria Institute* 58 (1926): 255.

35. Vincent of Lerinum, "Commonitorium Primum," in *PL* 50:637, 638; cf. O. Chadwick, 16–17.

36. Hilary, *Tractatus in LIV Psalmum*, in *PL* 9:352; *Ad Constantium Augustum* II, in *PL* 10:570.

37. Hilary, *On the Trinity* IV, 14, in *PL* 10:107; *Prologue to Tractate on the Book of Psalms* 7, in *PL* 9:237; *Tractate on Psalm* 14, in *PL* 9:295.

38. Hilary, *On the Trinity* IV, 14, in *PL* 10:107; *Ad Constantium Augustum* II, in *PL* 10:569, 570; cf. Hilary, *Tractate on Psalm* 1, in *PL* 9:247; *Tractate on Psalm* 134, in *PL* 9:758. For the rule, Hilary, *On the Trinity* IV, 2, and X, 1, in *PL* 10:282, 344.

39. This is the theme of Chadwick's book, note 32 above.

40. N. Nagel, "The Authority of Scripture," *Concordia Theological Monthly* 27 (1956): 702.

41. Emily Blackman, "The Task of Exegesis," in Davies & Daube, 18–19.

42. A. E. Harvey, *The Listener* (August 14, 1958), 241.

43. Denzinger, No. 1605–06.

44. Frederick Powicke, "The Christian Life," in *Legacy of the Middle Ages*, C. G. Crump ed. (Oxford, 1951), 54.

45. C. F. DeVine, "The Consequent Sense," *Catholic Biblical Quarterly* 2 (1940): 145.

46. F. X. Pierce, "Mary Alone is 'The Woman' of Genesis 3:15," *Catholic Biblical Quarterly* 2 (1940): 252.

47. Thomas Aquinas, *Summa Theologica* (Turin: Marietti, 1932). Question I, Article viii.

48. Ibid.

49. G. Florovsky, "Eschatology in the Patristic Age," *Studia Patristica* 2, in *Texte und Untersuchungen* 64 (1957): 246.

50. H. Clavier, "Les sens multiples dans le nouveau testament," *Novum Testamentum* 2 (1958): 185–86.

51. Blackman, 25.

52. Albert Dufourcq, *Histoire de la fondation de léglise* (Paris, 1909), 240, 248.

53. Clarence Craig, "Sacramental Interest in the Fourth Gospel," *Journal of Biblical Literature* 58 (1939): 32–33.

54. Harold Rowley, *The Relevance of Apocalyptic* (London: Lutterworth, 1944), 78.

55. E.g., W. A. Irwin, "Ezekiel Research Since 1943," *Vetus Testamentum* 3 (1953): 63, for the Old Testament; and Krister Stendahl, "Implications of Form-Criticism and Tradition-Criticism for Biblical Interpretation," *Journal of Biblical Literature* 77 (1958): 35, for the New Testament; cf. E. M. Good, "With All Its Faults," *Christianity Today* (January 16, 1961): 6–7.

56. Father Hebert, *Expository Times* 70 (1958): 33.

57. D. M. Mackay, "Divine Activity in a Scientific World," *Faith and Thought* 91 (1959): 75–76.

Chapter 32

1. Hugh Nibley, "Kangaroo Court," *Improvement Era* 62 (March, 1959): 145.

2. Eber D. Howe, *History of Mormonism* (Painesville, Ohio, 1840), 94; Jonathan Turner, *Mormonism in All Ages* (New York, 1842), 302; Thomas Gregg, *The Prophet of Palmyra* (New York, 1890), 35, 75, 95; John Reynolds, *My Own Times* (Illinois, 1855), 563.

3. P. J. Pierce, "The Origin of the Book of Mormon," *The American Anthropologist* 1, New Series (1899): 694. Italics ours.

4. William Linn, *The Story of the Mormons from the Date of Their Origin to the Year 1901* (New York: Macmillan, 1923), 90.

5. Samuel and Helen Fallows, *The Mormon Menace* (Chicago: Woman's Temperance Publishing Association, 1903), 16; W. E. La Rue, *The Foundations of Mormonism* (New York: Revell, 1919), 65. Italics ours.

6. Peter Meinhold, "Die Anfänge des amerikanischen Geschichtsbewusstseins," *Saeculum* 5 (1954), 86.

7. *Missouri Intelligencer & Boon's [sic] Lick Advertiser* (August 10, 1833.)

8. Ibid. (June 28, 1834.)

9. Charles Dickens, "In the Name of the Prophet—Smith!" *Household Words* (July 19, 1851): 385.

10. League for Social Service, *Ten Reasons Why Christians Cannot Fellowship the Mormon Church* (New York: 105 E. 22 St., 1898), 1–8.

11. H. A. Kelly, "The Silence of God: How is it to be Explained?" *Journal of the Transactions of the Victoria Institute* 58 (1926): 255–56.

12. See generally, Hugh Nibley, "The Passing of the Church," *Church History* 30 (1961): 131, 142–47.

13. M. S. Enslin, "A Gentleman Among the Fathers," *Harvard Theological Review* 47 (1954): 230.

14. G. W. Bromiley, "The Bible Doctrine of Inspiration," *Christianity Today* 4 (November 23, 1959): 139.

15. Heinrich Bornkamm, *Grundriss zum Studium der Kirchengeschichte* (Gütersloh: Bertelsmann, 1949), 14.

16. Paul Schlipp, *The Quest for Religious Realism* (New York: Harper, 1938), Chapter headings.

17. Harold H. Rowley, *The Relevance of Apocalyptic* (Cambridge: Cambridge University Press, 1944), 12.

18. N. Ferré, "Which Way British Theology," *Expository Times* 70 (July 1959): 305.

19. Alfred North Whitehead, *Science and the Modern World* (New York: Macmillan, 1962), 270.

20. H. D. McDonald, "The Conflict over Special Revelation," *Christianity Today* 5 (January 16, 1961): 306.

21. Ernst von Dobschütz, "Die Kirche im Urchristentum," *Zeitschrift für die neutestamentliche Wissenschaft* 28 (1929): 108.

22. N. A. Dahl, "Christ, Creation, and the Church," in *Background of the New Testament and Its Eschatology*, W. Davies and D. Daube eds. (Cambridge: Cambridge University Press, 1956), 440.

23. Frederick Grant, "The Economic Background of the New Testament," in Davies & Daube, 96.

24. F. Farrell, "Instability of Liberal Social Ethics," *Christianity Today* 6 (January 5 & 19, 1962): 308–12, 365–69; E. Cahn, "How to Destroy the Churches," *Harper's Magazine* (November 1961): 34.

25. See generally, Nibley, "The Passing of the Church," 131, 142–47.

26. J. R. W. Scott, "Christ and the Scriptures," *Christianity Today* 4 (November 23, 1959): 137.

27. C. S. Lewis, *The Case for Christianity* (New York: Macmillan, 1956), 45.

28. Dahl, in Davies & Daube, 422.

29. Edward Selwyn, "Eschatology in I Peter," in Davies & Daube, 400–401.

30. J. Rowland, "Science and Religion," *The Hibbert Journal* 60 (1961): 1.

31. Cyrus Gordon, *Ugaritic Literature* (Rome: Pontifical Institute, 1949), 3.

32. William F. Albright, "Archaeology and Religion," *Cross Currents* 9 (1959): 111.

33. Frederick Spencer, "The Second Advent According to the Gospels," *Church Quarterly Review* 126 (1938): 18.

34. John Walvoord, "The Doctrine of the Millennium," *Bibliotheca Sacra* 115 (1958): 106–8.

35. G. C. Berkouwer, "Review of Current Religious Thought," *Christianity Today* 4 (November 23, 1959): 168.

36. See generally, K. Prümm, "Dynamis in griechisch-hellenistischer Religion und Philosophie als Vergleichsbild zu göttlicher Dynamis im Offenbarungsraum," *Zeitschrift für katholischen Theologie* 83 (1961): 393–430.

37. Oscar Cullmann, "Rudolph Bultmann's Concept of Myth and the New Testament," *Concordia Theological Monthly* 27 (1956): 24.

38. A. Nygren, *Svensk Teologisk Tidskrift* 27 (1951): 1.

39. Emil G. Kraeling, *The Old Testament Since the Reformation* (New York: Harper, 1955), 133.

40. S. McCasland, "The Unity of the Scriptures," *Journal of Biblical Literature* 73 (1954): 7–9.

41. Miller Burrows, "Thy Kingdom Come," *Journal of Biblical Literature* 74 (1955): 8.

42. Hugh Nibley, "The Way of the Church—The Apocalyptic Background—II," *Improvement Era* 58 (December 1955): 902.

43. W. C. Klein, "The Church and Its Prophets," *Anglican Theological Review* 44 (1962): 17.

44. McCasland, 6.

45. G. W. Bromiley, 138; see also R. D. Crouse, "The Hellenization of Christianity," *Canadian Journal of Theology* 8 (1962): 32.

46. McDonald, 304.

47. C. F. De Vine, "The Consequent Sense," *Catholic Biblical Quarterly* 2 (1940): 145.

48. "Notes of Recent Exposition," *The Expository Times* 70 (1958): 34.

49. Martin Grabmann, *Geschichte der scholastischen Methode* (Graz: Akademische Druck, 1957), 1:275–78.

50. Ibid., 1:319–21, 333.

51. McDonald, 304.

52. H. A. Brongers, review of Adrianus Van Den Born, *Profetie metterdaad* (Roermond-Maaseik: Romen, 1947), in *Bibliotheca Orientalis* (1948): 34.

53. See generally B. M. G. Reardon, "The Relevance of Theological Liberalism," *The Listener* (May 30, 1957): 871–72.

54. Edwyn Bevan, *Hellenism and Christianity* (London: George Allen & Unwin, 1921), 214; see generally T. C. Vriezen, "Prophecy and Eschatology," *Vetus Testamentum Supplement* 1 (1953): 199.

55. Rowley, 35–36.

56. Solomon Schechter, "The Rabbinical Conception of Holiness," *Jewish Quarterly Review* 10 (1897): 11–12.

57. Bevan, *Sibyls and Seers* (Cambridge: Harvard University Press, 1929), 109.

58. Franklin Young, "Jesus the Prophet: A Re-examination," *Journal of Biblical Literature* 68 (1949): 297.

59. R. H. Charles, "Apocryphal Literature," in *Encyclopaedia Britannica*, 11th ed. (Cambridge: Cambridge University Press, 1910), 2:175; M.-J. Lagrange, *Le messianisme chez les Jiufs, Etudes Bibliques* (Paris, 1909), 40.

60. Olaf Linton, *Das Problem der Urkirche in der neueren Forschung* (Uppsala: Almquist and Wiksell, 1932), 101ff.

61. G. E. Ladd, "Why Not Prophetic-Apocalyptic?" *Journal of Biblical Literature* 76 (1957): 192; H. A. Kelly, "The Silence of God," and D. M'Intyre, "The Silence of God," *Journal of the Transactions of the Victoria Institute* 58 (1926): 253, 258. Quote is from W. Klein, 1.

62. E. Käsemann, *The Wandering People of God: An Investigation of the Letter to the Hebrews* (Minneapolis: Augsburg, 1984), 20–22.

63. Klein, 17.

64. Paul Tillich, "Die Wiederentdeckung der prophetischen Tradition in der Reformation," *Neue Zeitschrift für systematische Theologie und Religionsphilosophie* 3 (1961): 237ff.

65. A Erhardt, "The Birth of the Synagogue and R. Akiba," *Studia Theologica* 9 (1956): 111; Robert North, "Prophetismus ut Philosophia Historiae," *Verbum Domini* 29 (1951): 321–33; J. B. Agus, "The Prophet in Modern Hebrew Literature," *Hebrew Union College Annual* 28 (1957): 289–341.

66. Bornkamm, 74.

67. Linton, 51, 75–77, 189; E. Käsemann, *Zeitschrift für die neutestamentliche Wissenschaft* 41 (1942): 41ff, 71; G. Koch, "Der Gottesgeist und der Messias," *Biblica* 27 (1946): 255.

68. Erhardt, 111.

69. E. Käsemann, "Die Legitimät des Apostels," *Zeitschrift für neutestamentliche Wissenschaft* 41 (1942): 71.

70. Tertullian, *De Pudicitia* 22, in *PL* 2:1077–82.

71. J. Muilenburg, "Problems in Biblical Hermeneutics," *Journal of Biblical Literature* 77 (1958): 25–26.

72. T. W. Manson, "The New Testament Basis of the Doctrine of the Church," *Journal of Ecclesiastical History* 1 (1950): 1.

73. Titles of recent books by Marcel Simon, *Le judaisme et le christianisme antique d'Antiochus Epiphane à Constantin* (Paris: Presses universitaires de France, 1968); P. Parker, *Inherit the Promise: Six Keys to New Testament Thought* (Connecticut: Seabury, 1957); and S. Devan, *Ascent to Zion* (New York: Macmillan, 1942), respectively.

74. Eduard Schwartz, *Kaiser Constantin und die christliche Kirche* (Stuttgart: Teubner, 1969), 18.

75. E. Haible, "Die Vergegenwärtigung des Apostelkollegiums," *Zeitschrift für katholischen Theologie* 83 (1961): 80–87

76. John Davies, "Church and Ministry—Apostolic Succession Reconsidered," *The Expository Times* 70 (May 1959): 230.

77. A. G. James, "Apostolic Succession," *The Expository Times* 70 (March 1959): 166.

78. Peter Meinhold, "Geschichtskritik und Kirchenerneuerung," *Saeculum* 9 (1958): 1–21; R. Camacho, "Steps to Revival," *Reformation Review* 7 (1959): 1.

79. H. Cadbury, "Acts and Eschatology," in Davies Daube, 316–17.

80. Robert M. Grant, " 'Development' in Early Christian Doctrine," *Journal of Religion* 39 (1959): 121–22.

81. Rudolf Bultmann, *Zeitschrift für die neutestamentliche Wissenschaft* 27 (1928): 118–19.

82. W. Pauck, "The Idea of the Church in Christian History," *Church History* 21 (1952): 192.

83. R. E. Gahringer, "Toward a Reorientation in the Philosophy of Religion," *Journal of Religion* 38 (1958): 175.

84. Hugh Sellin, "The Crisis of Western Civilization," *The Hibbert Journal* 54 (1955–56): 168.

85. Grant, 121.

86. F. H. Marenck, *Glaubenlöse Religion* (Munich: Ernst Reinhardt, 1931), 7–8. Translation by the author.

87. Gustaf von Wingren, " 'Weg,' 'Wanderung,' und verwandte Begriffe," *Studia Theologica* 3 (1951): 111–12.

88. Bevan, *Hellenism and Christianity*, 81.

89. Whitehead, 190.

Scripture References

Index

Abraham and the true prophet, 11

Alexander of Alexandria and the Nicene Creed, 44-45

Alexandria, catechetical school of, 72

Ambrose, influence of, on Augustine, 93

Ammonius Saccus, founder of Neoplatonism, 101

Anthropomorphism: according to Augustine, 93-94; according to Mormon theology, 159-60

Anti-Mormonism and the belief of continuing revelation, 284

Antiquity as authority for religion, 218

Apologists on the limitations of paganism, 3

Apostasy: influence of gnosticism on, 63-70; influence of schools on, 71; influence of philosophy on, 80-88; influence of mysticism on, 102-3; influence of rhetoric on, 108-16; and the need for a restoration, 122; and the need for scientific method, 126

Apostasy, causes of: loss of spiritual gifts, 5, 245; loss of free agency, 182; closed canon, 200; loss of continuing revelation, 200; insistence on tradition, 216-23; loss of eschatological thinking, 269-83

Apostles, description of, by Eusebius, 30

Apostolic Fathers and the anti-resurrection trend, 157-58

Apostolic succession in orthodox Christianity, 295

Aquinas, Thomas, on revelation, 281

Arius and the Nicene Creed, 44-45

Athanasius: on ecumenical councils, 48; on knowledge of God, 56; on the veneration of relics, 217

Augustine: importance of, in world history, 80; as creator of Western theology, 81; influence of Neoplatonism of, 82; and the fusion of Classical and Christian thought, 83; and reconciliation of

paganism and Christianity, 84-85; and the importance of rationalism to Christianity, 87; and the use of intellectualism over revelation, 89-90; yearning of, for revelation, 89-91; biographical sketch of, 92-94; influence of, on the doctrine of the Trinity, 94-95; on the interpretation of scriptures, 205; and the organization of the early church, 244-45

Authority, divine: cessation of, in primitive Christianity, 248; as a sign of the true church, 251-52; rational foundations for claims of, 252-53; in orthodox Christianity, 296

Baptism for the dead, 168-69

Barnabas: on prophetic gifts, 4; and the conversion of Clement of Rome, 37-38

Barth, Karl, and supernaturalism, 128

Basil the Great on death, 166

Bible: need for interpretation of, 202-3; as inerrant and complete scripture, 278-79

Book of Mormon: as a window on other worlds, 209; as a witness, 209-13; as history, 210-11; and the Dead Sea Scrolls, 212-13; as scripture, 285

Browning, John, on the disappearance of prophetic gifts, 5

Bruno the Carthusian on baptism for the dead, 169

Canonical scripture, measures of, 281

Catholic Church, 292-93

Celsus, description of, of the birth of Christ, 18

Certainty, theological, and the influence of philosophy, 78

Charismatic gifts, 291-94

Christian as one who believes in Christ, 44